HANGING TOGETHER

Written under the auspices of the Royal Institute of International Affairs, London, and the Center for International Affairs, Harvard University

HANGING TOGETHER

The Seven-Power Summits

ROBERT D. PUTNAM
and
NICHOLAS BAYNE

'We must indeed all hang together or, most assuredly, we shall all hang separately.' BENJAMIN FRANKLIN, on the signing of the Declaration of Independence, 4 July 1776

Harvard University Press
Cambridge, Massachusetts
1984

Written under the auspices of the Royal Institute of International Affairs, London, and the Center for International Affairs, Harvard University.

The Royal Institute of International Affairs and the Center for International Affairs are unofficial bodies which promote the scientific study of international questions and do not express opinions of their own. The opinions expressed in this publication are the responsibility of its authors. Each author is responsible only for those chapters appearing under his own name.

Nicholas Bayne is a member of the British diplomatic service. His chapters of this volume are based on research conducted during a year's secondment to the Royal Institute of International Affairs. The opinions he expresses are entirely personal and should not be taken as reflecting official views.

Library of Congress Cataloging in Publication Data

Putnam, Robert D.
  Hanging together

Includes bibliographical references and index.
1. International economic relations—Congresses.
I. Bayne, Nicholas, 1937–   . II. Title.
HF1410.5.P87 1984   337   83–26480
ISBN 0–674–37225–5 (alk. paper)

Contents

Chapters 1, 4, 6, and 10–12 are by Robert D. Putnam.
Chapters 2, 3, 5, 7–9, and 13 are by Nicholas Bayne.

Preface

No Western country – not even the largest – can assure its prosperity by its own efforts alone. The countries of Western Europe and North America, together with Japan, need to collaborate if their own policies are to succeed. That is the relevance of Benjamin Franklin's cautionary advice that appears on the title page of this book. Yet cooperation among these countries encounters serious obstacles, rooted in national sovereignty and democratic politics. The history of the summit meetings held annually since 1975 between the leaders of the seven largest industrial democracies, joined by the European Community, illustrates both the prospects and the problems of managing an interdependent world.

Both in authorship and in content, this book aims to bridge the gap that often separates the world of scholarship and the world of affairs. The authors first met in July 1982 through the good offices of Dr William Wallace of the Royal Institute of International Affairs. We soon discovered that we shared an addictive curiosity about Western summitry. By background and experience, we brought contrasting perspectives to bear on this topic. Nicholas Bayne is by nationality British, and by profession a diplomat, although he has had some prior experience in scholarly research. Robert D. Putnam is an American and an academic political scientist, although he has served briefly in government. Hoping that our differing points of view, one European and one American, one practical and one more theoretical, might provide a deeper, more rounded image of the summit process, rather like a stereoscopic picture, we decided to join forces.

In the course of our collaboration we have discovered, somewhat to our own surprise, remarkably few differences between us, either in interpretation or in assessment. Despite the vicissitudes of transatlantic co-authorship in the face of tight deadlines, we have worked together closely and harmoniously. Nevertheless, each of us is responsible only for those chapters appearing against his own name; neither is bound by what the other has written, particularly as regards the assessments and recommendations in our two concluding chapters.

In those two chapters the distinction between our separate, but complementary purposes becomes manifest. Putnam is particularly interested in the process of summitry and in how the history of summitry can be used to improve our understanding of contemporary international political economy. Chapter 12 constitutes a prologomenon to that broader theoretical exploration. Bayne is more concerned with the substantive issues that have been addressed by the summits and with how the experience of past summits can be used to improve the practice of summitry in the future. Chapter 13 presents a range of tentative suggestions.

Truth, Karl Deutsch has said, lies at the confluence of independent streams of evidence. We have relied on several different sources in compiling this narrative. First, we have consulted most of the relevant published reports, as well as some unpublished material made available to us. Particularly important in this regard were the extensive press files from all seven summit countries that have been collected by the diligent and helpful librarians at the Royal Institute of International Affairs. The volume of press coverage has made it impossible for us to cite separately all the items used, and we have foregone citation with respect to events that were widely reported in the media.

We have also relied heavily on a wide range of personal interviews – nearly 300 between us – with participants and close observers of summitry in Washington, Tokyo, Bonn, Paris, London, Rome, Ottawa, Brussels, New York, and Geneva. Included among these interviews were encounters with nearly a score of past and present heads of government and cabinet members; more than two dozen 'personal representatives', who have conducted summit preparations; half a dozen central bankers, and scores of senior diplomats, domestic civil servants, political advisors, members of parliament, businessmen, journalists, trade unionists, and officials of international organizations. We are very grateful indeed to all those who so generously agreed to talk with us about their experiences and perspectives.

Two important problems inherent in this methodology deserve mention. First is the question of anonymity. Discussions involving the head of government are among the most sensitive topics in any political system. Given the delicacy of many of the issues and events that we were probing, we found it necessary to assure anonymity to all our interlocutors. We recognise that this derogation from the normal rigour of historiography imposes a special burden on us. We have tried to sift with special care what we have been told. Where it has been possible without violating confidences, we have indicated in general terms the source of our evidence ('a senior German aide', 'a leading Japanese politician', and so on). Often, however, we have had simply to assert, as fact, events or intentions for which we are unable to reveal our evidence.

The second methodological problem is that of reliability. Our dilemma is precisely that faced by Abraham Lowenthal in his study of the 1965 US intervention in the Dominican Republic.

Collecting reliable data through interviews is admittedly a tricky art based on an uncertain process of triangulation guided by inference. Personal rivalries and reputations, political convenience, psychological vested interests, memory lapses, and discretion combine to color what one can learn from talking to those who help shape policy, and there are always others with whom one cannot talk at all.[1]

We would add that similar problems of uncertain reliability afflict the press accounts on which we have relied.

The multinational character of the phenomenon we are studying is both an advantage and a disadvantage from this point of view. On the one hand, for many crucial events and issues we have been able to speak with participants from a number of different countries (as well as a number of different agencies within each country). We have also been able to cross-check accounts that appeared in press reports from different capitals. Triangulation and cross-confirmation have been thereby facilitated.

On the other hand, as we have wanted to discuss the national, as well as the international, face of summitry, we have had to delve into the intricacies of politics and bureaucracy in seven different countries, as well as a number of international organizations. We do not delude ourselves that we have become instant experts on each of these arenas, although we have tried to confirm all essential conclusions against a variety of sources. We have made special efforts to be comprehensive in our review of the evidence in those instances (such as the account of the 1978 German decision to reflate the economy) where our conclusions differ from standard interpretations.

Reliability remains a matter of degree, and in the text we have indicated degrees of confidence in our assertions. Whenever we are uncertain about the reliability of a source, we have used some qualifying phrase, such as 'reportedly' or 'apparently'. When different sources sustain equally plausible alternative interpretations, or when we go beyond the evidence to suggest hypothetical explanations, we have tried to so indicate. In most cases, however, independent sources have led us in the same direction, and in that sense, we are reasonably confident in the reliability of our broad conclusions.

Robert D. Putnam adds: for support for the research reported here, I am grateful to the Center for International Affairs, Harvard University; the Deutsche Gesellschaft für Auswärtige Politik; the Japan Foundation; and especially the Social Science Research Council. John Higginbotham, Karl Kaiser, Jean-François Verstrynge, and William Wallace were superb hosts and counsellors in Ottawa, Bonn, Brussels, and London, respectively. Hisashi Owada first stimulated my scholarly interest in Japan's relations with the West and then helped to make it possible to pursue that interest. Antonio Armellini, Christopher

Audland, Antonio Badini, Richard Cooper, Guido Goldman, Sir Derek Mitchell, and Wolfgang Wessels were very helpful to me, both in assisting with arrangements for my field work and in enlightening me about summitry. My fundamental perspectives on theories of international affairs have been formed in discussions with Robert Axelrod, Robert O. Keohane, and members of the Harvard seminar on international political economy. In addition, among those who offered helpful comments on draft chapters were Georges de Ménil, Randall Henning, Henry Nau, and Horst Schulmann. For research assistance and many other kindnesses, I am grateful to Nicola Ellis, John Goodman, Janet Helson, Lisa Lightman, Jonathan Putnam, Lara Putnam, Claudia Rader, and Masako Yasuda.

Nicholas Bayne adds: I would like to thank the Foreign and Commonwealth Office most sincerely for enabling me to spend a year at Chatham House conducting this research, to visit the countries concerned, and to publish the results in this form. I am deeply indebted to Chatham House for the warm welcome and the support I have received during my stay; to David Watt, William Wallace, Geoffrey Goodwin, Robert Belgrave, and Pauline Wickham for their encouragement and for reading draft chapters; and to Jean Pell for her impeccable typing. I also recall with gratitude all the help and hospitality given to me by my colleagues in Bonn, Brussels, Geneva, New York, Ottawa, Paris, and Washington.

We are both grateful to Sir Michael Palliser and I. M. Destler for their careful reading of the entire manuscript; to Judith Ravenscroft, our forbearing copy-editor; and to our colleagues in the Workshop on Summitry and European Policy-making at the European Institute of Public Administration, Maastricht, the Netherlands, and particularly to the director of that workshop, Cesare Merlini. We are pleased to acknowledge the permission of the EIPA to use here material that appeared in Putnam's chapter, entitled 'The Western Economic Summits: A Political Interpretation', in *Western Summits and Europe: Rivalry, Cooperation, and Partnership*, edited by Cesare Merlini (London: Croom Helm, 1984).

Naturally, none of the individuals or institutions listed above is responsible for errors of fact or interpretation that remain. The opinions expressed in this book are entirely our own. They should not be taken as reflecting any official views.

1 Abraham F. Lowenthal, *The Dominican Intervention* (Cambridge, Mass.: Harvard University Press, 1972), pp. vi–vii.

1 Introduction

For nearly a decade the leaders of the seven major industrial countries – the United States, Japan, West Germany, France, the United Kingdom, Italy, and Canada – together with representatives of the European Community, have met annually to discuss international economic and political issues. Regular summitry of this sort is virtually unprecedented in modern diplomacy. Proponents see the Western summits as providing collective leadership that is vital in a turbulent world. On the other hand, critics dismiss summitry as, at best, irrelevant. Some echo an even harsher criticism by Sir Harold Nicolson of high-level contacts in an earlier era: 'Nothing could be more fatal than the habit (the at present fatal and pernicious habit) of personal contact between the statesmen of the world.'[1]

This book analyses the history of these seven-power summits. We aim to answer several broad questions: Why has summitry emerged and persisted? How has the summit process evolved over time? What economic and political issues have been addressed? How has summitry fitted into the wider framework, comprising both domestic affairs and international relations? What have been the consequences of summitry, its successes and failures? How might it be improved? We begin with the first of these questions.

The institutionalization of summitry in the 1970s was encouraged by three structural features of contemporary international relations:
(1) the increasing entanglement of foreign and domestic politics that flows from economic interdependence;
(2) the waning of the US hegemony that had undergirded the long period of postwar prosperity; and
(3) the bureaucratization of international relations, a trend that some political leaders found particularly frustrating. Each of these factors deserves some explication.

Sovereignty versus interdependence
Economic interdependence among the industrial democracies has grown steadily and substantially over the past 30 years. International trade has accounted for a rising share of each national economy. Foreign direct investment is up. International capital mobility has accelerated. These developments have contributed to economic efficiency and prosperity, but they have also complicated economic

management. Everywhere, growing interdependence has gradually, but ineluctably dissolved the barriers between foreign and domestic economics and hence between foreign and domestic politics. Already at the beginning of the 1970s Richard N. Cooper had pointed out that 'increased economic interdependence, by joining national markets, erodes the effectiveness of [national economic] policies and hence threatens national autonomy in the determination and pursuit of economic objectives'.[2]

Early theorists viewed economic interdependence as a benign force that would induce international political integration. They believed that international trade and investment would create a web of mutual interests and mutual constraints, leading ultimately towards a 'world without borders'.[3] However, this view underestimated both the durability and the legitimacy of national decision-making. Neither elites nor their electorates are eager to relinquish national sovereignty. From this piont of view, interdependence conflicts with democratic responsiveness.[4]

How can the facts of international interdependence and national, popular sovereignty be reconciled? This basic dilemma confronts both students and practitioners of contemporary international affairs. Many have proposed to resolve the dilemma through international economic policy coordination. 'The growing interdependence of the world economy creates pressures for common policies, and hence for procedures whereby countries discuss and coordinate actions that hitherto were regarded as being of domestic concern exclusively.'[5]

Economists of various theoretical persuasions disagree about just what should be coordinated and how, but most believe that some kind of international coordination of policies is beneficial, if not necessary, for the achievement of national goals.[6] (Note that policy coordination does not necessarily mean the adoption of identical or even similar policies, but rather the adoption of mutually reinforcing policies or at least the avoidance of mutually inconsistent policies.) A decade ago, many expected that flexible exchange rates would liberate national policies from this constraint. However, it has become clear, both in theory and in practice, that international capital mobility frustrates that expectation. In an interdependent world, no exchange rate regime can obviate the need for attention to the policies of other countries when setting one's own.

On the other hand, the obstacles to successful international policy coordination are multiple. They include:

differences in national objectives (some countries give higher priority to price stability, for instance, or to social equality, than others);

differences in national economic structure (some countries are more trade-dependent, for instance, or more inflation-prone, than others);

differences in economic theory (some decision-makers may be more convinced Keynesians, for instance, or more committed monetarists, than others);

differences in national institutions (some countries have weaker trade unions, for instance, or a stronger legislature, than others); and

differences in national political climate (for example, the party pendulums in different countries swing with different amplitudes and periods).

Underlying these difficulties is the fundamental fact that governments and leaders are held responsible by national and subnational constituencies for economic circumstances that are conditioned by international factors. Interdependence has created an ever sharper dilemma for democratically elected politicians. The fate of a congressman from Youngstown depends on decisions taken in Brussels or Tokyo. The *projet* of a French socialist president is constrained by decisions of US monetary authorities. The tradeoff for price stability in Hamburg may be unemployment in Harlem.

In such predicaments governments and politicians must choose some mix of two broad strategies, one nationalist, one internationalist. They may try to regain control over their own destiny, by re-erecting protectionist barriers to international commerce and finance, risking the broader benefits that derive from integrated markets. Or they may seek instead to cooperate with their counterparts abroad in an effort to manage politically the mutual interference that is the price of interdependence. As Miriam Camps noted a decade ago,

the advanced, market-economy countries are reaching the point where they face a basic choice: either to move forward to new far-reaching forms of collective management of problems they can no longer handle separately or to put the brakes on their growing interdependence and, by more or less arbitrary measures, to bring problems once more within the span of national control.[7]

In short, economic interdependence is not an unalterable fact of life, immune from politics. Indeed, a precondition for the maintenance of a relatively open world economy is some degree of international coordination of policies once considered purely domestic. 'International policy coordination' sounds technically neat and politically antiseptic. But to suggest, as some analysts have, that only 'political will' is needed for governments to coordinate their policies internationally is disconcertingly like Molière's suggestion that all that is needed to cure sleeplessness is a 'dormitive potion'. The real question is this: Under what circumstances and through what mechanisms is the requisite 'political will' likely to emerge?

Economists and political scientists have recently begun to apply game theoretic concepts to the analysis of the international economy.[8] From a political point of view, international economic coordination can usefully be conceived as a two-level game. At the national level, domestic groups seek to maximize their interests by pressuring the government to adopt favourable policies, and politicians seek power by constructing coalitions among those groups. At the international level, national governments seek to maximize their own freedom to satisfy domestic pressures, while minimizing the adverse consequences of foreign developments. (Governments may also pursue certain 'state' interests, such as prestige or security, that are only indirectly related to pressure from their domestic constituencies.)

These two games are played simultaneously, so that national policies are in some sense the result of both the domestic and the international parellelograms of forces. Neither of the two games can be ignored by policy-makers, so long as their countries remain interdependent, yet sovereign democracies. A national political leader appears at both game boards. Across the international table sit his foreign counterparts, and at his elbows sit diplomats and other international advisors. Around the domestic table behind him sit party and parliamentary figures, spokesmen for the great domestic ministries, representatives of key domestic interest groups, and the leader's own political advisors. Domestic interest groups may be 'players' not because of their direct lobbying, but because of their anticipated reactions to possible moves, as interpreted by their bureaucratic patrons or by the leader's political counsellors. The absence of overt party or interest group involvement in international economic coordination by no means proves that the interests and preferences of those groups are irrelevant to the process.

The special complexity of this two-level game is that moves that are rational for a player at one board (such as raising energy prices or limiting automobile imports) may be quite irrational for that same player at the other board. Nevertheless, there are powerful incentives for consistency between the two games. Players (and kibitzers) will tolerate some differences in rhetoric between the two games – which is why each summiteer gives his own news conference after the summit – but in the end, either energy prices rise or they don't, either automobile imports fall or they don't. Moreover, rhetoric intended for one set of players may upset bargains struck at the other table; as we shall see, this is essentially what happened in the aftermath of the Versailles summit of 1982, causing the basic bargain on monetary issues and East–West trade to come unstuck.

It is natural to think that the conflicts in this process pit domestic interests against international pressures. For instance, most Americans (and most Japanese) want their national quota for petroleum imports to be as high as possible. Both steel workers and steel management in Pittsburgh (or Lille) urge their government to defend 'American' (or 'French') interests against foreign competition. On the other hand, economic interdependence and domestic diversity can sometimes produce powerful interests within each country that point in the same direction as certain international pressures. For example, American steel users and foreign steel exporters share an interest in low US import barriers. German trade unions might welcome foreign pressure on the German Government to carry out a more expansive fiscal policy, and Italian bankers might welcome international demands for a more austere Italian monetary policy. Thus, at least in principle, transnational alliances, tacit or explicit, might link foreign and domestic pressures. In fact, we shall discover some striking examples of this phenomenon in our review of Western summitry.

The political complexities for the players in this two-level game are staggering, quite apart from the technical economic complexities. Any key player at the international table who is dissatisfied with the outcome may upset the game board. Conversely, any national leader who fails to satisfy an adequate number of his fellow players at the domestic table risks being evicted from his seat. For example, the move by Canadian Prime Minister Joe Clark in 1979 to raise Canadian oil prices pleased his foreign counterparts, but contributed to his fall from power. Moreover, each national leader already has made a substantial investment in building a particular coalition at the domestic board, and he will be loath to try to construct a different coalition simply to sustain an alternative policy mix that might be more acceptable internationally. For example, as we shall see, international complaints about US interest rates did not cause President Ronald Reagan to alter his policies, despite domestic pressure in the same direction.

Economic adversity further complicates the game, by reducing the winnings available for side payments to disaffected participants. Even in theory there is no guarantee that any solution exists that will simultaneously satisfy the needs of the key players, and if such a solution exists in principle, the uncertainties of practical politics – the counterpart of Clausewitz's 'fog of battle' – may prevent the players from reaching it.

Western summitry, by bringing together those individuals who *par excellence* link the domestic and international games, represents an ambitious effort to resolve the sovereignty–interdependence dilemma. However, the complications of this two-level game are considerably greater than is characteristic of either 'normal' domestic politics or 'normal' international politics. Consequently, we should not be surprised to discover that summiteers have found the task difficult. We should expect agreements about international policy coordination to be hard to achieve and hard to make stick, usually imprecise and often 'lowest common denominator' in nature, and frequently suboptimal in terms of economic efficiency. As Keohane and Nye note,

Many of the most serious policy problems of complex interdependence result directly from this blurring of the distinction between domestic and international politics. Policy conceived as if the world consisted of billiard-ball states guided by philosopher-kings is not very useful. For international regimes to govern situations of complex interdependence successfully they must be congruent with the interests of powerfully placed domestic groups within states, as well as with the structure of power among states.[9]

Hegemony versus collective management

Even if all participants in the international economy shared identical goals and were free from domestic constraints, game theory reminds us, obstacles to successful coordination would remain. No unseen hand assures that the free play of peaceful competition will lead to optimal outcomes. To illustrate this point, Richard Cooper has used the metaphor of a crowd straining for a glimpse of a passing parade. Without shared rules, each individual rises on his toes, but none gets a better view, and all are uncomfortable.[10] International affairs are replete with so-called 'prisoner's dilemma' problems, in which every participant would be better off if collective action were taken, but in which each, individually, has a powerful incentive to defect from the collective action and become a 'free rider'.[11] In large assemblages, without mandatory coordination, public goods (such as the benefits of international economic cooperation) will tend to be undersupplied, since no individual wants to bear the full cost of providing a good that others could enjoy free of charge.[12]

One way out of this dilemma, as Hobbes explained, is for a single ruler to impose order in the interests of all. Translated into the lexicon of contemporary international relations, this approach is known as the theory of hegemonic stability. It is hardly an accident, defenders of this thesis observe, that the two golden ages of the liberal international economic order, one in the late nineteenth century, the second in the mid-twentieth century, correspond to periods in which a single power dominated the world economy, Britain in the Victorian era, the United States after World War II. The time of economic troubles between these two ages, and particularly the Great Depression, is traced by these theorists precisely to the absence of any single power willing and able to provide this sort of stability. 'For the world economy to be stabilized, there has to be a stabilizer, *one* stabilizer.'[13]

Entrepreneurship of a sort is required for the creation of public goods, including international economic order.[14] The hegemonic power has an incentive to create and sustain international economic order, because it benefits from that order so substantially, perhaps even disproportionately. It has the capability to provide stability because its power and wealth enable it either to induce or to impose cooperative behaviour on the part of the lesser powers, overcoming their temptation to 'free-ride'. Some theorists stress the tendency for the hegemonic power to exploit its special position, while others emphasize the benefits of the stability it provides for the other participants in the system. Almost all agree that cooperation and joint management are more difficult when many states have approximately equal power.

For the first quarter-century after 1945, the United States played this kind of hegemonic role as custodian of the world economy. In the aftermath of World War II, it was the dominant world power, both economically and militarily. It was powerful enough to be able to impose a new economic order, and it was wealthy enough to be able to induce consent to that order by opening its markets on a non-reciprocal basis and by providing financial assistance for reconstruction. The United States was willing to play this leading role, as it had not between the wars, because the postwar generation of leaders believed that US isolationism had contributed mightily to the disasters of the 1930s, and because they feared the political consequences of Western economic disarray. The counterpart of US leadership was the willingness of the Europeans and Japanese to follow the leader. On most important issues, the United States made the rules, while the others made the best of it. On the basis of this broad consensus, the Bretton Woods system was established and flourished.

By the 1970s, however, the economic and political presuppositions of this order had been transformed. Europe and Japan had grown to rival US power in economic terms, if not in political terms. The relative decline of the United States, inevitable as the rest of the world recovered from the anomalous postwar situation, was accelerated by economic mismanagement and military misadventure. Europeans and Japanese were no longer so willing to accede to US dominance, and Americans themselves seemed less willing to assert world leadership. The hyperbolic mood of the times was captured by one book title: *America as an Ordinary Country*.[15]

These developments were epitomized in 1971–3 by the collapse of the Bretton Woods monetary order, followed almost immediately by the first oil shock and the worst downturn in economic activity since the 1930s. The collective clipper of the Western economies had suddenly entered stormy seas, the captain had disappeared, and the ship's mates scuttled around the helm in wary confusion. In place of the hegemonic stability that US predominance had assured for a quarter-century, a new system of collective leadership for the world economy would need to be jury-rigged. For a generation of leaders who had themselves come of age during the Great Depression, the risks of a return to an alluring, but ultimately catastrophic economic nationalism were vivid.

The alternative of new international institutions with real authority and supranational sovereignty was logically appealing, but politically unrealistic.[16] Collective management would be difficult, but for reasons that game theorists understood, the problems would be somewhat eased if responsibility for sustaining the world economic order were borne by a few large states.[17] The seven-power summits emerged in part to address this dilemma, and their history reveals the tensions, the strengths, and the limitations of collective leadership.

Political leaders versus bureaucratic institutions

If interdependence and collective leadership involved novel problems, the third factor underlying Western summitry was more familiar. Scepticism about bureaucrats and their works has long been widespread among democratic politicians.[18] During the long postwar boom, this tension had rarely been manifest in the field of international affairs. But when the intrusions of interdependence combined with the economic upheavals of the early 1970s, this institutional and professional détente was called into question. For a chief executive whose political fate hung on his electorate's economic well-being, international economics could no longer be considered 'low politics', left to bloodless diplomats, to cunning central bankers, to distant international organizations, or to the haphazards of the market.

Another factor was also important – the increasing role played by functionally fragmented international networks of specialists. Financial issues were the province of the 'money mafia' of finance ministry officials, trade issues were handled by trade specialists, and so on. Moreover, despite the interconnection of economics and national security, these two sets of problems were in most countries handled by separate bureaucracies, linked only at the top. As we shall see in chapter 2, it was natural that the particular men in power in key countries in the mid-1970s would turn to summitry as a means for reasserting their power and responsibility. Given the stakes, it was probably inevitable that chief executives themselves would confront the task of re-establishing political and economic equilibrium.

Summitry as a microcosm of international relations in the West

Western summitry is, in sum, a response to three fundamental needs: to reconcile international economics and domestic politics, to supplement and perhaps supplant hegemonic stability with collective management, and to restore political authority over bureaucratic fragmentation and irresponsibility. Studying summitry thus helps us understand how these tensions are changing the character of contemporary international relations.

In analysing summitry from the point of view of international political economy, we must keep in mind that the summits themselves are merely one moment in a continuous flow of domestic and international discussion and bargaining about these issues. A foreign policy aide to one European premier warns, 'You cannot understand the summits without taking account of all the other ongoing international meetings. When we set out to influence another government – and I presume the same is true of anyone trying to influence us – we say, "We'll start off at the OECD Ministerials in May, follow up at the summit, and then hit them again at the IMF in September." '

Similarly, virtually all the items under discussion at the summit – from interest rates to East–West relations and from oil supplies to overseas development assistance – are the subject of continuing debate within the domestic arena. Consultation with businessmen, bankers, unions, and other interest groups is rarely, if ever, an important part of the national preparations for the summit, because, as summiteers say privately, 'We already know what they think about these subjects; we're talking about them all the time anyway.'

The stratagems and ploys, the convergences and divergences, the decisions and non-decisions that are visible within the summit process itself cannot be interpreted in isolation from this wider context. Our chronicle of the summits, therefore, must include the background of ongoing international negotiations, the ups and downs of the international economy, the domestic political circumstances of the individual leaders. On the other hand, just as a cloud chamber filled with saturated water vapour allows physics students to detect charged particles whose passage all around us ordinarily goes unnoticed, so the summit process condenses features of international political economy that are otherwise easier to overlook.[19]

One common misunderstanding of summitry must be avoided. The popular press, encouraged by over-enthusiastic government press agents, sometimes has cast the summit as a kind of grand assizes of the Western world, a supranational forum in which decisions on the great problems facing the industrial democracies are collectively rendered by the world's leaders. This image evokes a unity of purpose and a decisiveness of collective action that is inappropriate for this or any other international forum. 'You can't expect spectacular decisions from a meeting like that', says one of the founding summiteers, 'It's naive to believe that that is possible.'

At the centre of summitry are the leaders themselves. Sitting around the table reminds them of their collective international responsibilities. But we must not forget that they are, above all, national politicians, whose most enduring preoccupations necessarily arise from domestic politics. One of the most distinguished summiteers points out frankly,

You don't go to the summit with the idea of 'making policy', or usually of reaching any great conclusions about world economic problems. Every nation goes there, first of all, to explain its own problems, and secondly, to see how far it can get others to help it with its own problems. I doubt if many of us go there saying, 'Here is the central problem of world economic strategy. What measures should we all take to improve it?' We are all convinced of the value of an international trading system, so there is some attempt to take the world view, but basically we are most concerned about our own domestic problems.

On the other hand, summits at their most effective have represented precisely the recognition by national leaders that they cannot solve their own problems without attending to world problems – in short, their recognition that they must play at both game tables, unless they wish to retreat to costly economic autarky.

The summit meetings themselves have usually represented the culmination of a preparatory process that by the beginning of the 1980s had become a year-round exercise. As we will recount in subsequent chapters, as the summits became increasingly institutionalised, much of the preliminary negotiation was delegated to a small group of special representatives who met with their colleagues from the other summit nations in three or four preparatory sessions, to clarify agendas and issues and to explore possible resolutions of outstanding disagreements. Only occasionally have basic agreements actually been hammered out at the summit itself. Thus, our subject is not merely summits, but the broader summit process.

Moreover, as we shall see, it is crucial to examine successive summits not just as individual, isolated encounters, but as a series of attempts over a period of several years to address similar sets of problems. The developments in a single meeting take on added significance when seen against the background of prior sessions and subsequent developments.

These considerations have informed the organisation of this book. We seek both to recount a historical tale and to analyse its lessons. Narrative chapters are thus interspersed with analytic chapters that discuss the changing agenda and process of summitry. The successive summits are grouped in a way that corresponds to turning points in terms of both politics and policy, as well as to shifts in the agenda of economic ills. (For a statistical overview of the changing economic fortunes of the seven countries during the period covered by this book, readers may find it helpful to consult the Appendix.) We conclude by pulling together the implications of our story, both for refining our theories of international politics and for improving the practice of summitry in the years ahead.

2   The Origins of the Summits

In July 1975 thirty-five heads of state and government gathered in Helsinki to sign the Final Act of the Conference on Security and Cooperation in Europe. It was the zenith of détente. Both East and West could claim satisfaction with the results of the conference. These results could be added to the harvest of other agreements concluded over the previous five years on the same principle of reciprocal advantage. Although the military threat remained, it looked as if a satisfactory method had been found for conducting East–West political relations.

The leaders of the four Western powers met for lunch on 31 July 1975 at the British Embassy in Helsinki, together with their foreign ministers. Those present were President Gerald Ford and Dr Henry Kissinger; President Valéry Giscard d'Estaing and M. Jean Sauvagnargues; Chancellor Helmut Schmidt and Herr Hans-Dietrich Genscher; Mr Harold Wilson and Mr James Callaghan. Ostensibly this was a traditional meeting of the Four to discuss Berlin and German questions. But in fact the central item for discussion was the proposal that these four countries, together with Japan, should hold a summit meeting later that year to address economic and monetary problems. Though détente might be going well, the economic situation in the West was dangerous, a source of discord among the leading industrial countries and a threat to their political cohesion. These matters, no less than the East–West relations which had brought the leaders to Helsinki, demanded treatment at the highest level.

Economic problems of the 1970s

However they might have appeared at the time, the 1960s looked like a golden age from the vantage point of 1975. The economies of the OECD countries had grown on average by 5.5 per cent a year and international trade by half as much again, while inflation had been around only 4 per cent. The people of those countries had become accustomed to the steadily rising living standards, which derived in large part from the openness of the economic system, and expected their governments to provide them indefinitely. There had been strains in the system during the 1960s, especially over exchange rates, and errors in economic management, such as the inflationary financing of the Vietnam war. But the main impact of these tensions was not felt until after the end of the decade. The established bodies of international cooperation, such as the OECD, the IMF, and the GATT, had functioned steadily.[1] They had met only rarely at ministerial level in the 1950s and 1960s and never needed to involve heads of government. The more ambitious attempts of the European Economic Community to integrate domestic and external policies had brought ministers of the Six together regularly. But the European heads of government did not hold a substantive meeting until the Hague summit in the last days of 1969.

The 1970s opened with four events which, with cumulative effect, profoundly shook the system. These were, in chronological order: the collapse of the Bretton Woods monetary system; the first enlargement of the European Community; the oil crisis of 1973–4; and the ensuing economic recession.

The dollar ceased to be convertible into gold in August 1971; the European currencies floated against the dollar from March 1973. The rise of the European and Japanese economies in relation to the United States brought the Americans to demand the same freedom to adjust their exchange rate and to manage an autonomous monetary policy that other countries had. But the reform of the system set in hand late in 1971 was thrown off course by the first oil crisis. The rise in oil prices created such huge swings in external surpluses and deficits that a return to fixed, if adjustable, parities, which monetary authorities would defend in the market, was no longer plausible. Much looser arrangements, depending less on predictable rules and more on national discretion, were considered. But it proved hard to rediscover the interlocking balance of interests which had sustained the Bretton Woods structure and the negotiations dragged on.

With the entry of the United Kingdom, Denmark, and Ireland, in January 1973, the enlarged European Community now embraced all the leading West European powers. Its collective gross national product (GNP) was approaching that of the United States and its involvement in world trade was much greater. Here was potentially both a strong partner and a strong rival for the United States. Initial US complaints of trade discrimination were successfully channelled through the GATT and led, in due course, to the launching of the Multilateral Trade Negotiations (MTNs) at Tokyo in September 1973. But the definition of relations between the United States and the enlarged Community in a wider context proved far more difficult.

The Community had yet to discover how to operate as a unit. It tended, under French influence, to contrast its position with that of the United States as the means of asserting its own distinct identity. Dr Kissinger's idea for a 'Year of Europe' in 1973, intended to articulate the partnership between the United States and the Community, therefore soon ran into trouble. None of the principal leaders could generate the necessary effort of imagination or carry conviction. President Nixon was crippled by Watergate, President Pompidou was dying, Chancellor Brandt and Mr Heath both faced severe problems at home; within a year all four would have left office prematurely. With the disputes over the US response to the Middle East war in October, the Year of Europe ended in frustration and misunderstanding.[2]

After the Middle East war the OPEC countries launched the 'oil weapon': a temporary embargo on supplies and a surge in oil prices. Between October 1973 and January 1974, oil prices increased four-fold, from $3 to nearly $12 per barrel. This dislocated the economic policies of all the oil-consuming countries and led to sharp dispute about the correct response. The United States had its own substantial oil production which provided about two-thirds of its needs. The Americans advocated firm resistance to the OPEC cartel and collective action by OECD countries to conserve energy, develop new resources, and deal with emergencies. But the European countries and Japan were far more dependent on oil imports. France, in particular, argued against confrontation with OPEC and in favour of seeking an accommodation. The other Europeans leaned first one way and then the other. But although France opposed the United States directly at the Washington energy conference in February 1974, the Americans successfully carried through their initiative to set up the International Energy Agency (IEA). Late in 1974, after President Giscard had succeeded President Pompidou, France agreed that the European Community could cooperate with the IEA; and the Americans acquiesced in the French proposal for a conference to bring together a selection of OPEC, OECD, and developing countries to discuss energy and related topics. This eased the dispute considerably, though differences of approach persisted and France remained outside the IEA.[3]

The surge in oil prices caught the OECD economies in a dangerously exposed position. There had been a simultaneous boom in 1973, called in Britain 'the dash for growth'. Rising commodity prices, pressures on industrial capacity, and rapid expansion of the money supply had all stoked up the pressures for inflation. When the cost of oil suddenly increased four-fold, all recognised that this would both inflate prices further and depress activity in the oil-consuming countries. The OECD economies went into a steep recession during 1974, while average inflation reached 13.5 per cent, three times the normal level for the previous decade. Unemployment in the OECD area leapt up to reach 15 million by 1975, against 9 million two years before.

The leading Western governments were again divided on how best to respond. Germany, for example, had acted early in 1973 to restrain demand. It survived the first oil crisis in better shape than its neighbours. The German current account remained in surplus and inflation never rose above 7 per cent, while in nearly all other OECD countries it went into double figures. The United Kingdom, on the other hand, tried at first to sustain activity after the oil shock. But it ended with a larger external deficit, higher prices, and a deeper recession than the others.[4]

By mid-1975, therefore, the economic system which had run so well in the 1950s and 1960s was severely shaken. The Western economies were sinking into recession, in a disorderly fashion, apparently unable to adapt to the external threat posed by OPEC. The international exchange rate system set up after the war had collapsed and even modest alternative arrangements were in dispute. The enlargement of the European Community, which should have reinforced the Atlantic partnership, had instead increased frustration and bad feeling. The traditional organs of international cooperation – the IMF, the OECD, and the GATT – were all active and meeting far more often at ministerial level than in the past. They were reinforced by the newly created IEA. Even so, they were no longer able to reconcile the differences among the leading Western powers or to give them a sense of common purpose. In these conditions, many recalled the depression of the 1930s and feared a similar relapse into protectionist, inward-looking policies.[5]

The genesis of the summits

The events of the early 1970s had revealed all too clearly the severe difficulties of 'managing interdependence' in adverse conditions. The links between the industrial countries no longer suggested the image of climbers moving upwards securely roped together, but rather of prisoners shackled to one another deprived of their freedom of action. Furthermore, although there had been a visible shift in relative economic strength among the United States, Europe, and Japan, the United States still remained the single most powerful actor, and it proved hard for Europe to mobilise its new-found unity. These problems went beyond the competence of officials and even of departmental ministers; they seemed to call for the direct involvement of heads of government themselves. At this moment there appeared a team of fresh leaders in the principal countries, ready to move in new directions; in particular President Giscard, Chancellor Schmidt, and President Ford, all taking office in mid-1974.

The idea of a multilateral summit meeting to consider international economic issues had already been raised several times in the early 1970s, always from the US side, but without results. Dr Kissinger had thought of such a meeting in 1971 to deal with the international monetary crisis. But President Pompidou was clearly opposed to it and the Americans did not pursue it, preferring to work through bilateral meetings at summit level. In 1973, a meeting between President Nixon and the leaders of the European Community was considered as part of Dr Kissinger's Year of Europe, together with a NATO summit. The NATO meeting was eventually held in June 1974, but the summit with the Community was sidetracked at an early stage, again largely because of French resistance.[6] Meanwhile, the initiators of the non-governmental Trilateral Commission among the United States, Europe, and Japan also came out early in favour of multilateral summit meetings which, in their view, must also include Japan. Henry Owen wrote in 1973: 'The President might propose a meeting of the heads of government of Japan, the European Community countries and the United States to discuss common economic concerns.'[7]

In 1974, with President Nixon immobilised by Watergate, the initiative passed to the Europeans. Right from the time when he took office, President Giscard favoured the idea of a strictly limited meeting of heads of government to consider economic and especially monetary problems. He later explained his thinking to James Reston of the *New York Times*:

The capitalist countries seemed absolutely unable to manage their economic and monetary situations . . . but 'we never have a serious conversation among the great capitalist leaders to say what do we do now.' . . . The question had to be discussed between people having major responsibilities like the United States – a matter of conversation between a very few people and almost on a private level.[8]

President Giscard prepared the ground with care. He first broached the suggestion with President Ford and Dr Kissinger at the bilateral summit at Martinique in December 1974 and found a favourable response. A passage in the Martinique communiqué has a prophetic ring:

The two Presidents agreed that the governments of the United States and of the European Community . . . must adopt consistent economic policies in order to be effective in avoiding unemployment while fighting inflation. . . . And they decided to take the initiative in calling additional intergovernmental meetings should they prove necessary for the achievement of the desired consistency of basic economic policies among industrial nations.[9]

Chancellor Schmidt also believed that Western heads of government should involve themselves with international economic problems, though his approach was rather different. He considered that the leaders needed some alternative advice to that provided by their officials. He proposed the creation of a group of five distinguished persons, each one of whom should be personally nominated by a Western head of government and should not be holding public office at the time, even though they might have done so in the past. A group was formed in line with his initiative and began to meet to consider ways of dealing with the oil crisis and its consequences. Herr Schmidt's own representative was Dr Wilfried Guth of the Deutsche Bank. The others were Mr George Shultz, recently Secretary of the US Treasury; Professor Raymond Barre, lately French Vice-President of the European Commission; Sir Eric Roll, former Permanent Secretary of the British Department of Economic Affairs; and Mr Hideo Suzuki, who had just left the Japanese Finance Ministry to become an investment banker. This group met during late 1974 and the first half of 1975, in Germany, France, and the United States, and prepared reports for its patrons.

As so often, President Giscard and Chancellor Schmidt pooled their ideas. They promoted the summit together, though with President Giscard usually in the lead. But Herr Schmidt contributed the thought that Japan must certainly be present. President Giscard had originally preferred a four-power summit which could, if necessary, tackle political as well as economic issues.

By the summer of 1975 President Giscard judged that the time was ripe to float his ideas publicly. A further contact with Dr Kissinger, who breakfasted at the Elysée on 27 May 1975, still found the Americans positive.[10] In June he talked to James Reston; and in early July he gave an interview with the Hearst Press on the same theme, which was widely reported. Here President Giscard focused especially on monetary problems: 'What the world calls a crisis of capitalism is in fact a monetary crisis.' He suggested an informal summit meeting in Paris in the autumn to discuss economic and monetary problems, involving France, the United States, the United Kingdom, Germany, Italy, and Japan.[11]

The scene was now set for the crucial four-power meeting due in Helsinki at the end of July 1975. M. Giscard and Herr Schmidt had extensive economic discussions on 25–26 July; and two days later Herr Schmidt received President Ford in Bonn on his way to the Helsinki conference. After their meeting President Ford told the press: 'The Chancellor and I agreed that it was vitally important for the economic policies of Germany and the European Community to be integrated with our own economic policies.' Herr Schmidt let it be known that he expected the four-power meeting on 31 July to be concerned with economic and monetary matters and that he had prepared a paper setting out his ideas which he gave to all the participants.[12]

The Germans believed that the Helsinki meeting had agreed in principle to hold a summit of the four leaders present, plus the Japanese Prime Minister, to consider ways of reviving the Western economies. They said so in public; but Dr Kissinger denied it. There was certainly agreement to set up a small group of personal representatives to consider the matter further – and this gave the idea the necessary momentum.[13] Each personal representative should be chosen by virtue of his direct link with the head of government, like the members of the group earlier created by Herr Schmidt. Two members of that group were chosen also to prepare for the summit: Mr Shultz by President Ford and M. Barre by President Giscard. But the other leaders favoured people who, though close to them, were also more involved in government business. So Chancellor Schmidt picked Herr Karl-Otto Pöhl, State Secretary at the Finance Ministry, and Mr Wilson named Sir John Hunt, Secretary of the Cabinet. Immediately after the Helsinki meeting the Japanese Prime Minister was approached, welcomed the chance to take part in such a summit, and named as his representative Mr Nobuhiko Ushiba, former Ambassador to Washington.[14]

Four of the countries concerned were keen on the summit. But the Americans hesitated and were divided among themselves. Dr Kissinger was strongly in favour. The summit offered the chance to revive many of the ideas of his Year of Europe. As he later wrote, 'The current global crisis is too grave to be left to financial experts. The political and moral impetus to restore hope to Western economies must come from the heads of state and their Foreign Ministers.'[15] But Mr William Simon at the Treasury feared that President Giscard would use the summit to press for a return to fixed exchange rates. On this, French and American positions remained far apart and were not reconciled at the IMF meetings in early September.[16]

In mid-September President Ford, still uncommitted, sent Mr Shultz to Bonn, London, and Paris to find out more about the European leaders' intentions. His visit demonstrated the effectiveness, on this occasion, of a personal representative with direct access to the head of government. After several bilateral sessions, the climax of the tour was an informal dinner between Giscard, Schmidt, and Shultz, who had all been finance ministers together the year before. Mr Shultz had consulted Washington meanwhile and was able to convey President Ford's approval of the summit.[17] With US agreement secure, President Giscard was able, shortly afterwards, to invite his colleagues formally to meet on 15–17 November 1975 at the Château of Rambouillet, 30 miles from Paris, together with the Italian Prime Minister, a late addition to the list.

The distinctive features of the summits

The first essential feature of the summit was that it should be small, select, and personal. It should be limited to countries which carried weight and influence. It should bring together those directly responsible for policy. They should be able to talk together frankly and without inhibitions. As Herr Schmidt is reported to have said: 'We want a private, informal meeting of those who really matter in the world.'

The model in this respect was the 'Library Group' of finance ministers, later to become the Group of Five. This group first met in the library of the White House in April 1973, on the margins of the international monetary negotiations. It began with four members – the United States, Germany, France, and the United Kingdom – and soon added Japan. Italy attended one or two later meetings, but never became a regular member. Only the ministers were present, with a single official in support, and sometimes central bank governors. The subject matter at first focused on issues of monetary reform. But it was soon extended to cover a much wider range of economic matters of common interest – national policies as well as international issues.[18]

The Group of Five was both compact and influential. Its component countries made up over 75 per cent of the total GNP of the OECD and about 45 per cent of total quotas in the IMF. Within such a small group it was possible to work out finely balanced positions, which could form the basis for decisions in wider IMF bodies such as the Committee of Twenty and the Interim Committee.

The participants valued the group as a means of steering the monetary negotiations. But they prized it even more as an opportunity for frank, unfettered discussion of their major problems and preoccupations. Their meetings were very discreet and most of the proceedings were kept secret. They were not bound to a strict agenda or to papers prepared by officials. The participants could therefore express themselves with great freedom and build up strong mutual trust. They often found more common ground and understanding among their fellow finance ministers than among their own colleagues from other ministries back home. All this was a welcome change from more formal international discussions, even in bodies as limited as the Committee of Twenty or as homogeneous as the OECD. In those larger, more formal bodies national positions were set forth in prepared speeches. Any consensus tended to become vague and ambiguous in the effort to accommodate everybody.

Giscard, Schmidt, and Shultz were all original members of the Library Group. When Giscard became President of France and Schmidt became German Chancellor, they sought to recreate, at the highest level, the same sort of direct, informal, but highly influential exchanges. The summit was therefore, above all, a personal initiative by the leaders themselves, not prompted by others. President Giscard floated the idea without taking his officials into his confidence. Chancellor Schmidt backed it by circulating his own paper to the other participants. It was set up at the Helsinki meeting, which no officials attended, and prepared by personal representatives whose direct links with the leaders were more important than their place in the official hierarchy.

Giscard, Schmidt, and Kissinger in particular believed that the political qualities of ministers were superior to the technical attributes of officials. In their view officials, with their concern for precision and attention to detail, moved too slowly and were too easily discouraged, leading, in President Giscard's words, to 'built-in bureaucratic confrontations'. On the other hand, they considered that ministers – and above all, heads of government – owed their position to gifts of leadership, vision, and imagination, which could enable them to cut the Gordian knot of technical problems. The summits therefore had a strong anti-bureaucratic bias from the start; and Mr Shultz even asserted that '*all* of the national bureaucracies were opposed to holding a summit meeting'.[19]

This leads to the second essential feature in the launching of the summits: the strong conviction of the summit founders that international economic issues required treatment by heads of government, who could make an essential contribution beyond the capacities of other ministers, of finance or of foreign affairs. Briefly stated, the leaders would introduce a high-level political dimension; this can be broken down into several components, reflecting the analysis set forth in chapter 1.

First and simplest, the heads of government could integrate policies normally treated separately by departmental ministers. The competence of foreign, finance, and other ministers was limited; that of heads of government was all-embracing. The summit leaders were capable of integrating, for example, macroeconomic strategy, energy policy, and international trade issues. They could balance conflicting pressures and articulate 'packages' of ideas or actions which covered several different fields.

Second and more fundamental, the heads of government were best placed to reconcile the demands of foreign policy and domestic policy, having equal responsibility for both. On the one hand, their position at the head of democratically elected governments made them more strongly aware even than their ministerial colleagues of the obligation to devise and apply policies that commanded the support of the population. (This was especially the case in the United States and France, where the President was elected but his ministers were not; but even in the parliamentary democracies popular pressure often focused on the head of government.) On the other hand, they led countries each of which formed a pillar of the open economic system. They could recognise the responsibility to promote the system rather than weaken it and to adopt policies compatible with the actions of others; if they did not, they could both damage their neighbours and frustrate their own objectives. It was therefore the special role of presidents and prime ministers to fit together these elements and to look for policies in which domestic and international considerations could reinforce each other rather than conflict.

Third, the summit leaders carried an authority which their other ministers did not have. This authority might in practice be less than it appears. The leaders were circumscribed, for example, by the need to satisfy their legislatures (notably in the United States), other parties in a coalition (as in Germany), or colleagues within the Cabinet (as in the United Kingdom). But such constraints only partly diminished the impression of power and ability to get things done which was conveyed by a summit meeting – especially one which brought together the leaders of the seven largest industrial democracies. Summits could therefore command a degree of attention which other international meetings did not attain. Summit pronouncements would be studied with greater care and would remain texts for reference, while IMF or OECD communiqués, which covered the same ground, might soon be forgotten.

With the authority of heads of government went an awareness of unique responsibility. As Herr Schmidt put it: 'Heads of government are often solitary people, because they cannot leave to others those decisions which they must take themselves and answer for themselves.'[20] The only opportunity to share this responsibility was with other leaders bearing similar burdens. The summits would therefore serve not only to ease the loneliness of power but also to build up a sense of collective responsibility.

There were other consequences, however, which flowed from raising the level of informal economic discussions from finance ministers to heads of government.

The five finance ministers could preserve a high level of discretion, if with difficulty. They would normally come together on the margins of wider gatherings, which tended to distract attention, and would try to keep any other meetings secret. But there could be no question of heads of state and government meeting out of the public eye. When the leaders came together, this would arouse expectations of substantial achievements. Public opinion would look for progress where others had failed, since no higher level remained to which intractable problems could be referred. The summit participants would have to decide how far to try to damp down these expectations; how best to satisfy those that persisted; and what use to make of their meeting to educate public opinion. At the same time, they had to balance the value of face-to-face discussion of sensitive issues against the risk of leaks to the assembled press.

The Group of Five could also meet several times a year and its members were in periodic contact at wider meetings of the IMF and OECD. But the summits would meet only once a year, for 48 hours.

This would be the only occasion which brought together the leaders of the United States, Japan, Canada, and the major West European countries. The subject matter of the summits also went much wider than that of the Group of Five. In such a short time it would not be possible for the leaders, on their own, to conclude precise agreements and detailed measures. They would risk misunderstandings about what exactly was agreed in their limited personal exchanges. The danger of misunderstanding increased when the leaders did not share a common language; President Giscard and Chancellor Schmidt might be fluent in English but the Japanese and Italians often were not.

Before Rambouillet most of the participants stated that they did not intend to take decisions. They would instead work for broad consensus and for compatible approaches to economic problems, to be taken further in other, more formal bodies. This approach recognised the constraints of a short meeting. It also served to damp down undue expectations and to reassure those not invited, especially in the European Community. But right from the start – despite what was said in public – the summits moved into the ill-defined zone between consensus and general principles on the one side and precise, formal decisions on the other. From Rambouillet onwards the leaders joined together in statements of intent. They entered into commitments, either singly or collectively, which, though not legally binding, had strong political and moral force. Finally, some of the results of the summits, such as the monetary understanding achieved at Rambouillet, must be regarded as decisions. In general, the Americans tended to encourage this progression towards greater precision and formal decisions while the Europeans often tried to stem it. National differences soon became visible on other aspects as well.

Different national attitudes

President Giscard was the undisputed initiator of the summits. The reasons for this lay not only in his personal style and experience but also in French political structure and traditions. The institutions of the Fifth Republic in France have produced a concentration of power in the hands of the President which is not matched in any other West European country. The President of France is in office for seven years at a time. He does not have to justify himself to Parliament. He maintains his own personal staff which can work independently of the official apparatus. He can take policy decisions of wide effect without necessarily consulting his ministers in advance.

This wide personal authority made it natural for French presidents to favour summit meetings. General de Gaulle had proposed a 'directorate' of leaders in 1958. President Pompidou had initiated the first series of European summits, at the Hague, Paris, and Copenhagen in

1969–73. In the same way President Giscard's authority at home led
him to think in terms of the collective authority of the Western heads of
government and their joint responsibility for making the international
economic system work. 'We have seen a severe shock to the Western
economy. The striking thing is that, in the face of such a shock,
unknown since the war, there has been no joint consideration by those
responsible for the major Western economies. What France suggests at
Rambouillet is that the leaders there take to heart their economic and
political responsibilities and have an exchange of views on possible lines
of action.'

The purpose of this exchange, in President Giscard's view, would be
to establish what each leader had in his own mind, as opposed to
national positions conveyed through official spokesmen. 'In Rambouillet the real objective of the gathering was to engage in a direct
man-to-man discussion to try to know what each of our personal
convictions, aims and objectives really were.' If this process led to a
meeting of minds, the leaders could instruct that further work be done
by others, in confidence of success, and in this way the summit would
yield results. If not, there was no point in going further.

Both timing and participation should be governed by need. President
Giscard did not envisage a regular annual series. 'To maintain the
usefulness of the summit process and to protect it from bureaucratic
invasion, we decided . . . to let the next inviting country suggest a
meeting when the economic situation made it useful.' The participants
should be limited to 'people having major responsibilities' and President Giscard tried, more than any other leader, to keep the numbers
down. He admitted Italy with reluctance, turned Canada away from
Rambouillet, and strongly resisted the European Community.

As to the subject matter for the summit, his central interest was in
international monetary issues. He was ready to present the Rambouillet
meeting as intended to promote economic recovery, since this would
more easily gain support and allay US fears. But this did not change his
conviction, to which he always remained faithful, that greater monetary
stability was the key to durable recovery and more buoyant trade. He
preferred the summits to concentrate on a few salient topics and tried to
arrange for this in advance; especially exchange rates at Rambouillet
and energy at Tokyo in 1979.

The economic summit was only one of President Giscard's new
initiatives since taking office. He had already caused the intermittent,
prestigious summits of the European Community to be converted into
the European Council, meeting three times a year for less formal
discussions at the highest level. He had launched the Conference for
International Economic Cooperation (CIEC) to bring together industrial countries, developing countries, and oil producers. The Western

economic summits completed the pattern. The fact that President Pompidou had resisted similar proposals did not much concern him, as he owed few political debts to his predecessors. Each of his initiatives, however, was neatly differentiated from the other. The European Council was an instrument of management, meeting regularly to provide continuity. The CIEC was a conference of finite duration, intended to lead to precise measures. The economic summit was seen as an occasional meeting, for informal exchanges but not intended to produce machinery or to take formal decisions.[21]

Chancellor Schmidt did not share President Giscard's supreme authority and there was nothing in recent German tradition that pointed towards summits. Herr Schmidt led a coalition government and had often to appear before parliament. He successfully fought two elections during the eight years he attended the summits. It was rather his personal character and inclinations, together with his shared experience and close association with President Giscard, which made him a strong promoter of the economic summits. The sympathy between the French and German leaders was remarkable: 'Giscard d'Estaing and I knew each other so well that we could anticipate the reaction of the other and only needed to use the telephone as confirmation.' The two men often consulted each other on issues not yet thrashed out with their colleagues at home. Herr Schmidt had already backed President Giscard in launching the European Council and they worked together likewise on the economic summits.

Herr Schmidt saw the summits not so much as an occasion for discovering the personal convictions of the leaders – as President Giscard did – but as a means of inducing them to move towards compromise and of building up confidence among them. 'All participants were obliged, directly and personally, to seek answers to these questions . . . where and how can we unite over compromise solutions? . . . What can we do together to serve our common interests? . . . Summit meetings are not only designed to strengthen the readiness for compromise; they also create mutual trust and increase mutual predictability.' Herr Schmidt achieved this confidence not only with M. Giscard but also with President Ford and Mr Callaghan – though tragically never with President Carter. He put a special value on very intimate exchanges – 'fireside chats' – including bilateral sessions on the margins of the main summit.

His great concern was that the troubles of the 1970s would provoke a relapse into inward-looking policies of economic nationalism, with each country trying to solve its problems at the expense of others. The main purpose of the summits, in his eyes, was to counter that.

We have played our little part to keep the world economically together in a time when, rather easily, the greater economies, with wrong leadership from their respective governments, could have lapsed into the beggar-my-neighbour policies of the early 1930s. . . . There are still enormously strong tendencies for protectionism of all kinds. . . . The so-called economic summit conferences helped to avoid that. . . . They did not bring about much, but what they avoided was of enormous importance.

But Herr Schmidt did not focus on protectionism alone. He was a forceful advocate on many other themes – dealing with OPEC, managing capital markets, checking population growth in the Third World. He relished spontaneous debate across a wide range of topics. This suited his forthright and outspoken style, though sometimes he baffled the other participants with complex technical arguments advanced without warning.[22]

It is hard to detect any comparable UK influence on the conduct of the summits before the London meeting of 1977. Mr Wilson gave early support to President Giscard at Helsinki but did not claim to have himself influenced the launching of the Rambouillet summit. But both he and Mr Callaghan, who became Prime Minister in 1976, favoured informal exchanges among heads of government and compact, select meetings of limited groups. Mr Wilson had been active at the Commonwealth heads of government meeting held earlier in 1975. Mr Callaghan, as Chancellor of the Exchequer, had been host to a meeting of five finance ministers at Chequers in January 1967, a precursor of the Library Group. In the subject matter of the summits, the UK concern at this time was above all with unemployment.[23]

The chief objective of the Italians was to be invited to the summits on their own merits. This they achieved, but Sr Moro and his successors were inhibited by the short life and insecurity of Italian governments. Mr Trudeau, on the other hand, who joined the summit circle in 1976, stayed even longer than Giscard or Schmidt. He put a high value on direct, personal contact, partly based on his experience at Commonwealth meetings.

US attitudes are harder to disentangle, but they came to exert rather different influences. Like France, the United States had a presidential regime, which meant that the idea of summits came easily. But in other summit countries, including France, the head of state or government usually reached his position after experience in charge of one or more cabinet departments. This was not the case in the United States. President Ford's advisers – and especially the US Treasury – were therefore nervous that the President might be placed at a disadvantage in discussing economic issues with former finance ministers. These anxieties were not strong enough to keep President Ford away from Rambouillet. Even so, the US Administration was reluctant to see the President go into a summit, even for highly informal discussions, without a clear idea in advance what subjects would be raised and where the discussions were expected to lead, so that he would have the necessary advice.

A further difference concerned attitudes to the media. President Giscard, and to some extent his other European colleagues, could envisage a summit where the press were kept at a distance and given only a partial account of the proceedings. This, they believed, could help to damp down expectations. But this was much more difficult for the Americans, who judged that any attempt to restrict information for the press would only inflame their curiosity. Making a virtue out of necessity, the Administration saw the value of the summits in educating US public opinion about the merits of international cooperation and handled the media accordingly.

The key figures in the United States at this formative stage were Mr George Shultz and Dr Henry Kissinger. Mr Shultz – like President Giscard and Chancellor Schmidt an alumnus of the Library Group – saw the summit as a chance for direct exchanges and building up personal links. He commended it to President Ford in those terms: it would be useful for the leaders to get together as people to share their ideas and develop whatever common thoughts they could; then, as they went about making decisions about economic policy, they would have in mind the perspectives and the thoughts of the other parties. In line with this, Administration briefings presented the summit as a seminar or a retreat, not to be regarded as a decision-making group.[24]

But just before the summit a different approach was set out by Dr Kissinger in a speech at Pittsburgh on 11 November 1975. He set the summit in the context not only of economic interdependence but of the linkage between economic relations and security cooperation among allies – the same theme as his Year of Europe. The summit leaders should restore the confidence in the democratic process which was being eroded by present difficulties: 'They meet to give their peoples the sense that they are masters of their destiny, that they are not subject to blind forces beyond their control.' Dr Kissinger gave a detailed agenda for the summit, describing each of the subjects which the Americans wanted to discuss and the results they hoped to achieve. He called for 'common action to strengthen the basic structure of the international economic system' and for additional machinery: 'The United States will propose that ministers of our countries responsible for economic policy meet periodically to follow up on policy directions set at the summit and to review what further decisions may be needed.'[25]

Dr Kissinger's speech gave a vision of the summit as an established decision-making institution, with its own preparatory and follow-up apparatus. This was in contrast with the European presentation of the summit as an informal, occasional meeting, not designed to take decisions. Even at this early stage, the Americans had come to emphasise the public and systematic aspects of the summits, as opposed to the private and personal aspects valued by President Giscard and Chancellor Schmidt.

The Japanese inclined to the same approach as the Americans. Like the Italians, their first reaction was satisfaction at being invited. Mr Miki said: 'It is the first time that Japan takes part in a conference at such a level. The Japanese presence will bring new blood to international deliberations.' But the idea of spontaneous personal exchanges between leaders was unfamiliar to the Japanese and they were ill-equipped to profit from it, since the political structure in Japan tends to limit the freedom of action of the Prime Minister. In all forms of government business – domestic or international – the Japanese prefer careful and systematic work in advance to achieve predictable results and to avoid surprises. They therefore came quickly to support US ideas for preparation and summit machinery. From the start they suggested that Rambouillet should be the first of a regular series, not an occasional event.[26]

Before the leaders even met at Rambouillet, therefore, the tensions and contradictions of the summit process, later to become so familiar, were already appearing; between spontaneous debate and organised machinery, between simple consensus and precise decisions, between confidential exchanges and visible results. Nevertheless, despite Dr Kissinger's speech, the expectation was of a rather private and personal event. The leaders would confer together in congenial surroundings isolated, for a time, from the outside world. They would look not for spectacular results, but for a meeting of minds and a strengthening of their common ties.

3 Rambouillet and Puerto Rico, 1975–6

The leaders gathered at Rambouillet over the wet autumn weekend of 15–17 November 1975. The chateau was small and only the heads of government, with their personal staff, were accommodated there; the rest of their delegations were lodged elsewhere. The press were meant to stay in Paris, though some vainly gathered outside the chateau gates. Inside, President Giscard tried to preserve an intimate 'house party' atmosphere and to allow only ministers to take part in the discussions. But the chateau became uncomfortably crowded by the security men protecting President Ford, and the other leaders insisted on bringing their note-takers into the meeting room.[1]

Three of the leaders at Rambouillet were reasonably secure politically, which gave them confidence in the discussions. President Giscard, though elected in 1974 by the narrowest of margins, had largely reassured his Gaullist allies by his economic policies. Chancellor Schmidt had restored the morale of his coalition of Social Democrats and Free Democrats after Herr Brandt's departure, though he had yet to face the electorate. President Ford had earned respect at home, through his patent integrity, which contrasted him with his predecessor; but he too lacked any popular mandate. The other three were more vulnerable. The Labour Party was not united in support of the restrictive policies now in force in the United Kingdom – and Mr Wilson himself was planning to retire in March 1976, though few were then in on the secret. Mr Miki was under heavy challenge from other factions in the ruling Liberal Democratic Party and hoped to use the summit to restore his fortunes. Sr Moro's government was severely threatened by the advance of the Communists.

Advance preparations for the summit
The personal representatives of the heads of government had met three times to prepare for the Rambouillet summit. The representatives of the four Helsinki powers held a meeting in Paris in mid-September 1975 after Mr Shultz had conveyed President Ford's agreement. In early October they gathered again in New York, together with Mr Ushiba and with Sr Rinaldo Ossola as Sr Moro's representative, since Italy had meanwhile been added to the participants. They held a final meeting in London on 12 November.[2]

Their work before Rambouillet had been largely procedural. At the US request, the personal representatives agreed that foreign and finance ministers could take part in the summit, though President Giscard and Chancellor Schmidt would have preferred heads of government only. They worked out a list of topics, each to be introduced by a different leader. They discussed whether the summit should issue a final declaration. But though both Americans and Germans brought drafts of a declaration to the London meeting, the French insisted on leaving the question open till the summit itself.

The most contentious issue was the choice of countries to take part. The Italian government pressed for an invitation immediately after the Helsinki meeting, both in their own right and because Italy held the presidency of the European Community. After considerable French reluctance it was agreed to invite Italy, not so much on Community grounds but from concern that a refusal would weaken the standing of the Italian government and cause it to lose further ground to the Communists. When Canada bid for a seat at the table, however, with strong support from the United States, President Giscard firmly declined to enlarge the number further.[3]

But the most intensive preparation for Rambouillet had taken place in quite another context and largely unknown to four of the six participants. It concerned the reform of the international monetary system. At the IMF meetings in September, the latest stage in the prolonged negotiations, France and the United States had failed to reconcile their differences over the exchange rate regime. The Americans insisted that floating rates should be a legitimate regime; France would only admit floating as a temporary exception to fixed par values. At a Group of Five meeting on the margin of the IMF conference the other countries urged France and the United States to settle their differences bilaterally, confident that any consensus between the two would be acceptable to all.

President Giscard wanted the Rambouillet summit to resolve what he saw as the serious monetary crisis. But the issues were highly complex and positions were deeply entrenched. Furthermore, fixed exchange rates were an article of faith for a wide range of opinion in France and particularly for the Gaullists. Any retreat from this principle would be politically sensitive. With encouragement from Mr Shultz and M. Barre, talks therefore began in strict secrecy between Jacques de Larosière and Edwin Yeo, the senior officials concerned with international matters in the French and US treasuries, to work out a bilateral understanding. They held eight meetings during October and November, to hammer out a compromise on these delicate issues.[4]

The Rambouillet summit, 15–17 November 1975

Macroeconomic policies

The first topic for discussion among the leaders, on Saturday evening, was economic recovery from recession, introduced by Chancellor Schmidt. The recession in the OECD countries provoked by the first oil shock had begun in 1974. All the summit countries, except the United Kingdom, had reacted first against the inflationary impact of the oil price increase. They tightened monetary and fiscal policy during the year, while Germany had started early in the year before. But these actions made the downward slope of the recession even steeper. In the first half of 1975 GNP in the OECD area shrank at an annual rate of 4 per cent and unemployment rose to 15 million. Governments switched to stimulating growth, even though inflation still seemed dangerously high. Germany and the United States eased fiscal policy in early 1975 and public spending programmes followed in Japan, France, and Italy later in the year.

The United Kingdom in 1974 had tried instead to counter the depressive effects of the oil price rise and to sustain activity and employment. But this strategy could not succeed while its more powerful neighbours were doing the opposite. Prices leapt up, the external deficit widened, the pound fell; and the UK government was obliged to bring in restrictive policies in July 1975, just as the other countries began to promote recovery.

Being debarred from promoting growth themselves, UK spokesmen were strong advocates at OECD and IMF sessions during 1975, and at less formal meetings, of measures of stimulus by others. In this, they found allies in the OECD Secretariat, who were advocating differentiated policies between 'strong' and 'weak' countries as the way to avoid another synchronised boom, like the one in 1972–3 which had led to a synchronised recession. The OECD suggested:

Expansion should be led by those large countries which have comparatively favourable price and balance of payments positions – the United States, Japan and Germany – with countries such as Italy and the United Kingdom and a number of smaller countries, which are less well placed, concentrating primarily on reducing their inflation and relying on export-led growth.[5]

When the proposal for an economic summit surfaced in July 1975, the recession was at its worst. It appeared by then to have reached its nadir; most countries had launched or at least prepared their measures of stimulus; and the OECD judged: 'The area seems poised for a moderate recovery.' But this was only the promise of a recovery, not hard evidence. The future looked very uncertain and there was no postwar experience of such a sharp recession. The proposal for a high-level meeting, to restore confidence in the system and to reassure people that the leaders of the major economies were working together for recovery, had manifest appeal.

By the time the leaders met in November it was clear that the recovery had really started. The US economy had been growing very strongly since mid-year and President Ford gave a highly optimistic account to his colleagues at Rambouillet. The others were more guarded, as the revival in Europe was less visible. But Mr Wilson was reassured and did not press for additional measures of stimulus, though he urged that budget deficits should not be reduced precipitately. He could take satisfaction from the promise in the final declaration: 'We will not allow the recovery to falter.' In fact, most of the others – the United States, Germany, Japan, and France – were as much concerned to avoid 'another outburst of inflation'. Chancellor Schmidt and President Giscard believed they had done as much as they safely could in fiscal stimulus. They doubted whether this could produce a durable recovery and worried about the consequences of their swollen budget deficits. They attached more importance to maintaining the open trading system or to restoring international monetary stability. Meanwhile, one of President Ford's economic advisers remarked: 'Orthodox Keynesian methods for managing the economy no longer deliver the goods.'[6]

In short, the leaders at Rambouillet declared their confidence that existing policies were compatible and adequate to produce recovery. Beyond this, there was no coordination of policy and the idea of differentiated measures, favoured by the OECD, found no echo. The OECD, in fact, entered a note of dissent. In figures made available for the summit, and published later, they suggested that GNP growth in the United States, Germany, and France would be less than claimed by national governments.[7] But the OECD was mistaken on this occasion, at least for the first half of 1976. Growth picked up strongly in Europe and Japan while remaining buoyant in the United States. The confidence of the summit leaders was vindicated.

International monetary matters
On Sunday morning the summit turned to monetary questions, to be introduced by President Giscard. The summit was taking place very late in the cycle of the international monetary reform negotiations. After repeated postponements, the target date for the completion of these had been set for the IMF's Interim Committee meeting at Kingston, Jamaica, in early January 1976. Three issues had dominated discussion during the past year: the increase and adjustment of IMF quotas, arrangements for gold, and the exchange rate regime. Understandings on gold and quotas had been worked out during the IMF's

meetings in September – but only subject to satisfactory agreement on exchange rates.

The United States had come to regard floating exchange rates not only as tolerable but helpful. Floating rates gave them freedom to operate their own monetary policies, which was denied them under the Bretton Woods arrangements. In the turbulent conditions provoked by the oil crisis, floating seemed to them the only workable system. Other major countries did not all share the US enthusiasm for floating, but they too regarded it as inevitable in current conditions. Only France still resisted the idea that floating could be a legitimate long-term regime. In the French view, fixed rates provided an essential discipline, to which the United States should be subject like all other countries.

There appeared to be little room for compromise. But as the summit approached, President Giscard signalled a shift in the French position. In a public speech he admitted that in the past few years the fixed parity system had been too rigid. 'The goal to be aimed for at present is a viscous exchange system', he said, 'under which currencies would fluctuate in a medium that would put a brake on movements.' In a press interview he added: 'As compared with our traditional position, we have been brought to envisage limited flexibility in the system.'[8]

This prepared the ground for the cautious unveiling at Rambouillet of the compromise worked out with great labour between Larosière and Yeo. It took the form of a bilateral understanding, signed by the French and US finance ministers at the start of the summit. This was then discussed at length with their other four colleagues (though they were not shown the text) and endorsed by the leaders themselves. The understanding had two parts. First, it offered an amended version of Article IV of the IMF's Articles of Agreement covering exchange rate arrangements. This would begin with a statement of the obligations of IMF members to pursue economic policies conducive to monetary stability. It would provide for a range of permissible exchange rate regimes, including floating and cooperative arrangements like the European 'snake'. It would look forward to a possible future return to a fixed par value regime, though this would require adoption by an 85 per cent majority in the IMF, which would give the United States a veto.

The second part of the understanding envisaged that the monetary authorities of the United States, Japan, and the countries in the European snake would intervene in the markets to iron out erratic fluctuations in their exchange rates not caused by underlying economic factors. A complex system of consultation was provided: daily between central banks, weekly between senior finance ministry officials, and quarterly between finance ministers. The United Kingdom and Italy, whose currencies were vulnerable and outside the snake, were allowed to stay on one side for the time being. In short, the French had lifted their refusal to legitimise floating in return for a US undertaking to intervene to steady the dollar under certain conditions.

The monetary understanding was recognised, both at the time and subsequently, as the main achievement of the Rambouillet summit. It is clear, however, that this did not emerge from the personal exchanges between the leaders. On the contrary, it was meticulously prepared beforehand. The main discussion took place among finance ministers, with only brief and general treatment of the issue by the heads of government. Even the six finance ministers did little more than bless the bilateral deal between France and the United States, which was so finely balanced as to allow for little adjustment to meet the views of others. Nevertheless, the summit was crucial to the outcome in three ways, which well illustrate the impact which these meetings would have on other issues in the future. First, it provided a high-level political focus for the efforts of the French and Americans to resolve their difficulties. Without this, the dispute would have dragged on and the other strands of the monetary reform package could well have become unravelled. Second, the summit gave the understanding sufficient impetus to carry it through the final stages of the negotiations in the IMF. Third, the authoritative endorsement of the understanding by the summit helped to disarm political criticism, especially from Gaullists and others in France.

The follow-up to the first part of the Rambouillet understanding was extremely rapid and thorough. Within the next few weeks the finance ministers of the European Community, the central bankers at Basle, and the Group of Ten, both officials and ministers, worked over the understanding.[9] Joseph Gold, the IMF's legal counsel, had to adjust the language of the original Franco-American draft before it was suitable to become the IMF's new Article IV. But the way was clear for the adoption of all the elements of the monetary package – exchange rates, gold, quotas, and some special arrangements for developing countries – at the Interim Committee in January 1976. The new arrangements were unambitious and inelegant as compared with the Bretton Woods system. They were little more than an endorsement of the status quo as regards exchange rates and relied far more on administrative discretion than the discipline of rules. But the summit came too late in the process to bear the responsibility for that.

The second part of the understanding proved less durable. There was closer cooperation between central banks and finance ministries and some coordinated intervention in the first half of 1976. But the complex structure of consultation was never put into effect and the Americans seemed to lose interest once floating had been blessed by the Interim Committee.

Rambouillet endorsed, at the highest level, the principle that only the correct balance of economic and monetary policies can produce underlying exchange rate stability, though monetary authorities can usefully intervene in the markets to counter disorderly conditions. This principle has had a long life since then. It was restated at the 1976 and 1978 summits. After a period in which the Americans had ceased to intervene altogether, it was rediscovered at the Versailles summit in 1982 and formed one of the basic conclusions of the intervention study prepared before the Williamsburg summit of 1983.

But the summit participants always found it hard to convert this principle into a guide for action. In practice, it could only work if there was confidence in the markets that the major governments were giving priority to exchange rate stability in their policy choices. This confidence was never present, in part because governments did not do enough to earn it. All too often they pursued growth at the risk of letting their currency fall or fought inflation by methods which made their currency rise. Market sentiment then prolonged the upward or downward trend and this overshooting would frustrate corrective action over a long period. In those conditions it became impossible to determine whether or not an exchange rate movement was erratic and ought to be resisted. This in turn gave grounds to those, particularly in the United States, who argued that all intervention was ineffective.[10] Hence, the key exchange rates under consideration at Rambouillet – the dollar, the yen, and the currencies linked then in the European snake and later in the European Monetary System (EMS) – continued to move in a zig-zag fashion. The goal of exchange rate stability, or even M. Giscard's hope of a certain 'viscosity', would seem as far away at Williamsburg in 1983 as it was in 1975. But at least by then a new attempt had been launched to convert the principle into action, through the 'multilateral surveillance' begun at Versailles in 1982, to be described in chapter 10.

International trade

The other major problem tackled on Sunday morning at Rambouillet was international trade. World trade had contracted in the recession, falling in 1975 by 5 per cent in volume. Massive external deficits and rising unemployment generated pressures for trade protection. Italy, for example, had operated a temporary import deposit scheme from May 1974 to April 1975 to safeguard its balance of payments. In other countries, notably the United Kingdom, there were demands for measures to protect vulnerable sectors of industry such as textiles, footwear, and cars. In order to check these pressures, the OECD members had adopted in 1974 a 'pledge' to refrain from measures to restrict imports and they renewed this in June 1975. Furthermore, the MTNs in the GATT had survived the impact of the oil crisis, though they had not yet got very far, since the US Trade Act, which gave the

Americans their negotiating authority, was only adopted very late in 1974.

President Ford, Chancellor Schmidt, and Mr Miki (who introduced the trade item) had come to Rambouillet with the aim of strengthening the defences of the open trading system. Dr Kissinger declared at Pittsburgh: 'The President intends to propose that we reaffirm our common determination to avoid new barriers to trade. . . . The industrial democracies should use the summit to renew their resolve to pursue the Multilateral Trade Negotiations to an early conclusion.' Chancellor Schmidt likewise called for the rejection of protectionism, arguing that protective measures could not safeguard full employment. This approach was clearly reflected in the summit declaration. In addition, the leaders gave impetus to the MTNs by setting a deadline for their completion by the end of 1977. This had an immediate favourable effect in Geneva, where a procedural impasse between the Community and the United States over agriculture was resolved in mid-December.

In this debate the UK position attracted close attention. Mr Wilson was under pressure from domestic industry and the trade unions, and from some members of his Cabinet, to introduce measures of general trade protection. The imminence of the summit, however, strengthened the arguments in favour of observing international obligations. In parliament he rejected the idea of general protection and joined the consensus against it at the summit. But he did not rule out 'protective measures for particular industries suffering or threatened with serious injury as the result of increased imports'. At Rambouillet he sought his colleagues' understanding for this position.[11]

Mr Wilson believed he had carried his point. He quoted President Ford as permitting such measures 'in particularly acute and unusual circumstances'. But when a UK representative referred to this at an OECD meeting a few days later, it led to an immediate reaction. The British Ambassador in Washington was called in to be told that any exceptions must be severely circumscribed in scope and duration. Similar messages came from Paris and Bonn. These had their effect, in that the restrictions, when finally announced in December, were minimal, affecting only items of clothing and footwear from Spain, Portugal, and Eastern Europe.[12]

This episode is instructive, in two separate ways, in illustrating how the summits work. First, it demonstrates that the summits can strengthen the impact of international arguments in policy debates within participating governments. This can happen in the run-up to the summits and their aftermath, as well as at the meetings themselves. Second, it shows how different interpretations can arise of what has been agreed in the informal exchanges between heads of government. The leaders conceded the principle of Mr Wilson's exception, without clearly defining its scope. It was only when it was further discussed among 'experts' in an OECD committee that the risks of this loophole were recognized.

One other trade subject was treated at the summit, under East–West relations, introduced by Sr Moro. Since October 1974 the countries present, plus Canada, had been trying to work out agreed guidelines on minimum rates and maximum duration for export credits. The French had been reluctant participants in this. But when criticised at the summit for conceding cheap export credit rates to the Soviet Union, President Giscard agreed that negotiations on guidelines should resume among officials. This issue would recur at several future summits.[13]

Energy and relations with developing countries

Late on Sunday afternoon President Ford and Mr Wilson made a joint presentation of these two subjects. On energy, Dr Kissinger had forecast at Pittsburgh: 'The United States would urge the summit to recommit the industrial democracies to an even more forceful pursuit of the fundamental long-term goal of depriving the oil cartel of the power to set the oil price unilaterally.' President Ford explained the domestic measures that he proposed to reduce oil dependence by stimulating production, though in practice these were being blocked by the US Congress. He also spoke in favour of a minimum safeguard price for oil, as proposed in the IEA, and Mr Wilson supported him. But President Giscard was wary of endorsing IEA measures. He advocated instead seeking an accommodation with OPEC through the Conference on International Economic Cooperation (CIEC), which would open in Paris a month later. Chancellor Schmidt urged both strict conservation measures at home and negotiations with OPEC. But the outcome of a lively debate was closer to the French than to the US view, since no one wished to upset the prospects for their host's other initiative, the CIEC.[14]

The CIEC was also concerned with relations between developed countries and developing countries without oil. The latter had been badly affected by the higher oil prices and had grounds for attacking OPEC. But in 1974 OPEC, led by Algeria, had managed to persuade the non-oil developing countries that their best strategy would be to form a solid Third World front and demand the introduction of the New International Economic Order (NIEO). The West, they argued, weakened by its need for oil, would be obliged to concede this. The NIEO was intended to sweep away the existing system and bring in special advantages for developing countries: the indexation of commodity prices, assured transfers of resources from rich to poor countries, the right to expropriate foreign investment without compensation, and a much greater say in running organisations like the IMF and World Bank.

Resolutions which embodied the NIEO were adopted at the United Nations in 1974 in an atmosphere of confrontation between North and South. But since then Western leaders had launched several initiatives to show that, while they had serious doubts about the NIEO, they wanted to help the non-oil developing countries. President Giscard promoted the CIEC, where progress on energy could be set against progress on other problems of concern to the poorer countries. Mr Wilson introduced proposals for a world commodity policy at the Commonwealth Conference in May 1975 and restated them at the summit. Chancellor Schmidt advocated the stabilisation of export earnings from commodities. Dr Kissinger promoted a trust fund in the IMF for low-income countries and a development security facility. All these moves improved the international atmosphere, especially at the UN Special Session in September 1975.[15]

The Rambouillet summit, however, did not take the opportunity to shape the proposals of the various leaders into a coherent whole. Instead, it commended specific actions with immediate impact, notably stabilisation of export earnings and help in financing deficits. In line with this, the IMF's Interim Committee in January agreed to set up a trust fund, financed from the profits of gold sales, and to enlarge the scope of its facility for compensating for fluctuations in export earnings. But agreement on these moves was already close and the summit did not play the same decisive role as it had over exchange rates.

Assessment of Rambouillet and transition to Puerto Rico
This concluded the economic agenda. There was a brief exchange on political issues, kept strictly secret at the time and only revealed some years later, mainly about developments in Spain. Meanwhile, the French had agreed that a joint declaration should issue from the summit. A text had been prepared in the course of the meeting and was endorsed by the leaders after a brief discussion. The heads of government then moved to Rambouillet town hall for a closing press conference, which became a standard feature of the summits.[16]

The Rambouillet summit was an undoubted success. It was arguably the most successful of the entire series. Though less ambitious than the later summits at Bonn in 1978 and Tokyo in 1979, it was also less controversial. In some respects, as President Giscard said, the most important thing about the Rambouillet summit was that it was held at all. The heads of government found that they were able to meet and talk informally and to achieve common ground across a wide range of subjects. All the participants enjoyed it far more than they expected.

President Ford, who had been irritated beforehand by the refusal to admit Canada, was particularly enthusiastic.[17]

The leaders were also able to record some useful results from Rambouillet. Without any new departures in macroeconomic policy, they were able to impart some confidence to the recovery, which was justified by events. They made a clear stand against protectionism, with a visible impact on the policy of one participating country, and set a useful target for the MTNs. The monetary understanding was decisive in concluding the international monetary negotiations. It inaugurated a period of close cooperation on exchange rates, though this did not endure.

Altogether, the experiment of involving heads of state and government in international economic issues had proved its worth. Andrew Shonfield, then Director of Chatham House, called it 'the Rambouillet effect' and defined it in these terms:

Bargaining . . . needs to be prodded forward at intervals by political decisions taken at a high level. This is where the technique of economic summitry recently deployed at the Rambouillet meeting is particularly relevant at the present juncture of international economic relations in the West. It serves to galvanize national officials, and also some departmental ministers, who are inclined in present circumstances to become obsessed by the minutiae of narrowly conceived national interests.[18]

The question immediately arose: Would Rambouillet be repeated? The institutional ideas set out by Dr Kissinger beforehand and supported by Japan were not endorsed by the summit. The declaration indeed gave the impression that Rambouillet would be an isolated event and its consequences would be pursued elsewhere. This helped the European participants to reassure their absent Community partners. But this impression was not strictly accurate. In the aircraft which carried him back across the Atlantic, Dr Kissinger forecast to journalists that another summit would be held in about a year's time and that this could be brought forward if conditions became critical.[19]

President Ford did not in fact wait long before proposing a second summit meeting. The idea began to circulate in the US Administration towards the end of March 1976, at the suggestion of Mr Alan Greenspan, Chairman of the Council of Economic Advisors. The Americans sounded out the other participants in late April and in May. As word of his intentions began to leak out, a formal announcement was made, on 3 June, that President Ford had invited his colleagues to a second summit in Puerto Rico on 27–28 June 1976.

The principal economic reason given for calling another summit was concern that the revival was accelerating faster than planned. 'Economic recovery has come sooner and been stronger than expected,' said the US Secretary of the Treasury, Mr William Simon. 'Renewed inflation could abort recovery.' A second important reason was anxiety about developments in Italy. Heavy pressure on the lira had exposed the vulnerable state of the Italian economy. Elections were due on 21 June, in which the Communists were widely expected to gain so many seats that they would have to be included in the next government. The Americans saw the summit as a suitable occasion to consider both the financial aspects and the wider implications of events in Italy, since they were concerned at the growing influence of communist parties in Europe. Some other subjects were thought ripe for summit treatment, notably relations with developing countries after the fourth United Nations Conference on Trade and Development (UNCTAD IV) held in Nairobi during May.[20]

But alongside these reasons, a major objective for President Ford was to improve his prospects of being chosen as Republican presidential candidate and of winning the elections in November of that year. These political considerations influenced not only the decision to call the summit but also the timing, since it had to be held before the Republican convention began in early July. For other participating leaders, too, the political outlook had become less settled since the Rambouillet meeting. President Giscard was at odds with his Gaullist Prime Minister, M. Chirac, and would shortly replace him with M. Barre. Chancellor Schmidt had to face elections in Germany during October. Elections were also due in Japan during December and would cost Mr Miki the leadership. In Italy the Communists made substantial gains in the 21 June elections; not as many as had been widely feared, but enough to increase US anxieties, which Sr Moro was unable to dispel.

There was very little time to prepare the Puerto Rico summit. The personal representatives met only once, in the White House on 15 June. As before, they worked out an agenda, began preparing a declaration and allocated different items to different leaders, though more flexibly than at Rambouillet.[21] The early dispute over Canada's participation was settled by President Ford's using his prerogative as host to invite them. Though the public announcement said that they were invited because the 1976 summit was being held in the Western hemisphere, in fact Canada took part in all subsequent meetings. The number of countries attending was now fixed at seven and was not further enlarged. But the question of a European Community presence at the summit provoked a violent dispute – described below in chapter 5 – which was not resolved till the following year.[22]

The Puerto Rico summit, 27–28 June 1976

The Puerto Rico summit took place at the El Dorado Beach Hotel, 20 miles outside the capital, San Juan. Mr Callaghan and Mr Trudeau were the only newcomers. This was the shortest of all the summits, lasting just over 24 hours, though Ford, Giscard, Schmidt, and Callaghan lunched together before the main meeting began. Security was strict and the press were kept well outside the spacious hotel grounds. While the Rambouillet summit was meant to be an elegant house party, the atmosphere this time was more like a holiday weekend.

Economic policies and international monetary matters

The balance of economic policies was the most substantial item at Puerto Rico. Most of the OECD economies climbed out of recession in the first half of 1976 as fast as they had sunk into it the year before. World trade revived and unemployment in the OECD area fell back to 14 million in May 1976. Recovery had arrived; the concern now was to make it durable. Four days before the summit OECD ministers had endorsed a strategy drawn up by the Secretariat which aimed at achieving non-inflationary growth over the rest of the decade. The Secretariat outlined a scenario which envisaged an average growth rate of 5.5 per cent up to 1980. But this performance would be hard to achieve and even on the most optimistic hypothesis would leave inflation and unemployment higher than before the oil crisis.[23]

President Ford led the debate at Puerto Rico by stressing the need for cautious policies to check a revival of inflation. He argued for restraint in public spending and in the growth of money supply. This approach found strong support from Germany and Japan, as expected, but also from France, since the stimulus given to the French economy in 1975 had produced a large external deficit and driven the franc out of the European currency arrangement – the snake. President Ford also proposed that countries with large surpluses should allow their external balance to deteriorate, as was already happening to the United States. But the other two surplus countries – Germany and Japan – did not respond; this divergence was to cause increasing friction in the years ahead.

The United Kingdom and Italy argued for a less restrictive approach, with Mr Callaghan pointing to the dangers of prolonged high unemployment. But these views found little sympathy. Both countries were in a weak position, dependent on the goodwill of their more prosperous partners. Sterling had lost 10 per cent in effective terms since the start of the year and the lira had fallen by 20 per cent, obliging the Italian authorities to introduce strict monetary measures and to seek external finance from every available source. It was widely expected that Puerto Rico would be concerned with emergency financial support arrangements, linked with the IMF, for OECD countries in difficulty, notably Italy.

The Americans had earlier persuaded their partners to put together a Financial Support Fund in the OECD, only to see this blocked in the

US Congress. They now wished to see the IMF empowered to provide a super-tranche of extra finance to those countries which had exhausted their normal borrowing facilities. But the French in particular had doubts about this method; and when the summit met there were in fact no bids on the table. Italy's financial situation had eased with the opening of the tourist season and confidence was beginning to revive. The United Kingdom was propped up for the next six months by a package of $5.3 billion put together in early June 1976 by the central banks of the Group of Ten.

Without the pressure of a specific request, discussion was inconclusive, with agreement only that any special support should be provided multilaterally and that the borrower should adopt strict corrective measures. The 'strong' countries, while regarding their own policies as well judged, considered that the United Kingdom and Italy should do more to bring their public finances and monetary growth under control. Although Chancellor Schmidt warmly commended the United Kingdom's incomes policy, this on its own was not regarded as enough. The British were urged to make cuts in public spending and began to realise that, without such cuts, they could no longer count on US and German financial support. It was a foretaste of the strong pressure to be applied by the United States and Germany when the United Kingdom, later in 1976, sought a massive IMF loan and a safety net for sterling.

The Puerto Rico declaration asserted with confidence 'economic recovery is underway' and 'restoration of balanced growth is within our grasp'. In practice, the summit endorsed the restrictive policies being applied by the United States and Germany, policies which reversed the measures of stimulus introduced the year before, and with which the United Kingdom and Italy were obliged to conform.[24] In consequence, growth in the economies of the seven countries slackened off from an annual rate of 6.9 per cent in the first half of 1976 to 3.2 per cent in the second. This time the summit leaders had misjudged the staying power of the economic recovery.

Trade and energy issues
On these two subjects there was little advance at Puerto Rico. On trade, the summit again condemned protectionism and renewed the 1977 deadline for completing the MTNs in the GATT. But in practice these negotiations moved very slowly in 1976 and Puerto Rico was not able to impart a further impetus. The summit welcomed the guidelines on rates and duration for export credit which had been agreed among the seven countries since Rambouillet and urged other countries to adopt them too. But this provoked the Commission to take the four European summit participants to the European Court of Justice, to assert its claim that this subject fell within Community competence.[25]

Energy was barely discussed. President Ford had not overcome the congressional obstacles to his programme to increase energy production and was unlikely to do so before the elections. President Giscard still wished to avoid anything which would disturb the energy discussions at the CIEC or appear to endorse the policies of the IEA. On French insistence, the energy passage in the declaration was limited to one sentence.

North–South and East–West relations

Relations with developing countries were discussed at Puerto Rico mainly in the context of UNCTAD IV, since the CIEC was still in its early stages. At the UNCTAD talks in Nairobi the summit countries had appeared in some disarray, especially on the central issue of commodity arrangements. UNCTAD had endorsed a new Integrated Programme of Commodities, calling for commodity agreements to cover nineteen products and a well-endowed 'common fund' to finance price stabilisation for most of them. But the United States, Germany, and Japan had opposed the idea of a common fund as being wasteful and impractical. The United Kingdom had taken a similar view, disappointing those developing countries that hoped for support after Mr Wilson's initiative in 1975. France, however, had floated a compromise for a more modest common fund, which would set gains from intervention in one market against outgoings in another.

At the OECD meeting a few days before Puerto Rico Dr Kissinger had called for a united Western position towards the developing countries. But at the summit this common position remained elusive. The leaders were at one in favouring specific, practical measures of benefit to the developing countries, in preference to the comprehensive reforms of the NIEO. But they could not agree on the issues in question. The United States and Germany renewed their opposition to the idea of a common fund for commodities. Chancellor Schmidt, who introduced the discussion on this subject, circulated figures to show that commodity price stabilisation would benefit a limited number of mainly middle-income developing countries, as well as commodity-exporting developed countries including the United States and the Soviet Union; but it would be of no help to many of the poorest. In his view, export earnings stabilisation was a much more effective method of helping the poorer countries. But President Giscard argued the case for price stabilisation and for cooperating with the UNCTAD initiative, and he received some UK support. Despite intensive debate, the leaders were unable to reconcile these approaches.[26]

Dr Kissinger had also invited the OECD meeting to agree on what attitude they should adopt to economic relations with the Soviet Union and Eastern Europe. This subject too provoked lively exchanges at

Puerto Rico, both because of concern at the financial health of some East European countries and because of renewed political friction with the Soviet Union, notably in Africa. Mr Callaghan, who made the opening presentation, argued that the debt burden of East European countries needed watching, though he discounted the possibility of any defaults. Chancellor Schmidt expressed deeper anxiety about the financial outlook. But President Ford endorsed the general view that East–West economic links could be used to promote overall political relations – in contrast to the attitude of the next Republican administration in the United States, which would revive the subject at the Ottawa and Versailles summits in 1981 and 1982. In the intervening years it dropped from the summit agenda and the series of studies carried out by the OECD in 1977 did not attract the attention of heads of government.

Political subjects
Over lunch before the summit proper President Ford, Chancellor Schmidt, President Giscard, and Mr Callaghan discussed the sensitive issue of the Italian political situation. They considered whether they should provide financial help to Italy if there were Communist ministers in the new government. Their conversation was meant to be kept secret and was not suspected at the time. Two weeks later, however, Chancellor Schmidt told some American journalists that the leaders had agreed to provide no finance if the Communists were present. His revelation produced uproar in Italy and complicated Sr Andreotti's efforts to form a new government. Sr Moro was obliged to admit that he knew nothing of the matter. There was great embarrassment in Washington, Paris, and London, especially as Herr Schmidt seemed to have exaggerated the extent to which a firm decision had been taken.[27]

The matter was never in fact put to the test. Despite their gains in the 1976 elections, the Communists did not secure a place in the Italian government; and the economy improved so as to remove the expectation that special financial help might be needed. Furthermore, the angry reaction did not discourage the leaders of the four powers from using future economic summits as an occasion for coming together. They met in London in 1977 after the main meeting and breakfasted together at Bonn in 1978, though they were careful to avoid issues of direct concern to the other summit participants. That problem would not arise again until the Guadeloupe four-power meeting of January 1979, to be discussed in chapter 7.

Assessment of Puerto Rico and conclusions
Puerto Rico, like so many sequels, was a much less weighty affair than Rambouillet. There was, in fact, no real justification for it. It came too

soon after Rambouillet, was prepared with undue haste, and looked too much like an electoral gimmick. The confident message of economic recovery proclaimed in the declaration proved incompatible with the measures of restraint being adopted. It was not justified by events and thus looked complacent. The other economic discussions were largely inconclusive and added little to the results of Rambouillet, while the disclosure of the four-power exchanges made a bad impression both in Italy and elsewhere. But while Puerto Rico was much less productive, it was still harmonious. Though it too ended with no decision on a future meeting (despite a Japanese invitation), it was accepted that the leaders could meet again if one participant felt that this would be valuable and the others agreed. As economic growth slackened later in the year, President Giscard led the Europeans in proposing another summit meeting and did this even before President Carter took office.[28] The experimental period of the summits was over; they were now becoming a regular event.

These first two summits were intended to reproduce the direct, uncluttered format of the Library Group meetings. In this they were only partly successful, as the presence of more countries and more ministers made the circle wider and less intimate. Some of the founders were disappointed that 'bureaucracy' was already creeping in. Even so, these meetings came closer to the original aspiration than those which followed. As Mr Callaghan put it after Puerto Rico:

This was a substantial agenda for a two day meeting. The fact that we managed to cover it illustrates one of the features of this kind of meeting. The numbers attending are small and compact. Discussions are business-like and to the point. We do not make speeches at one another. We talk frankly but also as briefly as we can, and a lot of ground is covered.[29]

Some of the drawbacks of this format for a meeting of heads of government were now, however, becoming apparent. The achievement of the Rambouillet summit that made the most impact – the monetary understanding – was by far the most carefully prepared in advance. At Puerto Rico, where there had been very little advance preparation, the leaders could have an animated discussion among themselves, for example on North–South and East–West relations, but they ended with little to show for it and no means of carrying matters further. As a result, the participants and their advisers were beginning to give more thought to how to prepare for summits beforehand and how to follow them up afterwards. President Carter's arrival in office gave powerful encouragement to this process.

4 The Summit Becomes an Institution

Contrasting conceptions of summitry

The Library Group had marked its members for life. Meeting repeatedly, in a relaxed atmosphere, with no records kept, confident of their own expertise, extremely frank and even emotional, whether arguing or commiserating, they had come to share a sense of power and intense personal solidarity, sitting secretly at the controls of the world economy. As we have seen, Giscard, Schmidt, and Shultz envisaged summitry as an opportunity for conversation in the classic sense, 'the feast of reason and the flow of soul'.[1] Theirs was an image of summitry with little ceremony, little preparation, little substantive negotiation, little institutional underpinning, and as few pettifogging bureaucrats as possible – the summit (as one summiteer later put it) as 'an openhearted gossip among friends'.

Against this image, the new Carter Administration counterpoised a quite different, more institutional conception of summitry. The key positions in the new Administration were staffed by alumni, not of the Library Group, but of the Trilateral Commission.[2] These Trilateralists were acutely conscious of the tensions between interdependence and domestic politics and of the need to craft a system of collective management to replace US hegemony.

During 1976, Trilateral Commission task forces had considered how international processes and institutions could be reformed to address these problems. The key to increased cooperation, they concluded, was greater consultation among internationally inclined senior officials. 'Probably the most important element is the high-level expert, the official responsible for preparing the policy proposals which will be considered at the political level.' Consultation should be designed to strengthen 'transnational networks of like-minded officials', to foster 'transnational coalitions' among 'the outward-looking forces within each government'. 'Indeed, the economic officials of at least the largest countries must begin to think in terms of managing a single *world* economy.' To improve consultation among Europe, North America, and Japan, a 'Trilateral Staff Group' should be established, composed of 'senior governmental advisers with the personal confidence of the heads of government'. This group would oversee consultations among the trilateral countries, identify unresolved policy problems and seek solutions, and monitor the effectiveness of international institutions.[3]

The Trilateralists recognised the importance of 'political will': 'Political leaders must be brought to recognise that efficacious international policies, and increasingly, sound domestic economic policies, demand a common approach and, in certain areas, common action.'[4] But in this framework, summit meetings among heads of state should cap a process of intensive consultations among officials. For the Trilateralists (unlike the Librarians), bureaucrats were part of the solution, not part of the problem. A working group of the Atlantic Council, reporting at almost the same time, expressed a very similar conception of summitry: 'What is important is that such meetings become part of a continuous process of harmonization at all levels.'[5]

Not limited to atmospherics and warm fellowship, this Trilateralist image of summitry was more ambitious than the Library Group image.[6] The Trilateralist conception took seriously the prospect of international policy coordination, along with the necessity for hard bargaining, transnational coalitions, and package deals that might require substantive changes in national policies. If such coalitions were to be forged and such bargains struck, the roots of the summit process would have to reach deep into each government. The horizons of those charged with formulating 'domestic' policy would have to be broadened to include international concerns.

The Trilateralists did not believe that summits would necessarily take formal and mutually binding decisions, but they did believe that summits should seek to resolve differences over substantive policy issues, not merely 'exchange views'. 'We can't bring the President halfway around the world for a seminar,' Henry Owen, President Carter's personal representative, told his colleagues. The *New York Times* captured the US mood on the eve of the London summit: 'The most important thing [the leaders] can do is to agree on directives and follow-up machinery for closer coordination of economic policy. . . . [This summit] must produce results or begin a slide away from collaboration.'[7] A results-oriented summit, addressing tough, complex issues, would require more organisational infrastructure, perhaps something like the 'Trilateral Staff Group'. Intensive preparation and attentive follow-up were the most distinctive features of the new conception of summitry.

The international preparatory process

As we have already seen, careful preparations had been crucial for the monetary accord at Rambouillet, and deficiencies in preparation and follow-up had begun to concern some of the participants at Puerto Rico. Under the aegis of the Trilateralists, the summit process became increasingly institutionalised. Preparations lengthened, and their rhythm accelerated. Key to the process were meetings of the personal representatives, now dubbed 'sherpas'.[8]

For Rambouillet, the personal representatives had met three times, although the first meeting, two months before the summit, was concerned primarily with sorting out whether there would be a summit. For Puerto Rico, a single meeting, less than two weeks before the summit, had had to suffice. In 1977, with a new Administration in Washington, there were only two preparatory meetings, beginning two months before the London summit. For the first time, however, specific policy issues were discussed in detail among the sherpas, and language for a draft communiqué was debated at some length. Impartial observers noted with approval 'the more careful and intensive preparations'.[9] Moreover, at the summit itself the leaders agreed, at the urging of the Americans and the Japanese, to institute a follow-up meeting of the personal representatives.

In September 1977, the sherpas duly met to prepare a joint assessment of progress towards meeting the various pledges made at the summit. The fact of such a report implicitly acknowledged that summitry was expected to produce visible effects on the policies of the participating governments, not merely to improve mutual understanding among summiteers themselves. By 1978, the sherpas had settled into an annual pattern of three full preparatory sessions, the first at least three or four months prior to the summit, together with a follow-up session approximately six months afterwards. Summitry had become a year-round enterprise.

The sherpas inherited from the Library Group a unique sense of camaraderie, frankness, and corporate solidarity. One recalls that in his first meeting with the group he felt very distinctly like the 'new boy' entering a close-knit club. Another reports occasionally feeling a sense of loyalty to this anomalous international institution overriding his national loyalty. Though doubtless none could forget for long that he was present as a representative of his nation's highest authority, with the official obligations that necessarily followed, by most accounts the climate in the sherpas' group was (and remains) rather unusual in international negotiations.[10] Key to the special character of the group was a climate of sufficient mutual trust that each participant could be frank about pressures and divergences of view within his own government, reasonably certain that the others would not abuse or exploit these confidences. Such an atmosphere would be crucial to any successful solution of two-level, domestic–international games.

Advocates of the Trilateralist conception of summitry praised the collegiality and autonomy of the sherpas. Said one,

The sherpas' group became a new kind of international institution. It was the collective sense that emerged there about issues and priorities and bargains that determined the summit agenda. One of the values of the sherpas is that they developed a collective personality to some extent independent of their governments. In that sense, one can compare them a bit to the European Commission, whose members are nominated by governments, but then deal with governments. To some extent, the sherpas were carrying out national instructions, but to some extent, they had to use their own judgment as to how far their own governments would or would not go, in working out a common position that they could present to governments. Otherwise, one could not have had any negotiations for a successful summit.

On the other hand, this expansive interpretation of the role of the sherpas irritated domestic officials and frustrated some of the summiteers themselves, who wanted to do more than merely strike the final bargains on a limited set of issues. Some critics back home argued that the sherpas came to usurp the role of political leaders. 'They regard themselves as the junior board of trade for the world,' said one. Another complained that 'some personal representatives have tried to get in between the heads of government and their governments'.

Although the practice of using non-governmental figures as sherpas virtually disappeared after the first summit,[11] for the most part the notion persisted that the personal representatives should be 'personal', that is, very senior policy-makers close to the head of state or government. One experienced sherpa noted

It is important that the people around the table are not diplomats, but senior domestic officials, there because of their relationship with the chief executive, not because of any connection to the foreign ministry. The discussion is very frank, including our discussions about domestic politics, because we are closer to domestic politics than most diplomats.

In fact, however, not all of the sherpas fit this description equally well, and in some cases one can detect a trend towards 'depersonalisation' of the role. Helmut Schmidt's successive sherpas were all close personal aides, and when Horst Schulmann, for example, moved from the Bundeskanzleramt to the number two post in the Finance Ministry in 1981, he retained his role as personal representative. However, in 1983 Helmut Kohl, the new Chancellor, designated Hans Tietmeyer, Schulmann's successor in the Finance Ministry, as his sherpa, implying a more institutional criterion for selection. Barre's successor under Giscard, Bernard Clappier, the head of the central bank, did not have easy access to the President, but Mitterrand's sherpa after 1981 was Jacques Attali, the President's chief of staff and closest personal advisor. The British sherpa – there have been only two in the first decade of summitry – has always been the Cabinet Secretary, sometimes called 'the Prime Minister's Permanent Secretary'. The *Chef du Cabinet* of the President of the European Commission has always served as his sherpa.

The original sherpas in the United States and Canada, and even to some extent Japan and Italy, were chosen because of their personal standing with the head of government. For example, George Shultz under Ford, and Henry Owen under Carter, both had good access to the President; and Ivan Head was described by one of his colleagues as 'soul-mate' to Prime Minister Trudeau. More recently, however, in all of these four countries, the role of sherpa has become linked to a specific post with diplomatic responsibilities, typically the top official responsible for economic affairs in the foreign ministry. In these cases, turnover in the position of personal representative has been somewhat higher than elsewhere.

As the agenda of the summits became more regularised and the topics diversified, attendance at the sherpa meetings expanded from the original one per country. By 1977, the usual pattern was for each nation to send three representatives to the preparatory meetings, typically including a senior official from the foreign ministry, one from the finance ministry, and one from the office of the prime minister or president, although in some cases the third member of the troika represented another economics ministry.[12] With a few additional aides present, perhaps concerned with logistics, meetings of the full sherpas' group might include 25 people or more, which implied different group dynamics from the original, more intimate gathering of 5 or 10.

Formally speaking, this expansion corresponded to the fact that the foreign and finance ministers were part of the official delegation to the summit itself. More practically, the expansion reflected the increasing 'bite' of summitry into matters traditionally reserved to the departments and the consequent desire of those departments to keep a close watch on negotiations that might affect their interests. Significantly, this expansion was apparently sparked by the United States and Japan, the two countries in which bureaucratic rivalries most flourish. As we shall see, the French chairman in 1982 would convene a number of sherpa meetings restricted to one a side, in an attempt to curb the growing 'bureaucratisation' of the sherpa process. However, this practice would not reverse the tendency towards greater and more regularised involvement of representatives from various ministries in summit preparations.

During the sherpas' first meeting of the new year, agreement has generally been reached on which agenda items merit high priority (for example, macroeconomics in 1977 and 1978, and energy in 1979), and which can be dismissed with less attention (for example, monetary issues in 1979 and 1980, and energy in 1982). Often one or two summit nations have urged that attention be given to some special theme, and sometimes the inclusion of these novel items has been a matter of some controversy. For instance, in 1982 the Americans would press very hard for East–West economic relations to be included on the agenda for Versailles, as we shall see, but the French vigorously resisted this proposal until the eve of the summit itself, even though lively discussions about the topic among the summit nations continued throughout the spring.

Throughout the summit process, one common rule of thumb has been that virtually everyone seeks to avoid being left in a minority of one on any important issue. Formally speaking, any summit conclusion must be unanimous, and so there is no reason why any out-voted participant should not simply dig in his heels. To be sure, that has sometimes happened. However, participants often have adjusted their position, sometimes in advance of the meeting itself, in order to avoid complete isolation. Examples include the Germans on macroeconomics in 1978, the Canadians on energy in 1979, the Americans on North–South issues in 1981 and 1982, and the Japanese on trade in several years. Some sherpas report that the pressure to make key concessions to achieve unanimity is especially great on the host government, for whom the 'success' or 'failure' of the conference has a special domestic political resonance. (How substantial these adjustments have been in practical terms is a question addressed in subsequent chapters.)

From 1977 through 1982 the preparatory discussions centred on thematic papers drafted on the personal responsibility of one or another sherpa. During these years five topics became standard summit fare – macroeconomics, monetary issues, trade, energy, and North–South relations. Assignment of papers on these topics was sometimes a subject of genteel jockeying. In 1982, for instance, the macroeconomic paper, traditionally produced by the Americans, would be assigned instead to the less ideologically rigid British. Several times the Japanese volunteered to draft the paper on trade, on occasion provoking a counterdraft from the European Community. The preliminary papers served to focus the sherpas' discussions, and those discussions merged almost imperceptibly into the negotiations about the wording of the final communiqué. One participant compared the discussion papers to disposable stages in rocketry which fall away as the vehicle gathers speed.

The significance of the negotiations about communiqué language became itself a matter of increasing debate among participants. Some sherpas felt strongly that the preparatory give-and-take became substantively focused and precise only when participants were forced to confront language encapsulating alternative approaches to the underlying problems. In this view, communiqué-drafting became a vehicle for refining problems, clarifying points of view, and exploring new approaches that might reconcile divergent interests. Observed one participant, 'We are always pushing for the highest common factor.' Without something on paper, many officials felt, it was impossible to know what had been agreed, and impossible to implement the results of the meeting.

On the other hand, others dismissed communiqué-writing as the least productive part of the summit exercise, vitiating the advantages of frank, private discussion. Particularly when the domestic stances of governments on fundamental issues diverged, the communiqués tended to become what one official termed 'tossed salad' documents in which each summiteer could find a sentence or two endorsing his own policies. Another participant used a different culinary metaphor, speaking of the sherpas as producing different frostings that could be applied to the summit cake, according to taste. As we shall see, by the early 1980s, some heads of government, particularly those disenchanted with results-oriented summitry, would become increasingly restive about communiqués that were 'pre-cooked' by the personal representatives, leaving the principals only to add a few minor touches.

In some respects, the plenary sessions of the summit itself appeared somewhat anticlimactic in the Trilateralist version of summitry, for summit encounters are usually too brief for sustained discussion of any single issue. Typically, the first session was given over to formal statements of national positions, and the final meeting was consumed in a hectic haggling over a few controversial passages in the communiqué. Thus, no more than three to five hours were left for give-and-take among the leaders. (Until 1981 most of the summiteers were competent in English, but thereafter translation became a more serious problem.) The main substantive issues were usually resolved outside the conference chamber itself, and the occasional exceptions (for instance, the 1979 plenary discussions of oil import quotas) were deemed unproductive by most participants. This broader process reflected the Trilateralists' emphasis on detailed policy negotiations, but it increasingly irritated those summiteers drawn to the nostalgic Library Group image. They valued instead the informal opportunities that remained on the margins of the summit to exchange moods with their fellow politicians, to compare notes on broad questions of political and economic strategy, and to take one another's measure.

After 1976, summitry began to spill well beyond the confines of a single weekend gathering of heads of state and government, as we shall see in more detail in the chapters that follow. The process now involved most of the major international economic organisations, including the OECD, the IMF, and the GATT, as well as bilateral and multilateral contacts among the summit countries. In 1977–8, for example, the central summit issue of German fiscal policy was repeatedly discussed in all these channels. The range of issues at least potentially touched by summitry expanded, as officials and leaders sought to use the summit to force a reassessment of priorities or to strike cross-sector deals. As the one time each year during which national bureaucracies could be certain of gaining the attention of their chief executives, the summit preparations exerted a gravitational pull on virtually all ongoing discussions of any significant international issue. The line between preparation for the next summit and follow-up for the last one became blurred, as did the line between summitry and ordinary intercourse among governments. As these jurisdictional lines faded, more officials in each government acquired a role in summitry. Despite recurrent calls to limit the summit machinery, hundreds of officials came to be involved in the substantive preparations, not to speak of those working on logistical support. In short, for better or worse, summitry was becoming institutionalised.

The national preparatory process
As we have seen, the idea of unofficial preparations for the summit did not survive even the first round. One of the original personal representatives recalls: 'I learned very soon that it was not possible to act entirely on my own. Too many ministries were involved, and too many subjects on which I was not expert. I began to coordinate my activities with the regular departments – that's always a delicate thing in government.' With the advent of Trilateralist summitry, this coordinative process within each country typically became broader and deeper. The basic patterns of national preparations have tended to persist to the present, and it is convenient to sketch those patterns at this point.

The special role of the sherpas in organising the summit has imparted a basic similarity to the preparatory process within each national capital. In all cases the principal responsibility for coordinating preparations lies with the personal representative, even in administrative systems (for example, Germany, Japan, the United Kingdom, and Italy) where such 'one-man shows' are not traditional. Everywhere, participants report that as compared to the normal policy-making processes, summit preparations are more personalised, more centralised, more tightly held, and less bound by conventions of bureaucratic clearance. 'What counts in the preparation for the summit,' runs one typical account, 'is more the person and his relationship to the chief executive and less his job title.'

On the other hand, in every capital the unusual character of summit preparations has become more and more attenuated over the years, as the process has become routinised and assimilated to the normal practices of the administration. As one of the early sherpas remembers, 'We were originally all mavericks, but over the years the mavericks have lost the battles with the regular bureaucracy.' To some degree this trend reflects the greater range and complexity of the issues handled within the summit context, for sherpas everywhere have recognised their need to draw on the expertise – and maintain the goodwill – of the great ministries of state. Moreover, as the summit has become embedded in the multifaceted array of ongoing international negotiations, there has been less occasion for any special summit-linked policy review. 'The departments have position papers already prepared on all these issues,' explained one participant. This has been especially true in recent years, when (as we shall see) governments have become more reluctant to contemplate policy changes merely in response to summit pressures. Observed another official, 'It's the same people dealing with the same issues, whether it's for the summit or not.'

In most countries a summit 'team' or 'task force' has been established under the direction of the personal representative, often in collaboration with several 'deputy sherpas'. As indicated earlier, the most common pattern is a troika consisting of one person from the central executive agency (the White House, the Cabinet Office, the Bundeskanzleramt, the Elysée, and so on), one from the foreign ministry, and one from the ministry of finance, but sometimes other economics ministries are also represented. Below this trio there is usually a broader committee with representatives of other relevant agencies, including the departments responsible for energy, trade, and development aid.

The relative weight of the principal departments in the preparations varies a good deal from country to country. Where a central executive agency is well established, its role in summit preparations is always quite important. In the United Kingdom, Germany, and France, for example, the Cabinet Office, the Bundeskanzleramt, and the Elysée respectively exercise a degree of initiative on summit matters greater than would be characteristic of ordinary policy-making. Of course, the White House staff dominate the US preparations, even when the US sherpa is a State Department official. In Japan and Italy, on the other hand, the office of the prime minister is institutionally weaker, and more of the substantive preparations for the summit are handled elsewhere. Even in these countries, however, the prime minister is more influential on issues handled in the summit context than he would be normally.

The foreign ministry is always included in the core task force, but it is rarely in a dominant position. For example, the Auswärtiges Amt plays a subordinate role in German summit preparations, except on international political questions. At the other extreme, the Japanese Foreign Ministry has always provided the chief sherpa, and he typically clears his work within his own ministry before widening the circle of consultation to include bureaucratic rivals from the Ministry of International Trade and Industry (MITI) and the Ministry of Finance. Well-placed Japanese participants describe control of the summit preparations as 'the last trump' that the Gaimusho holds in bureaucratic politicking in

Tokyo. This contrast between Germany and Japan illustrates a more general pattern: the more that the personnel and the activities of major domestic ministries have become 'internationalised', the less prominent is the foreign ministry's role in summit preparations.

Given the historical antecedents of the summits, it is not surprising that representatives from the ministry of finance have always been in the inner circle for summit preparations. On the other hand, except on money matters, the finance ministry is almost never the lead agency.[13] The top officials responsible for international finance in these countries comprise a kind of informal international 'money mafia'. Finance officials have long been uneasy about summitry, believing that it tended to cut across existing networks of international collaboration. Summitry, they feared, undermined the institutional authority of finance ministries, bringing impractical outsiders into the act, particularly from the foreign ministry. From time to time finance ministries have used their independent channels of communication to exchange views about summit matters, and in recent years, as we shall see, they have tended to regain the initiative in international economic cooperation, via an expansion of the role of the Group of Five.

The role of central banks in summit preparations varies widely. Officials from the Banca d'Italia play a leading role in substantive summit preparations in Rome, although procedurally and politically responsibility for coordination lies with the Prime Minister's foreign affairs adviser, a career diplomat. (Strikingly, the regular financial and economic ministries in Rome played little part in summit preparations until recently, when certain key posts in these ministries were assumed by ex-officials from the Banca d'Italia.) The Bundesbank has played an important secondary role in German preparations, partly through representation on the inter-agency task force and partly because of personal ties between Helmut Schmidt and the top leadership of the Bank. In the three English-speaking countries, central bankers are occasionally consulted informally by the sherpas on monetary issues. Finally, at the other extreme, the central banks in France and Japan have no autonomous role in summit preparations at all, for these banks are institutionally subordinate to the finance ministries.[14]

The remaining economic ministries generally provide background briefings, without more direct involvement in summit preparations. The ministries of trade or energy, for example, provide papers on specific subjects, but officials from those departments are rarely involved in broader discussions of summit strategy and tactics. The two important exceptions to this generalisation are in Germany and Japan. Below the Chancellor's personal representative, most of the key officials involved in summitry in Bonn are in the Economics Ministry. In part, this fact has reflected a need for political balance, since both the

Chancellor and the Finance Minister have been drawn from the senior coalition partner (the SPD or the Christian Democratic Union), whereas the Economics Ministry has been led by a Free Democrat. Moreover, the particular officials responsible for trade, energy, and macroeconomics in the Economics Ministry have well-established international reputations. In Tokyo MITI has waged a long and partially successful struggle for a greater share of the status and influence that accompany involvement in summit preparations. In recent years MITI has become a basically 'internationalist' force in Japanese policy-making, but ironically, this shift closer to the Foreign Ministry's position on substance appears to have intensified the two ministries' rivalries over bureaucratic turf.

This rapid survey of summit preparations in the seven capitals has highlighted the role of government officials, for 'outsiders' have surprisingly little direct involvement. Despite pro forma consultation with business and union leaders in a few countries, interest group activity on summit matters is rare everywhere, and officials privately discount the significance of most of those few contacts that do occur. For example, a delegation of union leaders from the seven nations traditionally meets with the summit host just prior to the summit itself, but these encounters are dismissed by insiders as insignificant. This pattern contrasts sharply with the kind of intense lobbying that is characteristic of domestic politics in these countries.

'Only if the summits began to touch on particular sectoral interests would these groups become active and possibly influential,' observed one sherpa. The rare instances of interest group activity prove this general rule. In 1979, for example, Prime Minister Ohira consulted with business leaders before agreeing to unexpectedly stringent oil import targets. In 1982 the German Chamber of Industry and Commerce made strong public and private representations to the Chancellor, urging that he stand firm against US pressure to restrain trade with Eastern Europe. In both cases, however, the really decisive debates took place within the government itself.

Parliamentary and party involvement in summit preparations is equally scant, even where parties usually are key players in national policy-making, as in Japan, Italy, and Germany. Neither government backbenchers nor oppositions have shown much interest in summitry, apart from a handful of parliamentary questions and a perfunctory debate on the prime ministerial statement following the summit. Three exceptions illustrate the sorts of issues that can arouse greater interest among politicians. Following the 1978 summit agreement by Chancellor Schmidt to introduce an additional fiscal stimulus package, a lively debate preceded parliamentary approval. That same year, Congressional opposition to oil price decontrol seriously complicated

President Carter's summit negotiating stance. Prior to the 1982 summit, Liberal Democratic Party politicians from rural constituencies would take a strong interest in the proposed liberalisation of Japan's agricultural imports. For the most part, however, the political classes of the seven nations have been content to leave summit deliberations to their governments.

As a consequence, the controversies that have arisen in the course of national summit preparations almost always follow bureaucratic lines rather than conventional political cleavages. For example, the most common kind of dispute in summit preparations divides the foreign ministry from domestic departments, with the diplomats favouring a 'softer' line in the international negotiations. Of course, conventional domestic politics are not irrelevant to summit discussions, for senior officials usually follow what Carl J. Friedrich once termed 'the rule of anticipated reactions',[15] that is, they take into account the probable reactions of other key actors to proposed courses of action, particularly when those actors represent the special constituency of a given department. Officials are well aware of the positions of interest groups on the broad topics that appear on the summit agenda. 'We don't need to be told that the unions favour reducing unemployment, or that bankers are concerned about inflation,' pointed out one sherpa.

Ordinarily, a government's stance on such issues reflects a fairly stable equilibrium among the diverse groups within its supporting coalition. On the other hand, as we shall see, when this domestic equilibrium is unstable because of strong internal divisions, then the play at the domestic game board becomes more lively, and its connection with the international game becomes more visible. These occasional entanglements between domestic and international politics are particularly enlightening with respect to the sovereignty–interdependence dilemma.

If legislative politicians are largely absent from summit preparations, what about departmental ministers? The answer, strikingly similar in most countries, is that the key officials keep their ministers informed about the progress of preparations, but that ministers themselves are seldom directly involved. Sometimes the prime minister or president will consult privately with a few of his senior colleagues, often the foreign minister or the minister of finance. However, cabinet discussion of the summit preparations is at best brief and perfunctory everywhere, even in countries where the cabinet is supposed to be collectively responsible for government policy, such as the United Kingdom or Italy. The circle of effective consultation becomes wider only in the case of exceptionally assertive ministers, such as Secretary of State Kissinger or Economics Minister Lambsdorff, or ministers unusually close to the head of government, such as Chancellor of the Exchequer

Howe or Foreign Minister François-Poncet, or in the case of summit issues of exceptional domestic resonance, such as the 1978 German stimulus package.[16]

This description of the respective roles of politicans and bureaucrats belies the hopes of some of the founding generation of summiteers to perpetuate the anti-bureaucratic tenor of the Library Group. The bureaucratisation of summitry will be discussed at greater length later, but the evidence should not be interpreted to mean that the bureaucrats have escaped from political control. Officials rightly protest that if they were to deviate substantially from the main lines of their ministers' policies, they would be caught up short. However, the picture sketched here does imply that if political initiative is to be imparted to the national summit preparations, that impulse must come from the head of government himself and his personal political advisers.

The intensity of direct involvement of the chief executive himself and his top political aides in the substance, strategy, and tactics of summitry has varied widely. As we have seen, the founding fathers of Western summitry held a conception of the institution that reflected its Library Group origins, and their personal involvement in summit preparations was correspondingly great. President Giscard, for example, disparaged elaborate preparations. What counted for him were direct contacts among heads of state, and even his personal representative was kept at arm's length. Under Helmut Schmidt, despite increasing involvement by the ministerial bureaucracy in the detailed preparation of the German position, major strategic decisions were held within a narrow circle of Schmidt's most senior advisers and colleagues, including several senior ministers, a handful of aides in the Bundeskanzleramt, and several trusted outside confidants, particularly in the world of banking.

James Callaghan greatly enjoyed meeting with his foreign colleagues, and he invested a good deal of personal energy in summit preparations. Some observers felt that he took summits more seriously than many of his officials did, unlike his successor, who appeared less enamoured of summitry than her subordinates. Mistrustful of the regular civil service, especially in the Treasury, Callaghan relied heavily on his Cabinet Secretary and the staff of the Prime Minister's Office. Like Giscard, Schmidt, and Trudeau, Callaghan was disinclined to delegate much responsibility for substantive preparatory negotiations to the official machinery.

Preparations in Tokyo, Rome, and Washington represented a quite different pattern. In the Japanese case, rapid turnover in the office of Prime Minister, coupled with the linguistic and cultural isolation of Japanese politicians, tended to reduce the role of political leadership. Similar causes produced a similar result in Italy, but in no other capital have permanent officials so dominated summit preparations as in Tokyo. As one Japanese politician put it, 'The Japanese are bad at personal diplomacy but good at bureaucratic diplomacy, and the development of a summit *process* gives the bureaucrats a better chance.'

President Carter's personal representative, Henry Owen, had long been a leading advocate of Trilateralist summitry, based on extensive prior consultation among senior officials. Attached to the President's White House staff, he devoted virtually all his time to summit preparations and follow-up, unlike his counterparts abroad, all of whom had other administrative responsibilities. Owen used his role as sherpa as a springboard to wider involvement in the Administration's economic counsels. One enthusiastic account concluded that 'his role as one of the main, albeit lesser known, actors in the economic policy drama attests to the all-embracing character of the summit as an event that focuses on just about every major domestic, as well as foreign, economic issue'.[17] For his part, President Carter, a voracious reader, probably took the sherpas' paperwork more seriously than did his European colleagues. His successor, like most of the next generation of summiteers, would adopt a quite different approach to summitry.

Explaining the institutionalisation of summitry

Without question, the single most important factor that encouraged the institutionalisation of the summit after 1976 was steady pressure from the Americans. As we saw in chapter 2, American emphasis on 'co-operative decisions' and summit 'follow-up' was already evident in Henry Kissinger's remarks before Rambouillet in 1975. This more structured approach to summitry reflected both institutional features of the US presidency and a national desire to share the burdens of world leadership. The US propensity for institution-building received a powerful boost from the Trilateralists' carefully elaborated theory about how to manage interdependence collectively. Throughout the Carter years, it was the Americans who tended to press for more elaborate summit preparations and for greater specificity in the language of summit communiqués.

On the other hand, it was surely inevitable that in time the summits would become more formal, more elaborate, and more bureaucratised, regardless of the attitude of the US president. For reasons explored in the previous chapter, the weaknesses of the Library Group image of summitry were already becoming apparent before the advent of Jimmy Carter. An experienced participant in the Group of Five observed philosophically, 'Most institutions have started as a "library group", but almost all library groups, if they survive, become institutions.'

In later years, the disadvantages of elaborate preparations and results-oriented summits would become clearer. The ills of the summit process would be blamed on the innovations of the Carter years, and even some erstwhile Trilateralists would begin to complain about bureaucratisation and formalism. In assessing these innovations, however, it is important to recognise that during the late 1970s, the Trilateralists' more systematic approach to international policy coordination was widely hailed. As we shall see in chapter 6, the notion of carefully prepared package deals of mutual policy concessions, like that struck at Bonn in 1978, was clearly congenial to Schmidt, Giscard, and Callaghan, as well as to the Americans and the Japanese. Even the sceptical French acknowledged the merits of the new approach. *Le Monde*, for example, cautiously welcomed what it termed 'institutionalised Trilateralism'.[18] The editorialist added, 'the tree will be judged by its fruits', a task of historical assessment to which we shall turn shortly.

'Inside every small informal gathering,' wrote the *Times* leader on 11
June 1976, 'there is a large plenary session struggling to get out.'
Alongside the development of procedures among themselves, as examined in the previous chapter, the summit participants had to decide how
to deal with countries which were not invited. The heads of government
sought to cope with this problem without compromising the unique
features of the summits: the compact and selective format; and the
ability to integrate different strands of policy, both external and domestic. It involved them not only with other individual governments but
also with collective pressure from the European Community.

Other governments

The summits were always bound to arouse anxiety and suspicion
among those who were kept out. These feelings were keenest among
those just outside the circle, whose right to participate, on grounds of
economic weight or international influence, seemed only slightly less
than those inside. But many other governments were worried at seeing
the most powerful countries getting together on their own, for a
number of reasons. The summit might take decisions on matters of
equal concern to them, without consulting them or fully reflecting their
interests. The summit countries, trusting to their own power, might
conspire to set aside existing international rules or circumvent the
wider existing organisations where summit participants and non-
participants sat down together. Some commentators even argued that
the sense of exclusion among non-participants could alienate them from
international cooperation, making them no longer ready to support
collective actions, in political as well as economic fields; 'exclusion
breeds irresponsibility'.[1]

In two respects the private, personal format of the summits aggravated this problem. First, the leaders wished not only to limit the
numbers, but to be able to speak directly about their own concerns, not
on behalf of others.[2] This excluded devices used elsewhere to make
limited groups more acceptable, where each participant would speak
for a 'constituency' as in the IMF or on behalf of a group, as in the UN.
Second, the exchanges were meant to be confidential. In practice the
lively media interest meant that much of their content became public

through national press briefings. This was unsatisfactory to non-participating governments who found themselves less well informed than the media on issues which concerned them directly.

There was, by definition, no perfect solution to this problem. But the limited summits could be defended, and non-participants reassured, in a number of ways. The basic defence was a simple one and its force was admitted even by those most sensitive to exclusion. In short, it was better for the leaders of these countries to meet than for them not to meet. The summits were conceived, at a time of severe difficulty, as a means of bringing together the United States, Japan, and the leading countries of the European Community at the highest level, in a way which had not proved possible before. By this token, as long as the summits gave evidence of improving relations among the leading economic powers or helping to reduce tension between them, they provided their own justification.

The best available method for reassuring non-participants has been defined as follows:

In a measure this circle can be squared if, first, sufficient time is allowed for the process to work; if, second, the conclaves of the major powers are informal, not institutionalised; if, third, consensus rather than decisions are sought; and, fourth, if actions are reserved for and subsequently carried out within the appropriate international body.[3]

This method of reassurance was very largely adopted by the early summits and continued to be used for years to come.[4] It drew strength from the fact that at first the summit leaders themselves, for the most part, wanted an informal, non-institutional summit for their own reasons, not simply to reassure non-participants. But in several respects this presentation of the summits soon became unconvincing. The summits did not stick simply to consensus. Even at Rambouillet there was a 'decision' on monetary issues and comparable actions would become more frequent after the arrival of President Carter, with Henry Owen as his sherpa, because of their attachment to specific, quantified results. With the years the summit would come to look more and more like an institution, pursuing issues through its own apparatus instead of handing them on to an existing international body of wider membership.

In any case, the question of participation already proved highly controversial in the early years. The initial plan was to limit the summit to the countries of the Group of Five. But Italy and Canada pressed their claims with the greatest vigour, profiting from special considerations which applied at the time. Italy held the presidency of the Community at the moment of Rambouillet; the Puerto Rico summit was held in the Western hemisphere. Both Italy and Canada ensured that, once invited, they could not be left out in future.

Australia also bid for membership and was backed by Japan as a fellow Pacific country. If the Japanese had been host to a summit in the early, formative years, as they wished, they might have used their prerogative as host to get Australia added. But Tokyo's turn would not in fact come till 1979 and by then it was too late.[5] The Netherlands and Belgium had also a claim to be present; though slightly smaller than Australia in terms of GNP, both were much more active than Australia in international economic and financial matters, being members, for example, of the Group of Ten. But they did not bid for national membership, choosing instead to concentrate their efforts on Community participation.

The European Community

Within a few hours of the four-power meeting at Helsinki, which launched the first summit, President Giscard and Mr Wilson found themselves under attack from the other European leaders.[6] The idea of a summit attended by some Community members, but not all, raised a whole series of difficulties. First of all, there was a potential clash with Treaty obligations. Under the Treaty of Rome certain economic subjects, principally international trade, fell within Community competence. Member states did not have the right to act alone on these subjects, but only on the basis of a common Community position presented by the European Commission on behalf of all. Even where there was no legal obligation to act as one, the convention was growing that the Community members would coordinate their positions for international discussions and their joint view would be put across by the country holding the presidency. This was particularly the case in North–South relations.[7] Where Community member states still spoke independently in international gatherings – as they did, for example, on international monetary matters – there remained a requirement to consult together on major policy aspects.

But the fundamental issue was that the presence of some Community members at the summit, but not all, would be politically divisive. It would suggest that there was first-class and second-class membership in the Community. 'There is no more certain method of breaking up the Community,' said the Dutch Prime Minister, Mr Den Uyl, in 1976, 'the Community is thus put on one side and the Four will act more and more like a directorate.'[8]

For the Rambouillet summit these concerns were met by the participants suggesting – not entirely honestly – that it would be an isolated event, not one of a series. The success of the meeting and the promise in the Declaration to pursue matters further through existing institutions disarmed criticism. But a violent row broke out when the Puerto Rico summit was announced in early June 1976, without any advance warning being given to the other Community members. There were angry exchanges in the European Parliament and urgent discussions in Brussels. The smaller members of the Community were united in attacking France, Germany, the United Kingdom, and Italy for agreeing to a second summit without consulting their European partners.

But they were not unanimous in their views on what the Community should do. Belgium, Luxembourg, and the Commission argued for a Community presence at the summit, provided by the presidents of the Commission and the Council of Ministers alongside the four 'large' member states. The Netherlands, Denmark, and Ireland at first resisted this solution, as giving permanence and legitimacy to limited summits. As the summit was evidently going ahead, the Dutch moved to support the idea of a Community presence, provided this applied not only to Puerto Rico but to all subsequent summits. The French, however, rejected this condition. The arrangement collapsed and there was thus no Community presence, as such, at Puerto Rico.[9]

After inconclusive efforts to settle the matter, the dispute broke out with renewed vigour as the London summit of May 1977 approached. President Giscard, in advocating this summit, proposed that it take place in the United Kingdom, which held the presidency of the Council of Ministers at the time. It should be preceded by a meeting of the European Council, at which all Community members could express their views on relevant issues.[10] This suited the participants well, but did not satisfy the smaller countries at all. They insisted that Mr Roy Jenkins, the President of the Commission, should also take part and carried the matter to the European Council on 25 March 1977.

This European Council was intended to commemorate the twentieth anniversary of the Treaty of Rome. It was also to consider the subject matter for the summit in early May. But it looked like being a stormy and highly divisive meeting, dominated by what the British press called 'the war of Jenkins' seat'.[11] President Giscard had written to Mr Jenkins two days earlier, saying that, as the Commission was not a government, he could not come to a meeting of heads of government. The Dutch Prime Minister was instructed by his parliament to walk out if the European Council did not agree, at the outset, that Mr Jenkins should attend the summit. But at the last moment a confrontation was averted. Mr Jenkins, who visited Bonn shortly before the Rome meeting, had won the backing of Chancellor Schmidt. This left President Giscard rather exposed in opposition and he offered a compromise. This was accepted by all and the European Council therefore ruled:

The President of the Council and the President of the Commission would be invited to take part in those sessions of the Downing Street summit at which items which are within the competence of the Community are discussed. Examples of such items are negotiations about international trade and the North–South dialogue.[12]

It was not the end of Mr Jenkins' troubles. At the London summit he was admitted only to the second day of discussions, not to the first; though he was invited to the opening dinner for the leaders, President Giscard stayed away; at a later meal he was seated with the foreign ministers, not the heads of government; and at the closing press conference he was given no chance to speak.

Nevertheless, this would prove to be the turning point in the Commission's fortunes. Within a year, Commission participation in the summit and its preparations was extended to cover all the economic items, not just those within Community competence. Before the 1978 summit the Commission became deeply involved in promoting the EMS, a coordinated economic recovery programme, and a Community energy policy. Mr Jenkins' presence throughout the economic discussions would therefore be uncontested at Bonn and would not be challenged thereafter. He was never admitted to the political exchanges among the leaders. But in 1981, at Ottawa, Mr Thorn would gain access even to these, with the Commission joining the preparations in the following year.

Even so, the three European instigators of the summits – France, Germany, and the United Kingdom – agreed only after considerable reluctance to enlarge the summits' membership and dilute their personal character by letting in the Commission. President Giscard made no secret of this reluctance; and while Mr Callaghan preserved strict neutrality when presiding over Community debates, he did not make matters easy in London for his political rival Mr Jenkins. Though the Commission was admitted, the convention became firmly established that the summits would always take place when one of the four regular European participants held the presidency of the Council, so as to avoid enlarging the numbers further. This would not be possible in 1982, when the year was divided between the Belgian and Danish presidencies. Mr Martens would therefore be invited to take part for the Belgian presidency at the Versailles summit. Even then the French, as hosts, tried to keep down the numbers at restricted meetings by allowing only one seat for the Community. Presidency and Commission had to exert some pressure to be given a seat apiece.

Once participation was settled, the Community became capable of exercising a visible impact on the discussion at the summits and their outcome. From 1977 to 1981 a meeting of the European Council would always be held shortly before the economic summit. The key items for the summit were thus considered by the Community in advance, at the highest level. Although no formal mandate was given to those Community members attending the summit, common positions agreed at the European Council – on North–South matters in 1977, on economic policy in 1978, on energy in 1979 – would be carried forward to the summit and exercise a significant influence on the outcome. In later years Community procedures would become less transparent, with the habit of linking the European Council with the summit falling into disuse. This was partly a reflection of the move away from 'results-oriented' summits after 1980, partly due to the inability of the Community to break new ground in economic policy coordination, energy policy, or monetary cooperation. But even without this, the Europeans at the summit would always be able to draw on an extensive capital of Community positions and views on the economic issues, as well as on the parallel work done on foreign policy matters in political cooperation among the member states.

The link between the summits and the Community was untidy and imperfect, better in some ways than others. For the smaller Community countries it was still a second best, a poor alternative to taking part. The Commission and presidency, after all, were there not to put across the views of the non-participating countries, but of the whole Community and all its members, whether present or absent. Sometimes the process of consulting the non-participating member states seemed rather perfunctory. Even so, from 1977 onwards, the non-participants were kept regularly in touch with summit preparations and were far better placed to influence events than, say, Australia or Sweden.

For the Commission, the effect was strongly positive in one respect. Its presence at these select discussions at the highest level increased its standing and its influence, both within the Community and on those occasions when it dealt direct with the United States or Japan, principally on international trade questions. The personal qualities of Mr Jenkins and his sherpa, Crispin Tickell, impressed the other participants. They thus became accepted as members of this select circle and were able to exert considerable influence behind the scenes (though this would become harder for their successors after 1980). Nevertheless, the Commission was always at something of a disadvantage in the summit process. Only the President of the Commission had the right to attend, as against three ministers from each participating government. The Commission was reluctant to take too forceful or independent a line, since if it were not backed by the other member states its credibility would suffer.

The larger Community members retained a good deal of flexibility. They could act with the weight of the Community behind them if they so wished. But in practice they almost always spoke as independent powers, in the spirit of the personal format of the summits. In summit preparations, too, parallel work in the Community tended to exercise very little influence on their attitudes, except where Community competence manifestly applied, as in international trade. The country holding the presidency would operate as freely as the others, seldom assuming the role of spokesman for the Community and leaving all the liaison with the other member states to the Commission. There would even be occasions – conspicuously on the second day at Tokyo in 1979 – when the presidency would set aside or play down aspects of the Community position in the interests of reaching agreement at the summit itself.

The non-European summit members accepted the Community presence without difficulty at first. President Carter was disposed to welcome it and the Americans began by attributing to the Commission a more central role than it played in fact. In due course, some sources of irritation appeared. At times the Europeans would reach a common position in the Community context only with extreme difficulty and thus use up all their margin of manoeuvre, most conspicuously again at Tokyo, on the first day. But in general this would be much less of a constraint at the summits than in other contexts of EC-US or EC-Japanese relations. The different degrees of Community competence attaching to trade and financial matters would occasionally cause bewilderment and frustration. The Japanese sometimes felt that the Community presence tilted the balance unfairly in favour of the Europeans. The Americans would later react strongly against suggestions that the European sherpas should concert before they met their colleagues. But despite this sense that it introduced a rather cumbersome element into the summit format, the Community presence would never be challenged by the non-Europeans.

Despite all the drawbacks and imperfections, the Community/summit link should be judged a success. The arrangement joined together two very different instruments in a flexible way, which could adapt both to the changing format of the summits and to developments in the Community. It was only achieved at the cost of bitter disputes in the Community and would need constant attention over the years to keep it in balance. But it would enable the Community to work together with the United States and Japan at the highest political level, thus promoting one of the fundamental aims of the summits.[13]

Summary assessment
The strong suspicion of the summits prevailing among non-participants at the beginning gradually died away. There was no real evidence to suggest that exclusion bred irresponsibility among those not invited. The assurances provided by the summit countries that these were informal gatherings for consensus, not decisions, had some effect, though this was weakened when the summits too often departed from this model. Non-participants would remain quick to criticise suggestions which would extend the institutional aspects of the summit. The

most potent factor in allaying fears was the enlargement of the membership from the original five to accommodate not only Italy and Canada
but also the European Community, through an untidy but still effective
procedure. The cost of this was to make the summit less personal and
more cumbersome than its founders intended. But the benefit was that
it rendered the summits, with their highly selective format, acceptable,
or at least tolerable, to a wider circle of influential nations. Other
non-participating Western countries gained some sense of being
involved in events through the practice, which began in 1976, of
holding the annual ministerial meeting of the OECD just before the
summit. However, the summits' links with the OECD and other bodies
would not always prove easy or straightforward; they will be analysed in
chapter 9.

These select, exclusive summits thus became a recognised feature of
the international landscape. The finance ministers of the Group of Five
would continue to meet unobtrusively. The foreign ministers – and the
leaders – of the Four Powers would be punctilious in maintaining the
position that the agenda for their meetings comprises questions relating
to Berlin and Germany. The economic summit, with seven members
plus the Commission, would become the smallest non-regional
grouping which has general responsibility, operates openly, and is
accepted by all.

6 London and Bonn, 1977–8

As conceived by the Trilateralists, summits were to be neither house parties nor holiday outings, but rather occasions for transacting practical business. Appropriately, therefore, summits under their aegis were held in such work-a-day sites as Downing Street in London and the old Chancellery in Bonn. As the leaders foregathered in the first week of May 1977, several of them – Carter, Fukuda, Andreotti, and Jenkins – were new to this select club. The entire cast of characters would remain unchanged for the next two years, and so it is worthwhile glancing at each.

Since the previous meeting in Puerto Rico, the new host, Prime Minister Callaghan, had had to endure a prolonged, politically divisive negotiation over budget cuts as a price for IMF support for sterling. He hoped that a successful summit, particularly one that sanctioned more rapid economic recovery, might boost his sagging fortunes. President Giscard and his newly appointed Prime Minister, Raymond Barre, faced parliamentary elections in less than a year, and the outlook was daunting. On the eve of the summit, their austere new look in economic policy had been the target of severe criticism, not only from the ever stronger Socialist and Communist opposition, but also from their own Gaullist allies. Chancellor Schmidt had emerged victorious from parliamentary elections the previous autumn, but his margin had been thin, and his coalition was now riven by scandals and internal squabbling. Although he had campaigned as the self-assured manager of *Modell Deutschland*, he was not yet the dominant figure in Western diplomacy that he would become over the next year or two.

Prime Minister Fukuda had gained power in December 1976, only after serious electoral setbacks for his party. He now feared that criticism of Japanese trade policy by the other summiteers would add to his troubles in upcoming elections. On the other hand, he had had more Western experience than most Japanese politicians, and he would play a more active role at London and Bonn. Prime Minister Andreotti held office at the sufferance of an increasingly assertive Communist Party in a country ravaged by terrorism and inflation. Like most of the others, Prime Minister Trudeau presided over a slackening economy, and in addition he faced a powerful challenge from Quebec separatists. Roy Jenkins, newly elected President of the European Commission, had been offered a humiliating 'back row, one-day-only' ticket of admission to the summit, and that grudgingly.[1]

President Carter's mandate was fresh, but barely twelve months earlier he had been 'Jimmy Who?' and he remained an enigma to his new colleagues. Elected on a wave of discontent with the Washington establishment and with the Ford Administration's economic policies, he had already overloaded Congressional circuits with ambitious programmes on economic recovery and on energy. Moreover, he had disconcerted his allies abroad – particularly, though not only, Helmut Schmidt – with a flood of new initiatives on human rights, nuclear non-proliferation, arms control, and international economics. Unlike six of his seven fellow summiteers, Carter was not a former finance minister, but he had assembled a team of self-confident Keynesians with firm ideas about how to revive the world economy. As we noted in chapter 4, Carter and his Trilateralist aides were convinced that results-oriented summits could help resolve the dilemmas of national decision-making in an interdependent world. His emphasis on careful preparation of summit business meshed well with Callaghan's views, and his policy initiatives would provide much of the grist for this and ensuing summits.

Preparations for London

Macroeconomics: ending the 'pause'

Just as the Puerto Rico summit had been expressing confidence that 'recovery is underway', the recovery had entered what the OECD in December 1976 labelled (still with implicit confidence) a 'pause'. By summit-time in London, 15.6 million people were unemployed in the industrialised West, a postwar record.[2] The OECD, the Callaghan government, the Carter Administration, and many private economists in the summit countries shared a clear prescription for this problem. The view was well-expressed by a group of economists from Europe, Japan, and the United States, meeting at the Brookings Institution in early November 1976, who recommended that

Germany, Japan, and the United States should now adopt domestic economic policies geared to stimulating economic activity. Stronger economic expansion in the three countries, each of which has recently experienced a lull, need not intensify inflation problems, but should reduce domestic unemployment and provide benefits to other countries, both developed and developing.[3]

By allowing the weaker economies to benefit from expanding export markets, the three stronger economies would serve as 'locomotives' for global recovery. International Keynesian analysis indicated that this coordinated fiscal stimulus would have a more significant multiplier effect than could be accomplished by any single government, acting alone. At the same time, this programme would reduce the substantial and growing payments imbalances among the Western economies – in particular, by shrinking the surpluses of Japan and Germany – and would thus relax the balance of payments constraint on economic policies within the deficit countries, as well as contribute to exchange rate stability. This thesis was to be at the heart of international economic diplomacy and Western summitry for the next two years.

Denis Healey had carried this argument to regular meetings of finance ministers ever since 1974, and James Callaghan had apparently raised the issue during the 1975 Helsinki lunch that launched the summits. However, the others had refused to go along, leaving the UK economy in an exposed position, and by November 1976, stern measures had been necessary to halt sterling's free fall. A powerful faction within the Labour Party argued for an 'alternative strategy' that would go for growth behind new protectionist barriers. Callaghan and Healey had decisively defeated that faction in the November struggle, but the two were more strongly convinced than ever that their political dilemma could be greatly eased if only the three locomotives could be stoked up. Although the Germans' usual response was reluctance and even scorn, the British had sensed occasional hints, most recently at a bilateral summit in October 1976, that Schmidt would not mind being pushed into additional expansion. Nevertheless, German policy remained austere, and the German trade surplus grew.

Under Ford, the Americans had been quite unsympathetic to the UK pleas, but with the arrival of Jimmy Carter in the White House, Callaghan and Healey gained a powerful new ally. In economic terms, the new Administration was convinced that a coordinated global reflation, led by the United States, Germany, and Japan, was a quintessentially positive-sum game. In terms of foreign policy, the strategy would address the economic weakness in Europe that exacerbated both protectionism and the Eurocommunist threat. In political terms, Carter's electorate – disproportionately poor, Black, and unemployed – demanded accelerated growth. The President's new $30 billion domestic stimulus programme was designed to fit into a broader international package. As Treasury Secretary Blumenthal testified to Congress,

By adopting this stimulus program, the United States will be asserting leadership and providing a better international economic climate. We will then ask the stronger countries abroad [Germany and Japan were cited] to follow suit. This program itself implicitly calls on them to undertake stimulus efforts of proportionately similar amounts to ours.[4]

Immediately after his inauguration, the President dispatched Vice-President Mondale and two key aides, Under-Secretary of State Richard Cooper and Assistant Secretary of the Treasury C. Fred Bergsten, on a tour of allied capitals, aiming to impress upon the stronger economies their international responsibility to accelerate their growth and reduce their payments surpluses. In most of their stops the US proposals were received favourably, but after their talks in Bonn, Schmidt disparaged the Americans' advice as an ill-considered economics lesson from inexperienced academics. The Americans thought they had detected a different signal from one German official, who suggested that Schmidt might welcome foreign pressure for more stimulus. Officially, however, the German rejection was unambiguous. The political-economic gap that had opened between the Americans and the Germans with the advent of the Carter Administration was reflected in an exchange between Schmidt and Mondale about Ford's tight-fisted Treasury Secretary, William E. Simon. 'We owe a lot to Bill Simon,' noted Schmidt, admiringly. Mondale agreed: 'We owe Bill Simon everything – without him we wouldn't have won the election.'[5]

The barricade of counter-arguments erected by the Germans was to become familiar over the following eighteen months, and was often echoed by Japanese officials. In their view, the locomotive theory gravely underestimated the continuing dangers of inflation and the consequent threat to business confidence. (Despite the 'pause', inflation in the economies of the Seven persisted at an 8 per cent annual rate in 1976 and 1977, though it was barely half that in Germany.[6]) The Western economies faced not classic cyclical unemployment, but structural unemployment, rooted in the jump in energy prices and the rise of competition from the newly industrialised countries. Structural adjustment on the supply side was required, not risky fine-tuning of demand. Moreover, the German propensity to save meant that fiscal stimulus would not have the same expansionary consequences as might be expected elsewhere. In any event, it was recurrently argued, the effects of recent German stimulative actions were yet to be felt, and there were constitutional and administrative limits to any further budget deficits. Moreover, the locomotive theory overestimated international multiplier effects, particularly under flexible exchange rates; according to a Citibank estimate often cited by the Germans, a rise of 1 per cent in German growth would cut UK unemployment by only 50,000–100,000 people, while risking a renewal of inflation in inflation-allergic Germany.[7] Germany was already bearing its full international responsibilities by exporting capital and raising imports. In short, the Germans concluded, prudent and successful economic managers should not be asked to bail out irresolute and spendthrift governments. The deficit countries must put their own houses in order.[8]

The Americans recognised that under flexible exchange rates, the dollar would tend to fall and the Deutschmark to rise, so long as US macroeconomic policy was more expansionary than German policy. Carter's men contemplated the prospect of Deutschmark appreciation with equanimity, since it represented an alternative, though more circuitous, path to their goals of faster Western growth and reduced payments imbalances. Given German export dependence, they believed, the prospect of a stronger Deutschmark would encourage the Germans to adopt more stimulative measures. But even by itself, appreciation would tend eventually to correct the payments imbalances, though less efficiently than the locomotive proposal. Thus, it was of some importance that the Germans and Japanese were reported to have agreed during the summit preparations, and to have confirmed at London, that they would allow their currencies to float upward, if necessary, to reduce their trade surpluses.[9]

At meetings of the OECD in February 1977, and of the sherpas in March, the Americans continued their pressure on the Germans, with strong support from the British. Similar demands were made on the Germans in meetings of the European Community finance ministers. In addition to the battery of arguments already outlined, the German representatives insisted that German growth for 1977 was in any event likely to be in the 4.5–5.5 per cent range, considerably stronger than forecast by the OECD. The Germans reportedly expressed willingness to consider additional measures in the autumn, if growth fell below expectations.

The shift from an argument about German policies to an argument about German growth forecasts marked an important tactical turning point in the debate, even though it meant no shift in policies in the short run. Forecasts defended hard enough tended to become targets. If the Americans and their allies could extract from the Germans (and the Japanese) a commitment to a specific growth target, and particularly if the commitment included the notion of reviewing policies in the case of undershooting, then the reluctant engine drivers would have given a significant hostage to fortune. Although this dynamic took eighteen months to unfold, it played an important role in the story of the summits of London and Bonn.

In the short run, however, the US strategy for Downing Street was suddenly short-circuited. On 15 April 1977, under pressure from Congressional conservatives, the business community, and even some of his own advisors, fearful of re-igniting US inflation, the President announced that he was withdrawing his proposed $50 individual tax rebate, an $11 billion element in his own domestic stimulus package then before Congress. Chancellor Schmidt and his colleagues lost no time in claiming vindication by this recognition of the dangers of inflation.

Prime Minister Callaghan and other advocates of the locomotive strategy were once again isolated. To be sure, at the final preparatory meeting of the sherpas in Washington on 25–26 April renewed scepticism was expressed about German growth forecasts, and Carter's final pre-summit statements continued to stress his hopes that Germany and Japan would join the United States in leading Western expansion: 'When we are selfish and try to have large trade surpluses, and a tight restraint on the international economy, then we make the weaker nations suffer too much.'[10] But the President had undercut his own bargaining position, and the prospects for significant movement at Downing Street were dim. On the eve of his departure for the summit Chancellor Schmidt noted with brutal frankness:

I do not believe that the French or the President of the United States will ask us in London to make more inflation. The English might like to see others make a bit more inflation, but I think it would be desirable for the rest of us to help them, as we have been doing until now, to come down from their inflation rate of 18 per cent.[11]

Nuclear energy, trade, and other issues

An even more heated topic of controversy during the approach to the summit stemmed from President Carter's strong commitment to reduce the risks of nuclear proliferation, by dissuading other countries from proceeding with breeder reactors and plutonium reprocessing. Among the immediate targets of his crusade were German and French contracts to supply reprocessing technology to Brazil and Pakistan, respectively, both countries judged to be on the threshold of acquiring a nuclear weapons capability. Canada, which had already decreed an embargo on shipments of uranium to Europe in an effort to impose tighter safeguards, welcomed the US support.

The North Americans, however, were isolated on the issue. Callaghan, Fukuda, and Jenkins had each expressed serious concern about the new US policy during separate visits to Washington earlier in the spring, and Schmidt and Giscard were even more outspoken. With characteristic bluntness, the Chancellor termed Carter's stance 'a disaster'. The Europeans suspected that the Americans, like the Canadians, were holding back uranium shipments as a lever to force acceptance of the new policy. The US proposals, opponents argued, would strike at a technology in which Europe was believed to be ahead and which was of special importance to energy-poor industrial economies, like Europe and Japan.

On 29 April 1977, at a meeting of the fifteen-nation 'nuclear suppliers' club', the US proposals were roundly criticised, particularly by France, Germany, Japan, and even the United Kingdom. In the face of such allied reaction, Carter's advisors had been seeking privately to moderate the new policy, by proposing a joint study of the technical issues. Assurances were offered that uranium shipments to Europe would shortly be resumed. Nevertheless, as the President departed for London, he reaffirmed his intention to try to block sales like that planned to Brazil, setting the stage for a major confrontation with Schmidt and the others.[12]

Trade issues were also explored during the summit preparations. Here the international alignment was familiar: the United States, Germany, and Japan pressed for a strong condemnation of protectionism and a recommitment to a prompt completion of the Tokyo Round negotiations. It was generally conceded that the arrival of a new US Administration made it impractical to keep to the end-of-1977 deadline agreed at previous summits. However, the hard-driving, newly appointed US negotiator, Robert Strauss, insisted on joining the US summit delegation, and, arriving in London, he emphasised that 'I hope this meeting will tell people like me to get off our cans and out of the trenches.'[13]

As in the past, the French, British, and Italians were less enthusiastic. Fearing competition from the newly industrialising countries in older industries, like textiles, and from the Americans in newer industries, like computers, the French were now talking about 'organised trade', as distinct from 'free trade'. The British felt that in a climate of high unemployment the Americans were aiming too high in the GATT negotiations. In discussions of a draft summit communiqué during the final meeting of sherpas, the United Kingdom sought language calling for export restraint on the part of less developed countries, and linking protectionism and unemployment, the latter phrase presumably intended to remind the Germans and Japanese that the alternative to more rapid growth might well be new trade barriers. But all these suggestions were rejected, and the way seemed clear for a reasonably non-contentious discussion at the summit itself, although considerable unhappiness at Japanese trade practices persisted.

Even more preparatory time was spent on North–South issues. Representatives of Giscard and Trudeau pressed for a more forthcoming Western bargaining position for the concluding session of the CIEC in Paris. The main issues on the table there were the developing countries' requests for a debt moratorium and for commodity price supports, and the developed countries' counter-demand for continuing consultation on energy. Under pressure from their European partners, the Germans finally agreed at a meeting of the European Council in March 1977 to the principle of a Common Fund for commodity price stabilisation. (This agreement marked the first time that the Community members had achieved a common European position for summit purposes.) The Carter Administration was more sympathetic to the North–South dialogue than its predecessor had been. However, the Americans remained dubious about the Common Fund proposal, and the Europeans were unsure of the Americans' support for the CIEC. On the issue of the debts of the non-OPEC developing countries, the summit preparations coincided with moves to establish a new loan facility under the IMF (the so-called 'Witteveen facility') and to expand IMF and World Bank resources, and the summit would bless those initiatives. Perhaps because these North–South questions did not rouse the passions of most of the summiteers, or touch their vital political interests, the summit itself would not carry the discussion much beyond the point reached during the preparations.

The Downing Street talks, 6–8 May 1977

On Friday evening, the summiteers gathered for a get-acquainted dinner. As he had warned, President Giscard absented himself, in a show of indignation that Roy Jenkins should have been invited to the high table. Most observers thought that the French President's gesture was not unrelated to his current domestic difficulties with his Gaullist allies.

Much media attention prior to the summit had been devoted to the personal clash between Jimmy Carter and Helmut Schmidt. In the event, the often tense interplay between these two was at the centre of both the London and Bonn summits. The origin of the enmity between them lay in Schmidt's publicly stated preference for Gerald Ford in the 1976 elections. By summit time, however, each had accumulated a series of grudges, ranging from unanswered letters and barely veiled personal disparagement to substantive disagreements on vital matters of policy. A bilateral meeting had been scheduled for breakfast on Saturday in which the Brazilian deal might be addressed, but they began their debate on the nuclear issue over dinner on Friday, with a heated exchange. The breakfast session was cool, but not openly antagonistic; a German newspaper headline concluded, 'Not yet friends, but no longer opponents'. However, this guarded optimism turned out to be unwarranted. The antagonism between these two proud men seemed visceral and persisted throughout their terms of office and beyond. It provided a debilitating source of tension in transatlantic relations and a jarring note of discord at four successive summits.

Prime Minister Callaghan opened the first formal session on Saturday morning, stressing the social costs and political risks of slow growth. He noted the current economic forecasts of the German and Japanese governments, and he urged them to redouble their efforts to make sure those targets were actually met. He welcomed the US reflation and noted that it would inevitably cause an adverse balance of payments for the Americans over the next year. President Carter supported Callaghan's concerns about the surplus countries and promised continued US growth. Later in the meeting, Denis Healey was blunter, discussing the problems of deficit countries and (from his recent personal experience) excessive IMF-imposed rigour. He hinted at protectionist responses to continued recession, and singled out Germany and Japan for special criticism. In response, Schmidt restated his concerns about inflation, but pledged 'great efforts' to achieve the German growth targets. Fukuda, the oldest of the summiteers, movingly recalled his attendance at the 1933 London 'world economic conference', whose failure had opened the floodgates to protectionism, depression, and war, and he said Japan would do its share to stimulate growth.

Meanwhile, the sherpas worked on language to balance the conflicting concerns about inflation, unemployment, and growth. Over US objections, Karl-Otto Pöhl, the German representative, succeeded (with the help of the French, who were seeking language that would be helpful in defending Barre's austerity plan at home) in inserting the phrase that 'inflation does not reduce unemployment. On the contrary, it is one of its major causes.' This endorsement of Schmidt's basic stance on economic policy was quoted in all German press commentary following the summit, and would be hailed by Germans years later as one of the most significant achievements of German summit diplomacy.

On the other hand, the Americans and British obtained their tactical objective in the very next sentence, in which the summiteers agreed 'to commit our governments to stated economic growth targets or to stabilisation policies which, taken as a whole, should provide a basis for sustained non-inflationary growth, in our own countries and world-wide, and for reduction of imbalances in international payments'. Although the Germans and Japanese avoided the inclusion of specific figures in the communiqué itself, it was widely acknowledged that the Germans were aiming for 5 per cent, the Japanese for 6.7 per cent, and the Americans for nearly 6 per cent.

The outcome fit the pattern of previous summit communiqués, for both sides could cite language confirming their positions. On the other hand, in the days that followed, some authoritative German observers drew attention to the apparent German commitment to growth targets that seemed to many (including, privately, some officials in the Economics and Finance Ministries) already out of reach. For example, the *Frankfurter Allgemeine Zeitung* noted with foreboding that Germany had

committed itself to reach real growth of 5 per cent this year. That is surprising and dangerous. . . . Perhaps the Government is saying to itself that the commitment does not mean much, since new stimulus measures have already been introduced and the year is already half over. But even if the practical significance for this year is modest, a regrettable precedent is established for the future. Must the Federal Republic commit itself again next year?[14]

In that pertinent question lay the seeds of controversy.

On Saturday afternoon, discussion turned to two of President Carter's most controversial initiatives, on nuclear energy and human rights. The latter irritant was dispensed with fairly briefly, as Carter expounded his forthright policy, and Schmidt defended the quieter approach of his government.

The nuclear issue was thornier, and it occupied much more of the summit than the host had hoped. Fukuda, anxious to avoid the appearance of joining an anti-US front, had met privately with Carter seeking confirmation that the United States would allow the Japanese to go forward with reprocessing at their Tokaimura plant. In the plenary session Schmidt and Carter resumed their heated debate of the previous evening. Both sides recognised, as President Giscard succinctly summarised the next day, the dilemma of how to reconcile 'two necessities': to develop nuclear energy in a world where energy resources were limited; and to guard against the danger of nuclear weapons spreading to countries which did not have them. But on such practical issues as the German-Brazilian reactor deal, the dispute remained open. As expected, Carter suggested a joint study group on nuclear energy and non-proliferation but Giscard and Schmidt expressed reservations about the membership, mandate, and authority of such a group.

After further discussion on the following day, a complex procedural compromise was reached, including an initial study group to work out the terms of reference for a subsequent international inquiry. German and French sources repeated their reservations about the scope of this inquiry, and Schmidt and Giscard made clear their intention to proceed with their planned exports. Carter publicly restated his concerns about this 'very difficult and sensitive question'.

Nevertheless, though it was not clear at the time, the controversy that had roiled the Atlantic Alliance for months had been transformed by the summit into a cooperative endeavour. The short-term study was completed more or less on schedule, and the 'International Nuclear Fuel Cycle Evaluation', or INFCE, as the longer inquiry was called, opened in October 1977, with broader participation and a programme of work spreading over two years. In retrospect, it is clear that the London agreement allowed Carter to back off his demands that the Brazilian and Pakistani deals be revoked, and that commercial use of plutonium be renounced. At the same time, as the inquiry proceeded, other governments became more sensititve to the perils of nuclear proliferation. In the end, the French deal with Pakistan did not go forward. German commentators noted that despite Bonn's unbending public stance, the climate of opinion was shifting, and the Brazil deal 'in any case will be the last deal of this sort'.[15]

In short, INFCE represented a procedural solution to gain time to address a problem that, at least at the moment, defied substantive solution or genuine compromise. Broadly similar techniques would be used in 1982–3 in a belated attempt to defuse the even more controversial summit issues of East–West economic relations and currency intervention. In the case of non-proliferation, the success of the procedural approach was signalled by the fact that the issue occasioned no controversy at all at the Bonn summit.

Some passages in the communiqué on energy were intended as much to help with domestic difficulties as to resolve international disagreements. President Carter, who had just submitted to Congress an ambitious and unpopular energy programme, was pleased with language that committed the participants to 'conserve energy and increase and diversify energy production, so that we reduce our dependence on oil'. This seemingly innocuous sentence embodied what would become a major item of contention during the 1978 summit. Facing growing 'Green' opposition to their domestic nuclear energy programme, the Germans were pleased with the endorsement of 'the need to increase nuclear energy to help meet the world's energy requirements'.

Trade issues were on the agenda when discussions resumed on Sunday. Giscard and Barre had already stressed the structural changes under way in the world economy, and the consequent need for levelling trade barriers in an 'organised' way. (Japanese participants later expressed surprise at the intensity of these attacks on free trade.) The Americans, Germans, and Japanese succeeded in getting a commitment to 'seek this year to achieve substantial progress' in the Tokyo Round negotiations, but French, UK, and Italian resistance led to a certain dilution of the communiqué language on trade, and French briefings afterwards stressed the qualifications that had been introduced. Nevertheless, though no progress had even been attempted on the substantive issues in the GATT negotiations, Robert Strauss had received what he chose to interpret as his marching orders, and in July the Geneva talks moved into a more intensive phase.

When the discussion finally arrived at North–South issues, the summiteers moved briskly, but without much enthusiasm, to agree on a package of Western counter-offers and counter-demands that they said represented a commitment 'to do all in our power to achieve . . . a successful conclusion of the Conference on International Economic Cooperation'. The package included support for the idea of a common fund for commodity price stabilisation, as well as $1 billion in special aid, though the Americans and Germans continued to mutter their unhappiness. In the end, the North–South gap at the Paris meeting proved to be much too wide to be bridged by this Western initiative, and on 30 June CIEC ended in stalemate.

During Vice-President Mondale's initial tour of capitals, the Americans had pressed for the summit agenda to be expanded beyond economic issues to include such topics as arms control and mutual security. However, this proposal encountered the standing French and Japanese objections to broadening the formal agenda. While such 'political' issues were, as in past summits, addressed over meals and in corridors, the principle that the summits of the Seven were economic in character persisted. A meeting of the leaders of the Four Powers was publicly announced for the day after the summit of the Seven. Although this meeting was called nominally to address questions regarding Berlin, President Giscard revealed beforehand that it would cover broader political issues, including East–West relations and Soviet encroachments in Africa.

Post-mortem on Downing Street

Immediate reactions to the Downing Street summit were generally positive. The *International Herald Tribune* went so far as to conclude that 'the meeting itself was easily the most successful of the three industrialised-nation economic summits held up to now', a judgment echoed, for example, by the *Neue Züriche Zeitung*.[16] However, this satisfaction proved short-lived. Within less than four months, the host himself, under pressure within his party to accelerate UK growth and peeved that the locomotives were not pulling as strongly as had been expected, described his summit as 'a failure'. By spring 1978, with unemployment still climbing, protectionism still rising, and the Americans and Germans still bickering, the London gathering was viewed in most capitals as having achieved nothing at all – 'a fiasco', said *The Times*.[17]

However, this judgment too was premature. Summits must be seen as episodes in a continuing process of international accommodation, rather than as climactic moments of decision – as stages in a marathon, rather than as separate sprints. In this longer perspective, the Downing Street summit cultivated a number of important initiatives that would come to fruition in the next several years. As we have noted, the procedural compromise on non-proliferation enabled both sides to back away from a useless confrontation. In the hands of able and energetic negotiators, the summit's endorsement of the Tokyo Round proved to be a useful prod to entrenched interests that had long stalled the negotiations. Within twenty months of Downing Street, agreement would be reached at the GATT in Geneva, thanks in large part (according to key participants) to the stimulus provided by the London and Bonn summits. In the macroeconomic field, as the German press had foreseen, the growth targets accepted at London would provide leverage for a renewed offensive by advocates of coordinated world reflation, leading to a substantial agreement in Bonn. Even Roy Jenkins' rather humiliating admission to summitry through the servants' entrance would prove to be an adequate precedent from which fuller participation by the European Community could emerge. Only on North–South relations would the fruits of London wither, but no summit has been very productive in that field.

Following up London

The Carter Administration lost no time in attempting to consolidate what they saw as their gains from the London discussions. On 25 May 1977, Treasury Secretary Blumenthal declared pointedly that 'we are all committed to adopt further policies, if needed, to achieve stated [growth] targets and to contribute to the adjustment of payments imbalances'. In the first of a series of comments widely interpreted as an attempt to 'talk the dollar down', he asserted that Germany and Japan had agreed not to resist market pressures for the appreciation of the yen and Deutschmark.[18]

The US economy boomed ahead throughout the spring and summer of 1977, and as Prime Minister Callaghan had predicted at the summit, the US balance of payments moved into the red. On the other hand, German and Japanese growth continued to taper off. At a meeting of the Economic Policy Committee of the OECD in June, the pre-Downing Street expansionist alliance among the Americans, the British, the OECD Secretariat, and the smaller countries re-emerged, their offensive fortified by the London-sanctioned growth targets. By the time of the follow-up meeting of sherpas in September, it was apparent that neither Germany nor Japan was likely to meet its target. Representatives of those two countries pointed to modest additional stimulus packages that had just been introduced, but the Americans and the British pushed for further action. Gloom about world economic prospects had deepened by the time of the November meetings of the OECD. The Germans and Japanese, on the defensive because by now even they had to acknowledge that their growth was well below forecast, nevertheless once again rejected calls for additional expansionary measures. The German representative counter-attacked, terming the locomotive theory 'naive'.

But if most criticism in these international gatherings was directed at the German and Japanese trade surpluses and low growth, the ballooning US trade deficit and the falling dollar were also beginning to attract unfavourable attention. By the end of November, the dollar had fallen 18 per cent against the yen and nearly 16 per cent against the Deutschmark in less than a year. The US external deficit would reach $18 billion in 1977 and was expected to continue climbing in 1978. Many observers were beginning to agree with the Germans that currency instability (that is, the weak dollar) itself undermined business confidence and world trade, and that the US deficit was to be interpreted, not as a praiseworthy contribution to global recovery, but as the result of the United States' uncontrolled appetite for imported oil.

All sides conceded that the world economy was in serious trouble. But was the fundamental problem the tight-fisted German and Japanese fiscal policy, or the slack-jawed US energy policy? In effect, this debate had already fixed the parameters for the basic deal at the Bonn summit.

The winding road to Bonn

More than any of its predecessors or its successors, the Bonn summit illustrates the potential (and the limits) of institutionalised summitry as a way of reconciling interdependence and sovereignty. Substantive preparations began earlier and were more intensive than in the past. Nevertheless, one week before the summiteers arrived in Bonn, *Die Zeit* headlined 'A crisis without end? On the eve of the fourth world economic conference deep pessimism reigns', and the *New York Times* warned that 'the summit promises little beyond public relations manoeuvers. We should count ourselves fortunate if the personal and diplomatic irritations in the alliance are not exacerbated.'[19]

Yet, in the end, the agreement announced at Bonn would represent the clearest case, by far, of a summit deal that left all participants happier than when they arrived. The Germans and Japanese would promise (and deliver) significant additional reflation. The Americans would promise (and deliver) anti-inflationary policies and lower oil imports. The others would concede (and later ratify) a significant liberalisation of world commerce. As the participants concluded, 'The measures on which we have agreed are mutually reinforcing. Their total effect should thus be more than the sum of their parts.' It was apparently a textbook case of international policy coordination.

On the other hand, in the aftermath of Bonn many commentators said that the coordination was fictitious, that each participant was in fact just 'doing his own thing', that each was disguising predetermined, self-serving actions as 'concessions' made in the interests of international cooperation. Again, the *New York Times* spoke for observers in many capitals: 'In effect, each nation agreed to pursue policies that in large part, they had already accepted.'[20]

National autonomy or international cooperation – which did Bonn represent? As we shall see, the answer is 'both'. Each leader was, in the end, doing what he believed to be in his own and his nation's interest, although not all his advisors agreed. On the other hand, without the summit, he probably would not (or could not) so readily have done what he was doing. In that sense, whatever its substantive economic merits, the deal struck at Bonn represented a successful meshing of domestic and international pressures.[21]

Surprisingly, this unexpectedly successful deal was struck between two men, Jimmy Carter and Helmut Schmidt, who despised and distrusted each other. Indeed, as we shall see, the fundamental bargain was framed at the very moment when tension between them was greatest. The most intriguing question about the Bonn deal, therefore, is why it was possible. Before addressing that question, however, we must trace the tortuous path that led there.

The Japanese contribution

In November and December 1977, US foreign economic diplomacy was focused, not on the multilateral effort to achieve coordinated recovery, but on bilateral relations with Japan.[22] By now, it was clear that Prime Minister Fukuda's London targets were going to be badly underachieved. Growth for the year would be, not 6.7 per cent, but 5.3 per cent, and in place of a predicted trade deficit of $700 million, Japan's exporters would rack up a trade surplus of $10 billion, despite the yen's appreciation. Pressures to restrict trade with Japan were building in the US Congress, as they were in Europe.

Within Japan, a coalition of business interests, the Ministry of Trade and Industry (MITI), the Economic Planning Agency, and some expansion-minded LDP politicians pushed for substantial additional domestic stimulus, using US pressure as one of their prime arguments against the stubborn resistance of the Ministry of Finance (MOF). Prime Minister Fukuda, despite his background as a 'stingy' MOF bureaucrat, was by all accounts eager to be accepted as a responsible world statesman, conscious of his unfulfilled promises of London, and concerned about trade frictions with the Americans and (less vitally) the Europeans. In late November, he reshuffled his cabinet, bringing in several of the LDP expansionists and charging Nobuhiko Ushiba, the original Japanese sherpa, and now Minister for External Economic Affairs, with the task of seeking an accommodation with the Americans.

Within six weeks, Ushiba and Robert Strauss had reached formal agreement on a 7 per cent Japanese growth target for 1978, to be attained through additional fiscal stimulus, in addition to the settlement of outstanding bilateral trade issues. In return, the Americans pledged in general terms to bring down oil imports and control inflation. This agreement was a crucial building block in the package deal later in Bonn, where Prime Minister Fukuda reconfirmed (and in certain respects, amplified) the Strauss–Ushiba understanding.

Particularly striking about the Japanese decision was the interplay between domestic politics and international pressure. Without the internal divisions in the Japanese government, it is unlikely that the US demands would have been met. However, without the US pressure, and the legitimation added later by the multilateral summit commitment, it is even more unlikely that the Japanese expansionists could have overridden the powerful Ministry of Finance. 'Seventy per cent foreign pressure, 30 per cent internal politics', was the private judgment of one MOF insider. 'Fifty–fifty,' guessed an official from MITI. A senior politician, closely involved on the expansionist side of the dispute, explained how summit pressures and domestic politics became intertwined:

When the bureaucracy is unanimous, their position cannot be beaten at the summit, because the other heads of government are not audacious enough to engage in harsh criticism [of one another], and national sovereignty survives. But in some cases the arguments within Japan could go either way, as in the locomotive case, and then one can 'draw authority' from the summit.

A stormy Atlantic springtime

As 1978 opened, unemployment queues in Europe were longer than they had been in decades, with 7 million people jobless, as compared to 4.7 million at the time of Rambouillet. With the exception of the United States, virtually all the major Western economies were growing more slowly than had been expected only a few months earlier. In January, the Germans announced that the next summit would be held in Bonn, but Chancellor Schmidt again rebuffed international pressure for additional German stimulus. Germany could not serve as a locomotive to pull the others out of the recession, he said, adding elliptically, 'together with others this can be done, but not on our own'. World recovery required a strengthened dollar, and the key to that was the reduction of US oil imports.[23]

In February the German–American economic debate became more heated, although by now, both sides were replaying well-worn records. Treasury Secretary Blumenthal visited Bonn, driving home US views by threatening that the Americans might skip Schmidt's summit, unless a prior understanding could be reached on German growth. 'We don't need a new economic summit that would only send empty platitudes floating down the Rhine,' he was quoted as saying.[24] The Americans calculated, correctly, that in domestic political terms the summit was more important to Schmidt than to Carter. As Schmidt probably recognised, however, the Americans were bluffing. Summitry had become so institutionalised that none of the leaders could get off the merry-go-round without creating a major crisis within the Alliance.

Meanwhile, drumfire criticism of German and Japanese trade surpluses and inadequate growth continued in virtually every international forum, accompanied now by increasing uneasiness about US neglect of the dollar. Johannes Witteveen, Managing Director of the IMF, for example, termed past German and Japanese expansionary moves 'quite disappointing' and urged them to do more, but also called for more active US intervention in defence of the dollar to offset its payments deficit.[25] The OECD staff, hoping to mollify the Germans and Japanese, while convincing the United States that support of the dollar would not be a waste of money, unveiled its revised 'convoy' plan for moderate expansion by a number of 'convalescent' economies, not merely the erstwhile locomotives.

On 2 March 1978, the dollar fell below the symbolic DM2.00 level in Frankfurt, culminating a 20 per cent appreciation of the Deutschmark in twelve months. The Bundesbank had reportedly exceeded its monetary targets by nearly 100 per cent in the previous quarter in an effort to stem the tide of greenbacks. In effect, the US monetary expansion of 1977–8 was inducing monetary expansion in Germany (and Japan), as those governments sought to hold down their currencies against the dollar. Nevertheless, the dollar's decline created dilemmas for both US and German policy-makers. On the one hand, it threatened German exports, but on the other, some Americans began to fear, it increased inflationary pressures in the United States and raised broader questions about US leadership.

Despairing of effective action by the Americans, Chancellor Schmidt launched the first moves toward the EMS. The idea had been mooted by Roy Jenkins in October 1977 as a move toward European integration. But Schmidt became convinced of its merits only when the United States seemed incapable of action. He found immediate support from President Giscard, long convinced of the need for greater monetary stability. Disdainful of well-rehearsed opposition from the monetary experts, they broached their ideas at the Copenhagen European Council in April 1978, and the proposed EMS was the main theme of the European Council at Bremen ten days before the Bonn summit. Most of the other Community members welcomed measures to tie Europe closer together. However, Prime Minister Callaghan was hesitant, fearing that the EMS might reduce prospects for growth, by binding everyone closer to the German economy. He preferred measures which would involve the Americans actively rather than leave them outside.[26]

Others proposed alternative schemes to stabilise the dollar. Witteveen, supported by the British, pressed for a 'substitution account' to spread the dollar's 'burden' as a reserve currency. The Japanese expressed interest in a 'target zone' exchange rate regime. Some European bankers called for the United States to raise large foreign loans. But neither the Americans nor the Germans were much attracted by these ideas. Both preferred to address 'the fundamentals' behind the dollar's difficulties, although they could not agree whether the German (and Japanese) trade surpluses or US oil imports and inflationary pressures were more fundamental.

The Carter Administration did not contest the view that US dependence on foreign oil should be reduced. As one US observer noted,

In 1978 Americans were still paying prices well below world levels for energy; gasoline for automobiles, for instance, was less than half as expensive to American consumers than to their counterparts in Europe and Japan. US oil imports increased 20 per cent in 1976 and 18 per cent in 1977, so that by 1977 they amounted to almost 48 per cent of US consumption and cost a total of \$45 billion, compared with \$8.5 billion in 1973.[27]

It was just such facts as these that the Administration cited in support of the President's energy proposals that had been unveiled on 20 April 1977.[28] The complex programme included measures to promote conservation and encourage the development of alternative energy sources, but the centrepiece was a 'crude oil equalisation tax'. This proposal was intended to raise prices for newly discovered oil to world levels, thus encouraging production and discouraging consumption, while ensuring that oil companies would not earn huge windfall profits. However attractive this idea was intellectually, it was a disaster politically. By spring 1978, after a year's enervating struggle with Congress, the Administration's proposals seemed as far as ever from winning passage. Thus, many in the Administration sympathised with the Germans' complaints, particularly their insistence on the decontrol of US oil prices, although those complaints were also seen as an attempt to distract attention from the Germans' own responsibilities for global recovery.

As the German–American stand-off continued through the winter, bystanders became increasingly worried that they were caught in the middle of 'a dangerous game of chicken'.[29] This concern was particularly marked in London, in part because the government wanted desperately to relax the international constraints on UK growth in time for an autumn election, but also because Callaghan saw himself as an honest broker between Schmidt and Carter. In mid-March 1978, he visited Bonn and Washington to suggest the outline of a package deal for the summit: the Germans would accelerate growth, the Americans would agree to conserve energy and to share more broadly the burdens of managing the international monetary system, the French and British would agree to liberalise trade, and all would increase aid to the Third World. Neither the Germans nor the Americans liked the UK ideas on currency reform, but the notion of a package of offsetting concessions from the summit participants was attractive. The Americans suggested that their part of the bargain should include energy conservation and inflation-fighting, two issues on which the Administration could use some international support domestically.

Callaghan's initiative was an important step forward and contained virtually all the elements of the eventual Bonn settlement. It coincided with bilateral efforts by the Germans and Americans to cool their economic dispute. Following private assurances from Schmidt that he would move on the growth issue – 'if you do your part' – the United States announced on 12 March 1978 that they would attend the summit after all. By the end of the month, insiders in both Bonn and Washington sensed the outlines of a deal, although the specific content remained to be spelled out, including the size and timing of the German stimulus and the nature of the US commitment to cut oil imports. Already, the respective opponents of the proposed policy moves – in the German banking community, for example, as well as on the White House Domestic Policy Staff – were becoming uneasy.

At just this point, US–German relations were thrown into turmoil by an unrelated, but devastating development. On 27 March, President Carter dispatched a messenger to tell Schmidt that he had decided against production of the so-called neutron bomb. Foreign Minister Genscher raced to Washington on 3 April, but was unable to reverse the decision. He returned to Bonn, describing Carter disparagingly as a 'religious visionary'. Schmidt, blunter as always, termed the US president 'an unfathomable dilettante . . . incompetent to fill the shoes of the Western leader'.[30]

During this same week the sherpas, meeting in Bonn, reached agreement on the summit agenda and apparently confirmed the outlines of the package that had emerged over the previous month, although when it came to the all-important details the Germans temporised, saying that it was too early to assess the full results of their most recent stimulus measures.[31] Nevertheless, the timing of this incipient deal is striking confirmation that international policy coordination during the era of Trilateralist summitry did not depend on personal sympathy among the summiteers.

Pressure on the Germans for faster growth was mounting within the European Community as well. On 7–8 April 1978, the European Council endorsed in principle a 'concerted action' package aimed at accelerating European recovery. All recognised that the strategy entailed additional German expansion, and although the Germans promised nothing, they did not object to having the Commission work out further details. At the same meeting, Schmidt and Giscard put forward their startling proposal to create a 'zone of monetary stability in Europe'. Some observers thought they detected a link between the two initiatives: the Germans would agree to additional fiscal stimulus, if the others would agree to the monetary discipline implicit in tying their currencies to the Deutschmark and perhaps curb their protectionist impulses.

On the issue of oil imports, only the Canadians sympathised with the US position, but on the issue of growth, German isolation was clearer still. Giscard, Schmidt's alter ego, sympathised with his irritation at the Anglo-American 'bullying', but privately counselled him not to be unnecessarily insistent on fiscal orthodoxy. During a state visit to Tokyo by President Scheel and Foreign Minister Genscher, Minister Ushiba noted that Japan had voluntarily committed itself to a 7 per cent growth target and urged the Germans to make more effort.[32] After an IMF Interim Committee meeting in May 1978, the German press reported:

> Model pupil Bonn on the delinquents' bench

[Finance Minister] Matthöfer in Mexico City stood alone against (almost) everyone. . . . Neither in Mexico nor in his subsequent talks in Washington did he consent to new economic programmes. . . . But Matthöfer naturally knows that the Government will not be able to avoid additional measures, if the weakening of growth observable in the first months of this year should continue to mid-year.[33]

Publicly, Matthöfer conceded that 'pressure of this sort often has its effect in the long run, even if it is rejected at the time', and privately he confided to the Americans that he expected new stimulus measures to be introduced by the Federal Government.

The German decision: appearance and reality

It is worth pausing at this point to ask what had been happening in Bonn that could lead the Schmidt government to reverse its oft-repeated refusal to contemplate additional reflation. The simple myth, then and now, is that a reluctant government, led by a reluctant Chancellor, was forced to this unwise step by overwhelming international pressure. The facts are more complex and more interesting.

During the spring of 1978 a domestic political process, inspired by foreign pressures, but orchestrated by expansionists within the German government, led to a situation in which a revision of German economic policy would have been highly likely, even if the international pressure in the end had eased. In effect, those closest to Schmidt now say, the Chancellor 'let himself be pushed' into a policy that he probably favoured on domestic grounds, but would have found costly and perhaps impossible to pursue without the 'tailwind' provided by the summit.[34]

The German delegation had left London in May 1977, reasonably confident that they could meet their 5 per cent growth target. Almost immediately, however, it became clear that their optimism was misplaced. By mid-August Schmidt was sufficiently concerned about the latest indicators to call a number of senior colleagues to a private meeting at his home in Hamburg. 'I have been made to look ridiculous [*blamiert*],' he told them, as he asked their advice about possible policy adjustments.

By late winter, while the German public posture remained one of complete rejection of foreign entreaties for additional stimulus measures, several of Schmidt's closest economic advisors privately had concluded that just such a programme was necessary in Germany's own interest. Their line of argument was, in fact, strikingly similar to that of the OECD, the Americans, and their allies: German growth was proving slower than expected; unemployment remained stubbornly high, while inflation had dropped to quite tolerable levels; Germany's international surplus was dampening growth abroad, fostering currency instability and protectionism. In short, Germany had put on the brakes too soon. These advisors were not certain whether the Chancellor himself agreed with them, but all were aware of his domestic political needs, including the need to plan now for adequate economic growth in the approach to the 1980 elections, and there is reason in retrospect to believe that he shared their views.

But if the Chancellor's office was becoming convinced of the desirability of additional stimulus, the mood in the country and in the government itself was still decisively contrary. Building political consensus for a policy switch would take time, and an essential part of the process would have to be international pressure. Thus, in order to allow the domestic political situation to mature, the expansionists opposed suggestions from Callaghan and from some of the Chancellor's political advisors that the summit be held somewhat earlier than planned.

A second element in the strategy was firm resistance, both publicly and privately, by the government and the Chancellor, to the international pressures. This resistance served two purposes. Domestically, it protected the Chancellor's reputation as a sturdy defender of German national interests and, above all, a guarantor of price stability. Internationally, it powerfully increased his bargaining leverage vis-à-vis the Americans and their European allies. Assuming that international demands for German reflation continued – a good bet – the Chancellor might win energy restraint from the Americans and concessions on trade policy from the British and French, while assuring timely German expansion and reinforcing his stature, nationally and internationally. Rarely has a strategy in international political economy been played with such skill or success.

As 1978 opened, support within German domestic politics for additional expansion was visible only in the trade union movement and the SPD. Those forces were heartened by the international clamour for faster German growth, but alone they provided an inadequate basis for policy change. At the time of Blumenthal's February visit, for example, both the German Chamber of Industry and Commerce and the opposition CDU economics spokesman cheered the Chancellor's rejection of additional stimulus, as did virtually all the German press. Most senior officials in the Finance and Economics Ministries opposed further reflation, and indeed Finance Minister Apel had resisted foreign pressure in that direction for more than four years. An even more important adversary was Economics Minister Count Otto Lambsdorff, for given the coalition's narrow parliamentary margin, no significant policy change could be made without the consent of his Free Democrats. Finally, the powerful Bundesbank maintained its traditional defence of fiscal and monetary rectitude.

Within four months, however, each of these partners in German economic policy-making had become members – some reluctant, some enthusiastic – of a broad consensus for additional fiscal stimulus. In February 1978, the replacement of Apel by Matthöfer meant that the Finance Ministry was represented by someone less inclined to argue against reflation. Meanwhile, the mood in broader economic circles began to shift. Updated economic indicators, showing continued undershooting of growth targets and rising unemployment, encouraged these conversions to some extent. The appreciation of the Deutschmark, with its long-run threat to German export industries, may have played some role, although there is no evidence that this was decisive. By most accounts, the most important factor was the steady growth of international criticism of German responsibility for European and even global stagnation. As one reluctant convert pointed out later, 'In the end, even the Bank for International Settlements [the Basle organisation of central bankers] supported the idea of coordinated reflation.' Above all, there was a growing sense of inevitability – 'Well, after all, why not?'

As the US pressure mounted and as the domestic winds shifted, the Economics Minister appears to have concluded that if he could not fight the tide, he should turn it to advantage. Particularly after the FDP did poorly in several important local elections, and as his business constituents and his CDU rivals began to call for tax relief, Lambsdorff shifted his sights from the question of *whether* to the question of *how* to stimulate the economy. He signalled his conversion publicly in a June statement supporting tax cuts, made during a visit to Washington. Hearing reports of this, Chancellor Schmidt smiled triumphantly at one senior aide.

The Bundesbank seems to have been the last, most reluctant convert. Bundesbank President Otmar Emminger even called on Arthur Burns, a respected acquaintance of Schmidt's from Library Group days, to try to dissuade the Chancellor. Eventually, however, the Bank capitulated, having in mind particularly the international situation. In an unprecedented move, the Bank's leaders agreed to tell the government how large a fiscal deficit would, in the Bank's view, be permissible. In effect, the Bank was agreeing to monetary policy that would accommodate the stimulus programme. The Chancellor's right flank was covered.

By now the reaction in the chemistry of domestic politics was self-sustaining, no matter how crucial the initial foreign catalyst. Only the banking community and a number of more orthodox economists continued to hold out. During the final weeks before the summit, in fact, the Chancellor had to brake the internal pressure, so that he could use his growth 'concession' as a lever to extract commitments from the other summiteers. 'Let's wait a while, until after the summit,' he told his colleagues. 'Make them [the Americans and their allies] force me to do it, so that in the end, I can. . . .'

In short, the *fact* of a significant German stimulus programme was driven in the final analysis as much by domestic as by foreign pressures. The *composition* of the programme was clearly determined by domestic politics, and in particular, by Lambsdorff's tactical victory over those Social Democrats who wished to increase social spending and investment grants, rather than cut taxes. Whether the *size* and *timing* of the programme would have been the same without the foreign pressures is less certain, in part because the question involves conjectural history. Most German participants believe that without the international factor, it would have been very difficult for the government to put through the parliament so sizeable a boost to the budget deficit, and many believe that the Chancellor himself was persuaded of the specific numbers only at the summit itself. On the other hand, the figure agreed in the communiqué, 1 per cent of GNP, or approximately DM12 billion, had been used in internal discussions for several months prior to the summit. This fact might imply that the bargaining over numbers at the summit, like the pre-summit international bargaining over whether there would be a stimulus programme at all, was primarily shadow-boxing.

Trade and energy: the rest of the package

By May 1978, a more expansive German economic policy seemed increasingly probable. Meanwhile, the Carter Administration had shifted its foot from the accelerator to the brake, domestically speaking. On 12 April, the President had announced an anti-inflationary programme, and by 24 May, his Treasury Secretary was calling inflation 'public enemy number one'. German and US macroeconomic policies were beginning to converge.

The focus of international bargaining now shifted to trade liberalisation, on which the Germans and Americans were closely allied. The Germans were upset that several of their European partners, notably the British, seemed to be giving way to protectionism, as exemplified by trade-distorting subsidies to industry. The central trade question, however, concerned the Tokyo Round negotiations. Progress had been made at Geneva in the year since London. A detailed timetable had ensured that all bids for tariff cuts and non-tariff codes were tabled by January 1978, and active negotiation had ensued throughout the first half of the year. However, basic disagreements remained on the tougest issues:

agriculture, a special interest of the Americans, who were particularly critical of European Community export subsidies, and the French, who were concerned to protect the Common Agricultural Policy;

selective safeguards against import surges, a special interest of the British, who feared competition from the newly industrialising countries; and

tariff and non-tariff barriers to the Japanese home market, to which the European and Americans attributed a substantial part of the massive Japanese trade surpluses.

Behind these issues remained the fundamental scepticism of the French that this was the time for a major round of tariff cuts. At French insistence, but with occasional support from the British and the Italians, the Community negotiators had been dragging their feet in Geneva, as the Americans and Germans saw it. Privately, President Giscard recognised that a deal was unavoidable, given French isolation on the issue. However, he intended that his acquiescence would be accepted as his contribution to the Bonn package, and he was naturally also concerned to minimise the risks to French interests.

With the advent of the summit – and thus the deadline for 'substantive progress', in the words of the London communiqué – the indefatigable US negotiator, Robert Strauss, increased the pressure for reaching an agreement, threatening to lay all the outstanding issues before the summiteers themselves in Bonn, if no agreement had been reached by then. Meanwhile, the German Chancellor turned the screw another notch, letting it be known in the UK press that he considered a commitment to renounce protectionism to be 'the most important element' in a successful summit package deal.[35] Finally, after a week of intense negotiations, a 'framework of understanding' was reached in Geneva three days before the summit was to open. Though important questions remained unresolved, this framework would form the basis for the final Tokyo Round package.

Ever the able poker player, Helmut Schmidt sought to assure that everyone else's stakes were on the table before playing his final card. While suggesting to London that only trade concessions could elicit his commitment to growth, he hinted to his European partners that consensus on 'a stronger linkage among the European currencies' – the Schmidt–Giscard initiative that would eventually lead to the EMS – might have a place in the summit package.[36] But his 'main priority', as he told the US magazine *Business Week*, was the reduction of US oil imports,[37] and the evidence suggests that in fact this *was* the crucial part of the package for the Germans.

The Germans recognised that foreign pressure on the Americans to curb their thirst for imported oil might be useful to the Administration. Indeed, several senior US officials emphasised frankly to their German counterparts that foreign insistence on decontrol of the price of oil would be a welcome weapon in the Administration's struggles with Congress. However, higher oil prices were intensely unpopular among many of the President's constituents, and his domestic advisors in the White House had been troubled since early spring about the looming Bonn package deal. Moreover, as resistance to his energy programme hardened in Congress, the President's closest political aides became increasingly concerned that he not be made a fool of, by making commitments internationally that could not be kept domestically.

Barely three weeks before the summit, these worries suddenly became acute. Responding to continuing foreign demands that higher US oil prices be the centrepiece of the US contribution to the summit bargain, the President told a group of Congressmen that he was ready administratively to impose a surcharge on oil imports, if the Senate continued to stall his legislative proposals.[38] The Senate's response was swift and ominous: within a week, it approved a provision that (if confirmed by the House of Representatives) would annul the President's authority to act administratively as he had threatened. The Administration scrambled to repair the damage, exploring alternative means to limit oil imports, and sending the Senate Majority Leader to Bonn to assure Chancellor Schmidt that the prospects for eventual legislative success were still good. Nevertheless, as the US party departed for Bonn, they were privately more worried about their own part of the package deal than about the contributions of the other summiteers.

Bargaining in Bonn, 16–17 July 1978

The line-up of players for Bonn was identical to that for London, but their relative standing was not. Valéry Giscard d'Estaing had emerged remarkably strengthened from the March 1978 legislative elections; Helmut Schmidt's popularity had never been higher; and Roy Jenkins had just joined forces with the two of them at the Bremen European Council meeting on 6–7 July to win endorsement of a new European monetary system. Takeo Fukuda arrived bearing virtually all the 'gifts' that were expected of him: he had repeated his growth pledge for 1978 so often that in Tokyo he was nicknamed 'Mr Seven Percent', and three days before the summit Japan had announced that it would hold the volume of its exports constant in 1978, would spend $4 billion on an emergency import programme, and would double its development assistance within the next three years. Like his European counterparts, Fukuda was prepared for straight talk to the Americans.

By contrast, Jimmy Carter's honeymoon was over. At home, his approval ratings in the polls had plummeted from 75 per cent to 38 per cent, and abroad his credibility had been called into serious question. Nevertheless, any US president plays a central role in Western summitry, and a UK headline caught the mood: 'Weakened Carter holds key to Bonn summit'.[39]

Conscious of both the risks of exaggerated expectations and the attractions of high drama, official briefers underplayed the extent to which the summit had been prepared. One preview warned: 'Traditionally, Prime Ministers, Presidents, and Chancellors meet to put the final stamp of approval and authority on plans and proposals that have been worked out in detail by their staffs in advance. In this case the basic elements of those plans have failed to mature in the weeks of preparation.'[40] In fact, the prepared script was reasonably clear, although it was not certain whether the summiteers could summon the political will to follow it.

The first item on their agenda was macroeconomics. Following the failure of London's exercise in targetry, it had been agreed to focus less on economic outcomes and more on policy measures. As expected, Schmidt and Fukuda were exhorted to accelerate growth. Fukuda repeated his pledge of 7 per cent domestic-led growth, and promised to take additional fiscal measures in August or September, if that appeared necessary to meet the goal.

The outstanding issue, of course, remained the German commitment to additional stimulus measures. The German and US sherpas were asked to work out acceptable language on that question, as well as on the US energy commitment. (Ironically, during that session each negotiator privately favoured the policy being urged on his country by the other.) Senior members of the German Cabinet met to ratify the emerging deal, thus firmly committing both coalition partners. Poker-faced to the end, Schmidt resisted agreeing to a specific size for the stimulus programme until the last plenary session, when everyone's final offer was on the table, but the German delegation finally agreed to 'propose to the legislative bodies additional and quantitatively substantial measures up to one per cent of GNP, designed to achieve a significant strengthening of demand and a higher rate of growth'. After two years, 'the great locomotive debate' was concluded.

Formally speaking, each of the summit countries shared in the macroeconomic undertakings. France agreed that its 1978 budget deficit would be FF10 billion larger than earlier forecast. Italy repeated earlier commitments to cut public current expenditure, while increasing public investment. Canada restated its existing growth target of 'up to 5 per cent'. The United Kingdom reckoned that its budget announced earlier in the spring contributed to the concerted recovery. For the United States, Carter outlined his programme for battling inflation. In substance, only the Germans and Japanese promised new initiatives; the others simply reaffirmed measures already in the pipeline.

Meanwhile, the second item under discussion was energy. Fukuda, expressing a widely shared view with un-Japanese assertiveness, told Carter that most of the world's economic woes could be traced to the inability of the United States to restrict oil imports. In reply, the President explained in detail the domestic politics of the issue, expressing confidence that his energy programme would receive Congressional approval, but offering private assurances that if the legislation were unsatisfactory he would take unilateral action to cut oil imports. Schmidt had apparently been convinced during a pre-summit bilateral meeting with Carter that this approach was acceptable, assuming that appropriate language could be drafted, and the others expressed understanding for the President's political dilemma. The key phrases in the lengthy US pledge in the final communiqué – carefully cleared with the President's domestic advisers back in Washington – were commitments that 'by year end [1978] measures will be in effect that will result in oil import savings of approximately 2.5 million barrels per day by 1985', and that 'the prices paid for oil in the U.S. shall be raised to the world level by the end of 1980'.[41]

The most controversial topic turned out to be trade. The summiteers themselves spent a heated half-day on this subject, longer than at any other summit. The French were unhappy about the framework agreement reached the week before, complaining that the European Community negotiators had made excessive concessions to the Americans. Robert Strauss and his European colleagues turned up in Bonn during the summit, and a frantic round of bilateral discussions was held late into the night between the Americans and the French, the French and the Germans, the Americans and the Japanese, and finally the European Commission and the Americans. These sessions found solutions for a number of specific problems, including a procedural finesse for the contentious question of safeguards, although the communiqué noted that 'some difficult and important issues remain unresolved'. The leaders' commitment 'to conclude the detailed negotiations by December 15, 1978' served as a statement of political will that the bargainers subsequently were able to exploit to overcome internal obstacles. As one aide later put it, 'The summits created an atmosphere in which those of us working on the negotiations could legitimately say that it was unthinkable to fail.'   .

The discussion of monetary issues at Bonn was less satisfactory all around. Fukuda, Schmidt, Giscard, and Jenkins criticised US neglect of the dollar. Carter answered by restating the US view that world currency stability could be achieved only by addressing its fundamental causes, a view that was reflected in the final communiqué. The three Europeans explained the Bremen initiative for European monetary integration, asking for endorsement of that proposal from the others. With quiet encouragement from Prime Minister Callaghan, who was himself uneasy about the EMS idea, the Americans and Japanese closely questioned Giscard, Schmidt, and Jenkins about the details. While expressing general sympathy for the ideal of European unity, the non-Europeans did not provide the desired endorsement. After the year-long slanging match, international monetary policy was relegated somewhat incongruously to the tail end of the communiqué, ranking behind even some innocuous language on North–South relations.

One novelty of the Bonn summit was the emergence of a wholly unanticipated joint resolution condemning international terrorism and agreeing to suspend air traffic with any country that offered sanctuary to hijackers or terrorists. This idea arose in informal discussions over lunch and appealed to the summiteers, several of whom recently had endured airline hijackings and domestic terrorist episodes. Though a unique example of unscripted summitry, the lack of preparation was reflected in the fact that the resolution proved difficult to square with existing legal obligations. Many meetings were necessary over the next three years to work out implementation.

As always, foreign policy played a more prominent role in the summit talks than appeared in the final communiqué. An intriguing glimpse into the wide-ranging discussions was offered by Prime Minister Andreotti's subsequent catalogue of the topics touched on over dinner: Namibia, Cyprus, the Middle East, Rhodesia, Angola, Salt II, human rights, and even Callaghan's electoral outlook.[42] The 'Berlin Four' continued their habit of meeting privately on the margins of the summit, apparently focusing on East–West relations.

Reflections on Bonn

As the summit closed, the leaders seemed almost euphoric. They had discussed sensitive domestic issues frankly. They had recognised that national decisions had important international consequences. They had accepted mutual responsibilities that exceeded, they said, even their expectations. They had struck a bargain that seemed fair to all and yet politically realistic. Even the sometimes prickly French, who preferred less structured summitry, were pleased. Giscard proclaimed 'a new era of mutual trust among the seven'.

Given the fate of previous summit promises, press commentary on the Bonn commitments was justifiably cautious and even sceptical. In the end, however, virtually all the crucial pledges were redeemed:

1. In September 1978, the German Federal Government introduced a DM12.5 billion pump-priming programme, and two months later the programme was approved by parliament. Altogether, the German budget deficit for 1978–9 was in fact larger (probably by somewhat more than 1 per cent of GDP) than would have been expected on the basis of current trends.[43]

2. In September 1978, in light of an apparent shortfall in growth, Japan adopted an additional public works programme. By the end of the year, Japanese growth was a full point below Fukuda's 7 per cent target, although domestic demand was up to the mark. This was the only significant Bonn pledge that was not fully met, but the US sherpa, Henry Owen, testified the following spring that 'it is our view that Japan made a good-faith effort to achieve its Bonn target'.[44]

3. Japanese exports in 1978 were 2 per cent below 1977, while imports were 10 per cent higher. Japanese foreign aid in 1980–1 exceeded the 1977 levels by 130 per cent measured in dollars, or 90 per cent measured in yen.

4. The detailed Tokyo Round trade negotiations were successfully concluded within the deadline set at Bonn. Final approval of the entire package was delayed by a last-minute Franco-American procedural wrangle over action by the US Congress, but when this hurdle was cleared, the agreement was signed on 12 April 1979.

Bearing in mind the difficult domestic politics of energy in the United States, many recognised after Bonn that, as the *Frankfurter Allgemeine Zeitung* (no friend of the President) put it, 'Carter took on the biggest commitments'.[45] Back in Washington there were fierce debates within the Administration about how to keep the President's pledges. White House domestic advisors continued to argue for delaying oil price decontrol, but the Bonn commitment was a powerful trump in the hands of the proponents of decontrol. As one said later, 'If a president commits himself to something at a summit, and you can cite that in a meeting, that's a damn powerful argument. The rest of the government may not be impressed, but the President is.'

In October 1978, Congress passed a weakened version of Carter's energy package, thus meeting his summit commitment to have a long-range energy programme in place by the end of the year. As had been foreseen at Bonn, this legislation did not include decontrol, so the President was forced to resort to administrative action. His domestic advisors won a delay of several months in the effective date of full decontrol, thus postponing this politically costly move until after the 1980 presidential election, but in the end, virtually every one of the essential US energy pledges made at Bonn was fulfilled.

As we have seen, worries about the dollar played an important role both in the background to Bonn and in the plenary discussions, even though monetary issues were slighted in the final communiqué. In fact, during the second half of 1978, the US current account began to swing back towards balance, benefitting from the cheaper dollar, but this trend was not yet fully visible. In the meantime, currency markets were not satisfied that either the Bonn package or the several limp-wristed instalments of Carter's anti-inflation programme adequately addressed the dollar's problems. The dollar continued to slide throughout the summer and autumn of 1978, plummeting 12 per cent against the Deutschmark in October alone. Finally, on 1 November, the Americans grasped the nettle, sharply tightening monetary policy and putting together a package of international loans and swap agreements to support the dollar. The medicine was politically unpalatable, but the dollar rebounded smartly. For US monetary policy, it was, as Bundesbank President Emminger said, 'a fundamental turning point'.[46]

Market pressures, concern about the inflationary consequences of the dollar's decline, and perhaps Bundesbank insistence on tighter US monetary policy as a condition for taking part in the support package were probably the most important influences on this policy shift. On the other hand, exchanges with his summit colleagues at Bonn and again in the final days before the November measures may have sensitised the President to the need for decisive action. As Henry Owen later testified, 'the United States agreed [in Bonn] to give primary emphasis to fighting inflation, and in the view of our summit partners, the President's November 1 decision on fiscal policy and his support of the Federal Reserve decisions on monetary policy represent a satisfactory fulfillment of that commitment'.[47]

In historical perspective, the Bonn accords represent a rare and perhaps even unique example of international coordination of economic policies. Mutually supportive decisions were taken that probably would not have been possible otherwise. Several factors help explain this success:

1. Despite their differences of temperament and national interest, these particular summiteers and their administrations were fundamentally internationalist in outlook. Each sought the solutions to his country's economic problems in a global context. More clearly than at any other summit, all the central protagonists at Bonn aimed at a cooperative package deal, and each was prepared to compromise in order to achieve that outcome. As we shall see, the next generation of summiteers were more nationally oriented.

2. The political pendulums in the key countries were temporarily synchronised. Centrist and centre-left governments were in power virtually everywhere. In particular, despite much talk of a cleavage between Keynesian America and monetarist Germany, the Carter and Schmidt governments were not deeply divided in ideological terms. (The contrast with the analogous dispute between the Reagan and Mitterrand governments in the early 1980s is striking.) Quite apart from the long-standing German–American alignment on such issues as trade policy and North–South relations, economic officials in the two administrations shared many of the same analytic premises. For example, shortly before the summit Schmidt was being confidentially advised that:

Only with a more equilibrated balance of payments situation in the OECD area will there also be more calm in the exchange rates between the currencies of the deficit and surplus countries. Our economies have grown close together in recent years. For this reason, the idea of a concerted strategy among the industrialised countries has won more and more friends. If the Federal Republic takes part in such a concerted action, it does so, not out of altruism, but out of solid national interest. Given the export dependence of our economy, a higher employment level can be achieved only if our exports rise more strongly. This assumes that we put our partners in a position to import more goods from the Federal Republic. Essentially, that must happen through higher imports by the Federal Republic, and that in turn assumes that domestic demand here at home rises more sharply than is to be expected according to current trends.

Such an analysis could have been drafted almost as easily in the Carter White House (or the OECD) as in the Schmidt Chancellery.

3. The Bonn summit was meticulously prepared. In effect, the preparatory process lasted nearly two years, during which the respective governments came better to understand how their interests in a wide range of fields might be reconciled. Moreover, the summit process was well integrated with the conventional international organisations, such as the OECD, the IMF, and the European Community, so that in a procedural sense (as well as a substantive sense) the Bonn accords represented a kind of 'concerted action'. (It may also be relevant that even when personal relations among the summiteers themselves were embittered, the senior officials charged with preparing the summit shared considerable mutual trust and esteem.) Detailed preparation of summits has latterly acquired a bad name among several key governments, but preparation worked at Bonn.

4. Most fundamentally, the Bonn package effectively meshed domestic and international political dynamics. As we have seen, each of the three governments called upon to make the most specific contributions to the bargain – the United States, Germany, and Japan – was internally divided. Within each, one faction supported the policies being deman-

ded of their country internationally, but it was initially in the minority. In each case, the domestic advocates of the internationally desired policy were able to use the summit process to shift the internal balance of power in their favour. In effect, it was, one later explained half-jokingly, a kind of 'internationalist conspiracy', but if so, it was a conspiracy that took careful measure of domestic political realities. President Carter spoke for all his colleagues, when he insisted in the final press conference, 'Each of us has been careful not to promise more than he can deliver.'

It is less clear whether the Bonn accords were successful in strictly economic terms. There is little dispute that the US energy measures were long overdue, and no doubt that US oil consumption and particularly oil imports have fallen substantially thereafter. It seems quite likely that these improvements in the energy picture are attributable in some measure to the policy shifts agreed in Bonn.

The assessment of the macroeconomic measures is more difficult and more controversial. There is, of course, no question that in the years after 1978, government deficits in the 'locomotive' countries ballooned, global inflation rates shot up, and a recession of unprecedented severity ensued. On the other hand, the intervention of the second oil shock and the subsequent tightening of monetary policy in the United States and elsewhere make it very difficult to determine what role in all these woes was played by the policy decisions of 1978.

It seems plausible that the increases in the German and Japanese budget deficits are attributable, at least in part, to the fiscal decisions of 1978. This view is widely held in those two countries. On the other hand, here too the effects of the 1978 decisions are entangled with the effects of the subsequent recession on government receipts and expenditures.

In terms of direct effects, the inflation and recession of the 1980s must be blamed on the 1979 oil shock and the consequent reaction of monetary authorities. The fiscal measures agreed at Bonn were too modest to have caused those difficulties directly. However, a more subtle and more plausible criticism would be that the oil and monetary shocks themselves may have been exacerbated by the Bonn decisions. Several official and semi-official post-mortems, as yet unpublished, reach divergent conclusions on this question.

Monetary policy in the Seven during 1978 was, in retrospect, highly expansionary, in part because of US money growth and the weak dollar. Most of this predated the Bonn decisions, of course. However, it might be argued that the Bonn decisions allowed the Americans to postpone an overdue tightening of their monetary policy, although this argument would need to take account of the US decisions of 1 November 1978.

On the oil price front, the proximate causes of the later difficulties were the Iranian revolution, the exploitation of that supply interruption by the other oil producers, and misguided stocking decisions by the oil consumers. On the other hand, those factors would probably not have had the same effects if global demand had been slacker. In that sense, it is possible to argue that the architects of the locomotive experiment underestimated the downside risks of inflationary side-effects. In short, there is a plausible case that the Bonn decisions were a necessary, though not sufficient, condition for some of the subsequent woes. A related view is that

the budgetary stimulus enacted by Bonn in the summer of 1978 was 'a prime example of the classic fine-tuning mistake of organising a reflation when none was required'. According to this view, autonomous forces were already producing a recovery and a readjustment of trade disequilibria, and would have done so without the benefit of the Bonn programme, if the second oil shock had not intervened.[48]

It exceeds our scope (and our competence) to offer the kind of sophisticated econometric analysis that would be necessary finally to resolve these 'what-if' questions.

Nevertheless, it is arguable that in economic terms the Bonn decisions, both on energy and on fiscal stimulus, came a year late. If those policy changes could have been achieved in 1977, as their proponents originally hoped, the benefits would have been clearer and the risks of adverse side-effects substantially lower. On the other hand, as our story has shown, the politics of international policy coordination are so complex that timely action is difficult at best. Politically, the Bonn decisions could hardly have been reached much earlier, even if, economically, they may have come too late.

Whatever the economic facts, the political fact is that the Bonn accords acquired a very bad reputation of a *post hoc, ergo propter hoc* sort. It soon became the received wisdom in both Germany and Japan that the 1978 decisions were extremely ill-advised. The events of 1978–80 convinced most major governments in the West that only severe fiscal and monetary restraint could restore economic stability. By September 1979, Helmut Schmidt expressed the view that 'this ridiculous little "locomotive theory" has withered away now, and correctly so'.[49]

Thus, Bonn – no matter how successful it may have been as an example of international policy accommodation – represented the end of an era for the demand management school of economic policy within the summit process. By the next summit, the original Labour advocates of coordinated reflation had been thrown out of office by a sterner Margaret Thatcher, and Jimmy Carter had turned sharply towards more restrictive policies. Above all, the rise of the Ayatollah Khomeini and an emboldened OPEC had transformed the agenda of world economic problems and, with it, the nature of summitry.

Internationally 1979 was a bad year. It began with the fall of the Shah of Iran, leading to a renewed surge in oil prices. It ended with the US hostages trapped in their Embassy in Tehran and with Soviet troops invading Afghanistan. In the course of a single year, the entire economic and political context for the summits was altered fundamentally for the worse. Faced with this new context, the summits themselves were forced to change direction.

Macroeconomic policies
The first four summits had been recovery summits. They had begun after the recession which followed the first oil shock had touched bottom, and had been concerned with securing economic revival. The next four – or at least the three after Tokyo – were to be recession summits. They had to deal with the immediate crisis of the second surge in oil prices and with the extended recession which followed it. Only in 1983 would the cycle return to its starting point, with economic recovery once again in prospect.

The first quartet of summits, from 1975 to 1978, had come to focus with increasing complexity on the macroeconomic strategy of the participating countries. The basic premise of the summits had been that by working together the participating countries could achieve a stronger and better-balanced recovery than if they proceeded apart. But it had proved difficult to produce convincing results from this basic premise. The summits appeared, in retrospect, to have moved by trial and error. The commitments undertaken became more precise and more specific with each year. From the general statements of intent at Rambouillet and Puerto Rico the summits had moved to fix growth targets at London and to adopt measures for individual countries at Bonn.

In the process, three lessons were established. The first was that simultaneous action by the participating countries in one direction or another produced an exaggerated result which could frustrate their intentions. Measures calculated to have a particular effect in one country produced in fact a stronger impact because of the interaction with other countries doing the same thing. When all had brought in restrictive measures together in 1976, the momentum of the recovery had been checked in a way which belied the confident message of the Puerto Rico summit.

The second lesson was that no one country, even the largest, could successfully sustain policies against the trend of what the others were doing. The United Kingdom's experience in 1974–5 was one example of this. But even the United States had been unable to keep up its policy of reflation from 1977 onwards without parallel action by Germany and Japan. Hence the conclusion had been reached, by the Bonn summit, that the successful generation of a collective recovery meant different countries doing different things: harmony, not unison. This had been called the 'convoy' approach, to distinguish it from the unlucky 'loco-motive' concept of the year before. But a better image would be from a football team, where different players have different roles according to their position and their capacities.[1]

As the third lesson, the participants endorsed the principle that coordination of macroeconomic strategy alone would not bring suc-cessful results if other policies in the summit countries, for example energy policy, were incompatible with this aim. So the Bonn summit sought to conclude a 'five-point plan', relating together macro-economic, trade, energy, and other policies, through a multidiscip-linary process which only the summits were able to encompass.

The idea of a collective recovery was associated with a largely Keynesian economic philosophy. It involved the stimulus of economic growth through demand management, i.e. by government action to increase public spending or to cut taxes, which thus enlarged the budget deficit. This was often associated with incomes policy as the favoured means of keeping inflationary pressures in check. This approach had made it possible to demonstrate how the actions of governments would generate growth not only in their own countries but in others, so that the total stimulus achieved was greater than the sum of the individual measures. It had also matched the political concern of summit governments to create new jobs and bring down unemployment.

But the Keynesian, demand management strategy was already strongly challenged. The alternative school argued that governments should give higher priority in monetary and fiscal policy to checking inflation than to promoting growth. Growth itself was held to come not by government action on demand but by the removal of constraints on the private sector and the free market. Throughout the first four summits this debate continued. Neither Rambouillet nor Puerto Rico had advocated new measures to stimulate economic recovery, though they endorsed existing ones. But the United States under President Carter had favoured demand management, with strong support from the United Kingdom and some also, usually, from Italy and Canada. Germany was the spokesman for the anti-inflation movement, with backing from Japan, though this was seldom strongly expressed. The

French government took an intermediate position, adopting austere policies for itself but quietly supporting stimulus by Germany and Japan.[2]

Each summit declaration had reflected the rival strands of argument. The United Kingdom would welcome statements such as: 'The most urgent task is to assure the recovery of our economies and to reduce the waste of human resources involved in unemployment' (Rambouillet, 1975). Germany would stress: 'Inflation does not reduce unemployment. On the contrary it is one of its major causes' (London, 1977). After the London summit and the problems associated with the locomotive approach, it looked as though demand management had received something of a setback. But it had returned for a remarkable late flowering in 1978, with the European Community, the OECD, and the IMF unanimous in advocating collective economic stimulus, before the package of measures was finally agreed at the Bonn summit.

By the end of 1978, the OECD economies had largely recovered from the first oil price increase. The wide imbalances of external surpluses and deficits had been corrected. Unemployment was being reduced, especially in the United States; and though there had been less progress in Europe, there were now prospects for more buoyant growth. The OECD Secretariat was no longer calling for measures of stimulus and was trying to find a point of balance between the Keynesian and monetarist approaches.[3] The recycling of the surpluses of the oil producers through the commercial banking network had enabled many developing countries to finance essential imports and keep up their growth rates. But inflation remained stubborn in OECD countries. It only came down briefly below 8 per cent in 1978 (against an average of 4 per cent in the decade to 1973) and was edging up again. Incomes policies in several countries were under severe strain; and the money supply in Germany and elsewhere was swollen as a result of support given to the dollar.

The onset of the second oil shock turned everything upside down. Oil prices rose 150 per cent over the eighteen months from December 1978, an addition to the price equal, in real terms, to the quadrupling of 1973–4; a more detailed narrative of the second oil crisis will be given in the following chapter. The effect of this on the OECD economies, as with the first oil crisis, was both depressive and inflationary. Its effect on economic policy-making was to discredit the strategy adopted over the past five years. Whatever the merits and achievements of this strategy, its comparative neglect of inflation was judged to have left the world economy as vulnerable to renewed oil shocks as it had been in 1973.

After the first oil crisis most governments had moved within a year or two to counter the depressive effects, leaving inflation dangerously high. This time OECD governments were determined to contain the inflationary impact. They adopted 'non-accommodating' fiscal and monetary policies to prevent higher oil prices infecting the entire wage and price structure of their economies, and resolved to endure the depressive effects on output and employment while these lasted. There was again unanimity in the Community, the OECD, and the IMF, all of whom advocated this approach in 1979.[4]

This concentration on fighting inflation was not limited to containing the immediate impact of the oil crisis. It led to a comprehensive setback for the demand management approach to macroeconomic policy; and by the end of 1979 the anti-inflation school prevailed among all the summit countries. The central focus was on bringing down inflation by control of the money supply and reduction of public expenditure. Monetary growth targets had in fact become common in the summit countries during the 1970s, but they were exceeded as often as they were met, even in Germany. Now monetary control became a central instrument of policy, while governments moved in parallel to cut back public spending and to enlarge the role of the private sector. Under demand management an increase in the budget deficit had been a favoured method to promote growth. Under the 'neo-classical/ monetarist' philosophy now prevailing this was condemned from two directions. Financing a large budget deficit would put pressure on the money supply and drive up inflation; it would also absorb resources which would be used more productively by the private sector.

The shift away from demand management towards monetarism took different forms and followed different timetables in leading summit countries. It was most abrupt in the United Kingdom, where Mr Callaghan's government, which had relied too much on voluntary incomes policy to check inflation, was defeated in May 1979 by the Conservatives under Mrs Thatcher with an avowed monetarist strategy. In the United States the first turning point came with the introduction of control of the money supply aggregates by Mr Paul Volcker, President Carter's new Chairman of the Federal Reserve, in October 1979; but the arrival of President Reagan in 1981 would powerfully reinforce the trend.[5] In Germany the shift was less pronounced, since the Germans had always led the anti-inflation school. One effect in Germany, however, would be gradually to increase friction within the ruling coalition between the 'free market' FDP and the more interventionist SPD. The German budget deficit became swollen by the effect of the measures of stimulus brought in, following the Bonn summit, just before the oil shock. After the government struggled for years to bring it down, the FDP would finally make this the occasion for breaking the coalition and bringing down Chancellor Schmidt in 1982.

This compressed and over-simplified account of the shift in prevailing economic philosophy is necessary to explain how the treatment of macroeconomic policy at the summits changed after 1979.

The first change was to make the summits less ambitious. The prevailing sentiment was that governments in the past had tried to do too much. They would be wiser to do less themselves and to leave the market to do more. The summits therefore moved away from precise commitments in this field back to more general statements of intention and consensus.

The second change was to make the summit discussions and their conclusions simpler and more uniform. There was now no call for different measures by different countries, so as to produce a balanced pattern of growth. All were agreed to concentrate on the same objective – the control of inflation – and to use, by and large, the same methods. Even allowing for the preoccupation with energy matters, the discussion of economic policy at both Tokyo in 1979 and Venice in 1980 was unusually short and the message in the declarations simple and undifferentiated.

The third change was more complex. The summits became less concerned with cooperative action than with mutual encouragement and support. Collective measures to stimulate growth had involved a set of actions by the participants which had to fit together in order to work properly. The control of inflation, on the other hand, required measures which each country must take on its own – often called 'putting its own house in order'. Since such measures were painful and unpopular, it was helpful for governments to point to others who were making the same sacrifice. But the measures taken by others to check inflation could not substitute for the measures which each government had to take home, in contrast to the possibility for a government to achieve export-led growth of GNP when others stimulate domestic demand. (Although in theory governments should benefit from lower import prices resulting from the successful anti-inflation policies of others, in practice this was usually cancelled out by exchange rate movements.)

In its operation – and this led to a fourth, more controversial change – anti-inflation policy could prove competitive rather than cooperative internationally. If one country drove up interest rates or the value of its currency in order to check inflation, others had to follow suit or they would lose ground because of the exchange rate effects. In some circumstances this could prove a useful collective discipline. But in others it could provoke complaints that governments were not taking sufficient account of the impact of their policies on their neighbours. This did not emerge at Tokyo in 1979 or Venice in 1980. But the summits of the next three years – Ottawa, Versailles, and Williamsburg – all featured arguments with the Americans about the impact of their high interest rates and what was causing them. The content of summit discussion of macroeconomic and monetary policy changed from considering not so much what could be done together as how to avoid hurting one another.

Despite this different and rather simpler approach, the three lessons of the first quartet of summits would still prove valid for those which followed. First, it was demonstrated once again that individual countries could not successfully go against the trend – this time by France. While the government of M. Barre remained in power, it gave priority to checking inflation. But after President Mitterrand replaced President Giscard in May 1981, his new government tried to stimulate growth and to bring down unemployment by demand management methods. Like the United Kingdom in 1975 and the United States in 1978–9, France suffered a widening deficit, a weakening currency, and inflation which remained high when that of others was falling. The French government had to change over to strict measures of austerity and to maintain them in place even while recovery was beginning in other summit countries.

The second lesson – that simultaneous pursuit of a single line of policy leads to an exaggerated effect – was shown to hold good as well. The collective impact of the restrictive measures adopted in 1979 and subsequent years produced a much longer recession than was originally foreseen, with unemployment rising to 35 million in the OECD area. The depressive effects of the oil price increase itself were largely absorbed by the end of 1980; but the strict stance of policy in most summit countries kept growth down for a further two years. Although inflation was eventually reduced to its lowest level for a decade, this process took longer than most governments anticipated and the measures adopted to check monetary growth and reduce budget deficits did not always have their expected impact during the period of recession.[6] The summit governments, with the temporary exception of France, did not waver in the priority they gave to fighting inflation. But they did not expect the recession to last so long and began promising a revival from 1981, long before it actually appeared.[7]

The third lesson – that macroeconomic strategy must be compatible with energy, trade, and other supporting policies – was likewise demonstrated during this second quartet of summits. Because they did not anticipate the length of the recession, the summit governments endorsed policies in these fields which were compatible with the revival of growth from 1981, not with a prolonged period of reduced demand. The next section of this chapter looks at the consequences of this in greater detail.

Monetary relations, trade, energy, and the developing countries
The first four summits had from the start recognised the linkages
between economic recovery and other policies in the trade, monetary,
and energy fields. By the Bonn summit these linkages had been
wrapped up in a package of interlocking measures. The summits had
seldom discussed the issues in any depth of technical detail, seeing their
role as to give political direction. This was done mainly in three ways:
by endorsing general principles and strategies, such as energy conservation and resistance to protectionism; by promoting individual commitments by summit participants, such as President Carter's energy
undertakings at Bonn and the limitation of UK trade restrictions at
Rambouillet; and by giving impulses to wider negotiations in other
bodies.

These impulses were most effective in the monetary and trade fields.
Rambouillet provided the key to the monetary reform negotiations
concluded in early 1976; successive summits, up to Bonn, urged on the
MTNs in the GATT. These two important sets of negotiations, both
launched before the first oil shock, helped to counteract the protectionist, inward-looking trends which it provoked. The early summits
also contributed to establishing the export credit consensus. Energy
received less attention, because of early differences over the role of the
IEA, but the London summit helped to launch the INFCE studies.
In the North–South field the London summit made some progress
towards a common position for the last stage of the Conference on
International Economic Cooperation, though the conference itself
ended with an impasse.

But all the international negotiations stimulated by the early summits
– with the exception of INFCE – were already going on before the
summit cycle began. Furthermore, all had run their course by the end
of 1979.[8] The early summits, while urging on existing negotiations, had
not helped to originate a new series which might take their place in due
course. The subsequent summits were therefore faced with the problem of keeping the international system in good order, in the difficult
circumstances of the recession, without any negotiations in progress
which could serve as the antidote to economic nationalism.

Work in the international monetary field was directly affected by the
shift in economic philosophy. Those governments which attached the
greatest importance to control of the money supply – notably the
British and the Americans – became reluctant to accept international
obligations on their exchange rates which could distort their domestic
objectives. Only France consistently pressed for action in this field.
President Giscard promised a new initiative in November 1979, but this
never saw the light. There was no real movement in this field until the
Versailles summit of 1982 tentatively launched the process of 'multi-

lateral surveillance' of economic policy and a study of exchange rate intervention.

In international trade, too, there was little discussion in 1979 and 1980. The subject only received serious treatment at the Ottawa summit of 1981, which gave a strong impulse to the proposed GATT ministerial meeting. That, however, was deliberately seen as a single event by most participants, with only the United States contemplating the start of a new negotiating round. The expectation was that the preparation and holding of this meeting would serve to hold off protectionist pressures during the aftermath of the second oil crisis, until the arrival of economic recovery, which should be well under way by the time the meeting took place late in 1982. But the effect of prolonged and simultaneous deflation was to upset this calculation. The meeting was held at the lowest point in the recession and achieved less than had been hoped.[9]

The Tokyo and Venice summits of 1979 and 1980 were far more active in promoting international action in the energy field than the early summits. This was an inevitable response to the second oil shock. As the following chapter will show, the immediate political effects of these summits were helpful in checking the disunity in the West. They gave a useful boost to the activities and standing of the IEA. But the energy policies being promoted by the summits became irrelevant because they were not consistent with the macroeconomic strategy which the leaders had adopted. The energy targets and goals adopted at Tokyo and the longer-term measures prepared for Venice assumed that energy demand would exert continued upward pressure on oil prices throughout the 1980s. But in fact the long recession produced both by the oil price increase itself and by the austere policies adopted to cope with it caused oil demand and prices to fall away so that the targets and measures were no longer appropriate. Energy, after being in strong focus in Tokyo and Venice, virtually ceased to be a summit subject.

The first four summits had not achieved much in the way of stimulus to North–South negotiations. At the time of Rambouillet, in 1975, many of the leaders were personally promoting ideas in this field, but the summit missed the chance to launch a collective initiative. At Puerto Rico, London, and Bonn the leaders were responding, largely defensively, to proposals from the developing countries, and the results were disappointing. But the absence of progress in negotiations mattered less because many of the developing countries managed to keep up the momentum of their growth after the first oil crisis better than the OECD members. The oil-importing developing countries grew nearly twice as fast as the OECD members during 1973 to 1978, though often only by virtue of heavy external borrowing.[10]

From 1979 onwards the pattern was largely repeated. There was another brief opportunity, at Tokyo, for the West to regain the initiative after differences between the non-oil developing countries and OPEC had surfaced at UNCTAD V. But with all the distractions of the second oil shock the chance passed and thereafter the summit participants were back in their usual posture of reacting to proposals from the South. They gave their closest attention to the Cancun North–South summit held in October 1981. But this, like the GATT ministerial meeting, was to be a single event, not the beginning of a process. 'Global negotiations' in the UN raised many difficulties and ended in deadlock; progress in sectoral negotiations was uneven, with setbacks over new resources for the World Bank. This time the disappointing results from negotiations increasingly stood out against the very sombre background of economic conditions in the developing countries, which were hit much harder by the second oil crisis, with its prolonged recession, than by the first. Many of those which had borrowed heavily after the first oil shock were almost overwhelmed by their debts. In 1981 the growth of GNP in the non-oil developing countries fell below the increase in population for the first time in three decades and 1982 was even worse.[11]

The summits from Tokyo onwards achieved less in the way of lasting impetus to international negotiations than those which had gone before. Some of the reasons for this have already been indicated. First, while the initial summits helped to conclude some important negotiations begun earlier in the decade, the later ones had to start from scratch, as it were, in conditions where existing economic structures were under severe strain and it looked as though ambitious negotiations might end by making matters worse. Second, the summits misjudged the duration of the recession and adopted approaches to the major issues which proved inappropriate when recovery was delayed.

A third reason follows from the change in prevailing economic philosophy, already discussed. The participating governments, in international as well as in domestic economic policy, put less faith in government intervention and more in the operations of the market. They believed that undue international regulation was likely to distort and limit trade and financial movements. They saw a risk that international negotiations could distract governments from their national responsibilities to run their economies properly. This view was endorsed by the United Kingdom and Germany and was shared by the United States after the arrival of President Reagan – which explains the continuing US pressure to organise international energy policy while President Carter remained in office. But even here there was a progression from tightly drawn national targets to less precise long-term measures.

In the absence of wider negotiations in progress, to which they could impart momentum, the summits began to create, as a sort of surrogate, their own special groups composed of officials or ministers from the participating countries and the Commission. The 1979 and 1980 summits created (and re-created) an energy monitoring group and commissioned a special aid study from the sherpas. A group on hijacking, created after Bonn, was kept in being and extended to cover terrorism also. Further groups were created in later years, covering trade, technology, exchange markets, convergence of economic policy, and the monetary system. All these operated in addition to the regular work of the sherpas in preparation and review. In part the creation of these groups reflected the difficulty of launching full-blown international negotiations in such adverse conditions, especially when the summit countries found it hard to agree among themselves. A summit-based study group could determine what the prospects were for progress on a wider front. In part, it was a consequence of the summits' reluctance to become too closely linked to established international organisations, which will be considered in chapter 9. But apart from the anxiety it aroused in the other institutions and in non-summit countries, this practice produced very uneven results in resolving the problems at issue, at the cost of making the summit process more elaborate and 'bureaucratic', against the professed wishes of the leaders.

Political issues

There had always been some discussion of non-economic, foreign policy matters at the summits since they began in 1975. Two developments conspired to make political discussions rather more organised and more extensive from 1979 onwards. One was the deterioration of East–West relations; the other was the reaction to the Guadeloupe meeting of January 1979.

President Giscard, in his very first idea for a summit, would have admitted political alongside economic issues if the participants had been limited to four.[12] But once Japan and Italy were admitted, followed by Canada and the European Community, he had insisted that the summits were devoted to economic questions and prevented their extension to political matters. In his view the choice of participants made sense for economic exchanges, since it brought together the seven largest industrial powers. But there was not the same rationale for political discussions which, he believed, should be held in a much smaller circle. Political discussions would therefore be a deviation and a distraction from the summit's proper purpose.

The Japanese at this stage had shared the French view, though for different reasons. Reticence about engaging in international political discussion had been a basic rule for them since the war. They had hesitated to engage in formal political discussion at the summit, particularly on themes which would expose them to pressure to align themselves with positions adopted by the Atlantic Alliance.

President Carter, on taking office in 1977, had challenged the French view and suggested that the London summit should discuss political and security matters alongside economic ones.[13] In the event, this was narrowed down to the issues of nuclear proliferation and human rights. Nuclear proliferation was allowed by President Giscard, as having economic as well as political implications, and human rights were disposed of in barely fifteen minutes. Thereafter President Carter and his sherpa, Henry Owen, had come round to the position that economic issues should be the main subject matter for the summits. The general view in fact prevailed that foreign policy consultations, once admitted on the same footing, might well encroach upon and drive out the economic exchanges. Cooperation on economic issues, which touched on domestic preoccupations, was considered to be more difficult than foreign policy coordination and the leaders should not be distracted from it.

Nevertheless, active political discussion had taken place on the side, usually over meals. This was done sometimes among all seven countries, sometimes in separate meetings of the Four, though these were strictly meant only to discuss Berlin and German questions. Chancellor Schmidt, for one, would not have accepted the complete exclusion of foreign policy matters; in his view, the heads of government had to be free to discuss what they wished. But he preferred to deal with political matters in unscripted 'fire side' chats, which he regarded as among the most valuable elements in the summits. As he said: 'You do not realise how much time we spent exchanging views on political issues . . . we didn't mention the discussions we had on these issues in the communique, but they were very important.'[14] But there was no preparation for these exchanges and no provision for public statements or for follow-up. One consequence of this was that the leaders' decision at Bonn to issue a statement on hijacking took everyone by surprise, even their closest advisers.

When the summits started in 1975, the East–West political environment had been reasonably favourable. Thereafter it deteriorated steadily, beginning with Soviet-backed disturbances in Angola and Ethiopia. Then the Soviet development and deployment of the SS-20 intermediate range missile began to cause growing anxiety in Europe, even as the Americans and Russians were working to control long-range strategic weapons through SALT II. In October 1977 Chancellor Schmidt brought this issue into the open in a lecture given in London: 'Strategic arms limitations confined to the United States and the Soviet Union will inevitably impair the security of the West European members of the Alliance vis-à-vis Soviet military superiority in Europe if we do not succeed in removing the disparities of military power in Europe parallel to the SALT negotiations.'[15]

Throughout 1978 the NATO allies struggled to find an agreed response to this problem. At the NATO summit in May, President Carter gave his backing to work in modernising theatre nuclear forces (TNF) in Europe, while stressing the need 'to consider jointly the relationship of long-range theatre nuclear systems to arms control'.[16] But as recorded in chapter 6, confidence among the allies, especially between President Carter and Chancellor Schmidt, had been badly shaken by the earlier failure to agree on the stationing in Europe of the 'neutron bomb'.

The Guadeloupe summit between the United States, Germany, the United Kingdom, and France was, in its origin, an attempt to make a fresh start with this sensitive issue. Chancellor Schmidt floated the idea in terms which recalled those used by President Giscard to explain the economic summits to James Reston back in June 1975. According to Brzezinski's account:

Schmidt said it made him feel 'uneasy' that President Carter, Giscard, Callaghan and he never met together in informal, top level discussion of political-strategic issues. . . . What was lacking was a forum where the leaders of the four countries most directly concerned in security problems could meet and discuss frankly, openly, and flexibly matters of common concern.[17]

The others responded favourably to this concept. President Giscard took the initiative in inviting his colleagues to meet on 5–6 January 1979 at Guadeloupe.

The meeting was productive. On the central question of missiles in Europe, the four leaders agreed on what became known as the 'two-track' approach, linking the stationing of US cruise and Pershing II missiles in Europe with progress in arms control negotiations on intermediate range weapons with the Soviet Union. Both 'tracks' were worked out in detail during the coming year, with preparations for arms control talks beginning in parallel to the existing work on TNF modernisation, all leading to a formal NATO decision in December 1979. Meanwhile, the three Europeans at Guadeloupe gave unreserved backing to President Carter over the SALT II negotiations, then at a critical stage. In addition, the four leaders decided to promote a financial rescue operation for Turkey, whose economic collapse would threaten NATO's southern flank. They considered how new approaches to China should fit in with existing policies towards the Soviet Union, with President Carter giving his consent to UK military sales to China. They also discussed the prospects in Iran and the Gulf.[18]

This was a meeting very close to President Giscard's original aspiration for the economic summits. Only a very small group of countries with major responsibilities were present. The heads of government were supported by a single adviser each in the meetings, with no other ministers. There was very light advance preparation and no final declaration or communiqué. Those present – and especially President Giscard – would have dearly liked to hold future meetings in this highly restricted format.[19]

But the hostile reactions from those not invited made this impossible. Italy, Belgium, and the Netherlands resented their exclusion from the discussion on missiles. The Japanese considered, with good reason, that they should have been involved in the discussions on China and the Gulf, which were of equal concern to them. As a sign of their displeasure that the decision to aid Turkey was taken in their absence, they withheld for a long time any contribution to the financial package.

The consequence of the Guadeloupe meeting was thus to give the remaining members of the seven – Japan, Italy, and Canada – a strong incentive to develop the economic summit as a more formal and visible vehicle for political discussions, going beyond spontaneous exchanges over meals. This would ensure that they would not be excluded from high-level political discussion in future. Since each in turn would be host to the next three economic summits, they were well placed to exert influence on the matter.

The Japanese made only limited progress at Tokyo in 1979. They were still inhibited by their own reluctance to discuss matters of concern to NATO and the Atlantic Alliance. They tried hard to promote a declaration on the Middle East, but met with solid resistance from the French. However, President Carter's proposal to discuss Indochinese refugees helped to establish the precedent that the summits would habitually react to sudden crises or to political events too grave for them to pass by in silence. The refugee issue in 1979 was followed by that of diplomatic hostages in 1980 and the Lebanon crisis in 1981 and 1982.

The Soviet invasion of Afghanistan and the disarray in the Alliance which followed it gave the Italians, who were hosts in 1980, an excellent opportunity to ensure that political issues were established as part of the formal and avowed agenda for the Venice summit in June. They began the practice of bringing together senior officials from the foreign ministries of the seven countries shortly before the summit, who, in parallel with the sherpas, would work out an agenda on political matters and draft texts for possible issue by the leaders. This led to a half-day's discussion at the Venice summit on Afghanistan and East–West relations and the issue of a separate declaration on Afghanistan. At Venice there was no meeting of leaders *à quatre*, which had been customary since Puerto Rico in 1976.

As the third of the summit countries absent from Guadeloupe, the Canadians sought to expand the political content further when they were host to the summit in 1981. Some of their ideas, such as using the seven-power format for political crisis management, did not gain favour. But in general they found President Reagan, newly elected, well disposed to political discussions and the Ottawa summit issued a separate foreign policy document – a 'chairman's summary on political issues' – which covered the Lebanon crisis, East–West relations, Afghanistan, Kampuchea, and refugees. All this had been carefully prepared in advance, apart from the passage on the Lebanon crisis which had flared up during the summit. In addition the leaders at Ottawa had for the first time to deal seriously with hijacking issues covered by the Bonn declaration.

During this period the value of the seven-power summits for political and security discussions was also beginning to attract favourable public comment. A paper by the Atlantic Council of the United States, published just before Venice in 1980, argued 'for broadening the scope of the discussions of the summit leaders' who alone had the 'authority and responsibility for integrating political, economic, and security issues'. In March 1981 Mr Brzezinski suggested publicly 'the expansion of our yearly economic summit meetings into a strategic summit which would also address, at the highest political levels, the consequences of Soviet power projection and the mutual security requirements to meet that challenge'. About the same time a joint report by the directors of the UK, American, French, and German institutes of international affairs (known as the 'Four Institutes report') recommended that 'the seven nation summits should from now on be devoted at least as much to political and security concerns as to economic ones' and that political preparation might perhaps be supported by 'some type of a permanent, though small secretariat'.[20]

Throughout these developments, however, the French were maintaining their unshaken view that the central purpose of the seven-power summits was economic and not political discussion, with President Mitterrand taking exactly the same position on this as his predecessor. When their turn came in 1982 to be hosts to the summit, they reversed the trend of the three preceding years. At Versailles, foreign policy discussions were limited to meals; the political representatives met in advance but prepared no drafts for the meeting; and no declarations were issued apart from a brief reaction to the Israeli invasion of Lebanon, drawn up on the spot. Even so, to President Mitterrand's distaste, Versailles was dominated by an issue which was much more political than economic – East–West economic relations, pressed with great vigour by President Reagan. The Germans had wanted this issue on the agenda back in 1975 and 1976 for economic reasons, because they feared for the financial stability of Eastern Europe. But President Reagan's motives were political: to have Western economic relations with the Soviet Union – which were far less important to the United States than to Europe – reflect the strained political and security situation provoked by the introduction of martial law in Poland.

By Williamsburg in 1983, though East–West economic relations had been taken off the boil, the two-track approach on missiles in Europe, which had begun at Guadeloupe, reached a critical point. The summit offered an obvious opportunity to reaffirm, at the highest political level, the common Western commitment to negotiations with the Russians on withdrawing their SS-20s linked to the stationing of cruise and Pershing missiles in Europe from the end of the year. But because of customary resistance to political discussion from the French, who took advantage of the US preference, on this occasion, for minimal advance preparation on other issues, it was uncertain right up till the summit itself whether the opportunity would be taken. Chapter 11 will explain how the leaders only decided on the spot to issue a security declaration from Williamsburg.

This account serves to illustrate the growing place given to non-economic issues at the summits and the rather erratic and unpredictable handling of them. The foreign policy preparations, described at the time of the Venice summit as 'furtive and improvised', never became as thorough as the work of the sherpas.[21] The most careful preparations were those organised by the Canadians before the 1981 summit. Thereafter the scope of advance discussion was reduced, leaving the key decisions to be taken at the summit itself. This approach might suffice if discussion was not to go beyond spontaneous exchanges over meals or snap reactions to pressing events. But it would become a drawback should the leaders wish to have a more profound discussion of a complex and sensitive subject and to give public expression to any consensus which they might reach.

Summary and conclusion

This chapter has shown how the later summits came to differ from the early ones, taking 1979 as a watershed year when both economic and political conditions began to grow much worse.

The first summits had moved by trial and error towards precise commitments on specific economic measures. The later ones reversed this process, by stages. The oil shock of 1979–80 helped to dislodge the demand management approach, already under severe challenge, in favour of the neo-classical/monetarist philosophy which gave absolute priority to overcoming inflation and distrusted undue government intervention. The summits moved away from precise commitments towards simpler, less ambitious conclusions, and became concerned less with joint international action and more with mutual support for painful domestic policies. As Andrew Shonfield put it: 'International interdependence grows while the notion of international management of the world economy moves into disrepute.'[22]

With the unfair advantage of hindsight, the earlier summits could be faulted for neglecting the insidious effects of inflation and for failing to provide sufficient continuity to the process of international negotiation. The summits after 1979 could be criticised for not foreseeing the severity and persistence of the recession and adopting approaches to trade, energy, and other issues which presumed the arrival of a recovery which was not forthcoming. In these adverse conditions, it became difficult for the summits to give lasting impulses to wide-ranging international negotiations. Even energy policy, a highly active subject at the summits of 1979 and 1980, became inactive when the recession choked off demand and caused oil prices to slacken and then to fall.

The worsening political situation, especially after the Soviet invasion of Afghanistan, gave an incentive for more foreign policy discussion at the summit. This was encouraged by Japan, Italy, and Canada, to avoid any repetition of the Guadeloupe format from which they were excluded. Some advance preparation and some separate declarations on political issues became the practice after Venice, though the French would maintain their reservations about formal non-economic discussions at the summits.

Foreign policy questions thus became firmly established as a recognised part of the summit proceedings, alongside, if secondary to, the economic subject matter. But the two sets of issues tended to be treated separately, not in relation to one another (the exception, perhaps, being East–West economic relations, tackled at Versailles in singularly unfavourable conditions). Both the Atlantic Council paper and the Four Institutes report noted earlier in this chapter saw advantage in adding political to economic issues at the summits so that the leaders could look at them together, on the grounds that 'political and security issues have become increasingly inseparable from economic ones'. The summits themselves, however, neither attempted nor achieved this synthesis.

8 Tokyo and Venice, 1979–80

The Japanese, hosts to a major international meeting for the first time in their history, made meticulous advance plans for the Tokyo summit, fixed for late June 1979. They envisaged their meeting more or less as a replica of the Bonn summit, with the same five interlocking themes – economic policy, monetary issues, trade, energy, and North–South relations – and the same structure of preparations. A first meeting of the sherpas in Tokyo on 22–23 March 1979 commissioned papers on each topic and fixed further meetings in May and June to consider them.[1] But the onset of the second oil crisis ruined these plans and much of the careful advance work was wasted. For the only time, so far, the summit leaders would have to deal not with chronic economic problems, but with the abrupt and unpredictable twists of an immediate crisis, which was producing near-panic conditions back home, especially in the United States. Events moved so fast that the preparations were overtaken and the leaders had to hammer out the results at the table among themselves.

The second oil crisis
The oil shock began in the political confusion generated by the fall of the Shah. Exports from Iran were first interrupted for three weeks in autumn 1978, collapsed again at the end of the year, and never regained their previous levels. The total shortfall, after allowing for increases elsewhere, amounted to less than 2.5 million barrels per day, about 5 per cent of supplies to the IEA countries. But this interruption, compounded by uncertainty, confusion, and rumour, was enough to upset the whole balance of the oil market. By late 1978 oil prices had been falling in real terms for over two years. Stocks had been run down lower than their normal pattern for the time of year. Economic demand was rising quite strongly in Europe and Japan, and the European winter was unusually cold. In the United States, President Carter's anti-inflation measures and first energy package, implemented in late 1978, had yet to make an impact and anyway did not touch domestic oil prices. So the first sign of an interruption in supplies started a scramble for additional cargoes.[2]

The tension in the market was revealed by the steep rise in spot prices. In October 1978 these had been about the same as official prices, i.e. $12.70 per barrel; by mid-February 1979 they were double.

OPEC decisions to increase official prices, in December 1978 and March 1979, still left a huge gap, so that the unified pricing system broke down. While in Saudi Arabia ARAMCO still had the benefit of official prices, other OPEC members began to add premiums and surcharges, to cut back deliveries to contract customers, to demand new contracts at higher prices, and to shift supplies on to the spot market. As oil companies bought not only to meet current demand but also to replenish stocks, they drove up the price against themselves. By mid-June 1979, the spot price had risen to $36 per barrel, two and a half times the 'official' price, which then stood at $14.55.

Despite the rocketing prices, the drop in oil supplies was too small to trigger the emergency oil-sharing arrangement of the IEA, which required a shortfall of 7 per cent. The IEA, meeting on 1–2 March 1979, agreed that all members should reduce their demand for oil on the world market by a total of two million barrels per day, i.e. 5 per cent. The Community, at the European Council on 12 March, endorsed a parallel commitment to reduce demand for oil in 1979 from 525 million tons to 500 million tons, thus associating France, which was not in the IEA, with a 5 per cent reduction.[3]

Since these IEA and Community commitments accurately matched the shortfall provoked by the Iranian stoppage they should, by rights, have proved effective. But the IEA decision, in particular, was full of uncertainties: about the level from which the reduction should be made, about the methods to be used, and about the timetable. When the IEA met again on 21–22 May 1979, it reaffirmed the commitments to a 5 per cent saving and decided to extend similar action into 1980. But by that time these commitments had clearly failed to carry conviction. Several governments were taking actions on the supply side which were barely compatible with their undertakings and further disturbed the markets. Japan, for example, promoted direct purchases of crude from exporters to replace lost supplies. In the United States, anxiety among consumers and the weakness of the Federal allocation system had produced long queues at petrol stations – 'gas lines' – and threatened a shortage of heating oil. Under these pressures the US Administration reversed its earlier advice to oil companies to stay out of the spot market. A week after the IEA meeting it brought in a $5 per barrel subsidy or 'entitlement' on imports of heating oil from the Caribbean. Though this was intended to have limited local impact, the United States was bitterly criticised by the Europeans for distorting the world market and failing to consult its partners.

Before the summit

By the end of May 1979 the Western consumers were facing an energy situation which was manifestly out of control, while the disarray in their own ranks was sadly reminiscent of the quarrels of 1973–4. The Tokyo summit, fixed for 28–29 June, looked like the last opportunity to restore some unity to the West and some order to the markets. The sherpas had been wrestling with the energy issue, on the basis of a separate report from a group of energy experts, with the initial aim of reinforcing the work of the IEA. But events moved so fast that the last sherpas' meeting, in Paris on 15–16 June 1979, was unable to make clear recommendations about energy to the summit.[4] The Americans urged that short-term commitments be prepared for endorsement by the leaders, but the Europeans were not ready to agree to this. In fact, the key developments took place elsewhere, with the French and Americans working together, rather as they did before Rambouillet.

The energy crises of 1974 and 1979 confronted Western consumer governments with a 'prisoner's dilemma' of the sort defined in chapter 1. If all worked together to conserve energy, this should produce, in due course, a new balance of oil demand and supply at reasonable prices, and every government would benefit. But any individual government was under the strong temptation to contrive to assure its own supplies at normal levels, while others made the sacrifices. Two governments, in particular, had broken ranks after 1974. One was France, which stayed out of the IEA and tried to make bilateral deals with OPEC. But in fact the French gained no special advantages from this, either in supplies or price levels, so that they entered the second oil crisis much readier to work together with other consumers. The other was the United States, which, while being the most powerful advocate of collective international action, proved quite unable to organise its own domestic policy so as to save oil. The Community countries reduced oil imports by nearly 10 per cent in volume between 1973 and 1978, even before allowing for the effect of North Sea oil. Japan too managed a small reduction. But the volume of US oil imports rose by nearly a third.[5]

President Carter, for his part, was resolved to make the American people less wasteful of energy and to make good the neglect of energy policy by previous administrations. But he had the greatest difficulty in turning his convictions into effective action and – as chapter 6 has already shown – in reconciling domestic and international pressures. Only on 5 April 1979 was he able to honour his commitment from the Bonn summit to decontrol domestic oil prices, on a longer timetable than originally promised. This was the limit of what he could do on prices. Further responses to the oil shortage depended on actions to ration supplies and other administrative measures, which were very difficult to apply fairly and efficiently and very unpopular in domestic political terms.

The Europeans were agreed that not only must they conserve energy themselves but they must also bring the Americans to reduce their oil imports, or all would suffer. They differed, however, over methods. The Germans advocated reliance on market forces and rational pricing for oil, together with structural policies to reduce waste and promote alternative energy sources. In this they had the support of the new Conservative government in the United Kingdom, which did not allow North Sea oil to be used as a reason for keeping down prices, and set high conservation targets. Germans and British alike distrusted administrative action as being ineffective and distorting, whether this meant quantitative restrictions at home or attempts to control external markets. The French, on the other hand, traditionally relied on government regulation in all areas of energy policy, both domestically and internationally. They were openly critical of US efforts at conservation – 'They have not yet begun,' said President Giscard to *Newsweek* just before the summit.[6] But it was easier for the French than for the Germans to find common ground with the US Administration.[7]

In the hectic weeks before the Tokyo summit, the French took the initiative. They proposed an energy plan with four main elements. First – and most important in their eyes – was strict control over the oil markets, partly through setting a maximum price for oil imports. Second was national ceilings for oil import volumes over the next three years. Third was the development of new energy sources, particularly nuclear power. Fourth was the promotion of a dialogue with the oil producers themselves. President Giscard – as President of the European Council – transmitted these ideas in a memorandum to his Community colleagues on 14 June 1979.[8]

But already there had been consultation with the Americans, with visits by the French foreign and energy ministers to Washington early in the month.[9] From this it became clear that the policies being developed by the Americans closely matched two out of the four elements in the French plan. The first was national oil import targets, which the US Administration, after much internal debate, had decided to adopt as the central instrument of energy conservation. Henry Owen, the US sherpa, and Richard Cooper of the State Department were the strongest advocates of this approach. They argued that such targets, to be adopted first by the Tokyo summit and then by the whole of the IEA, would reinforce the commitment to achieve 5 per cent savings in oil demand; convince OPEC of the West's determination to use less oil; and give strong international backing to President Carter's conservation policies at home. The other element was investment in new energy sources. The Americans were reticent about nuclear power, which had been set back by the Three Mile Island disaster. But they had already, in summit preparations, proposed a new international fund to develop synthetic fuels and a new body to promote the greater use of coal.

President Giscard, having won a degree of support from the Americans, next sought to convince his colleagues at the European Council, which met in Strasbourg on 20–21 June, to agree a Community position before the summit one week later. The first two elements of the French energy plan – market control and import targets – were unattractive to Germany and the United Kingdom. But alternative proposals were tabled by the Commission, which provided the basis for compromise. The Commission was attached to long-term energy targets, up to 1985, and this had already found expression at the Bonn summit. It now recommended that the Community's total annual imports of oil between 1980 and 1985 should be no higher than in 1978, i.e. 470 million tons.[10] This collective target would allow the Community to benefit from rising supplies from the North Sea and would help countries like Italy which expected their national imports to expand. It was endorsed by the European Council to become the centrepiece of the Community position for Tokyo. On oil markets the European Council simply decided to set up a register of transactions to improve information, provided other countries did so. Promotion of alternative sources, especially coal and nuclear power, was readily agreed, since a Community commitment helped those countries, like Germany, whose nuclear programme was arousing strong local opposition. Contacts with oil producers were also endorsed, though not everybody shared the high expectations of the French.[11]

The outcome of the European Council was a setback for the Americans. They believed the collective European target for oil imports would serve as a screen behind which the other Community countries would escape any real sacrifice thanks to growing supplies from the North Sea. They doubted the value of precise targets as far ahead as 1985 (though they had promised oil import savings up to 1985 at Bonn on European urging). For short-term targets for oil imports they wanted to have 1977 as the base year, since they feared 1978 would be unusually low because of the arrival of new Alaskan oil. President Carter therefore came to Tokyo determined to oblige the Europeans to adopt national import targets for 1979 and 1980. He paid a bilateral visit to Japan before the summit, to agree a joint position with Mr Ohira.[12] The Japanese strongly disliked oil import targets as far ahead as 1985, fearing that these would constrain their growth, and believed the Americans would refuse them too. They were prepared to set short-term limits, though privately they hoped that European resistance to national targets would frustrate this as well.

The Tokyo summit, 28–29 June 1979
This was Mr Ohira's first summit as Prime Minister (he had been there as Finance Minister in 1975 and 1976). He had displaced Mr Fukuda

in late 1978 and did not have his predecessor's confidence in his Liberal Democratic Party backing nor the same long experience of international exchanges. President Carter was under severe pressure at home because of his energy policies and thus badly needed concrete results from the summit. While in Tokyo he received a depressing report from his domestic policy adviser: 'Since you left for Japan, the domestic energy problem has continued to worsen. . . . Nothing else has so frustrated, confused, angered the American people – nor so targeted their distress at you personally.'[13] In contrast, President Giscard and Chancellor Schmidt were at the height of their powers. Mrs Thatcher in Britain and Mr Joe Clark in Canada had only taken office during May. Sr Andreotti's government had just fallen and he was at Tokyo simply as caretaker.

The night before the summit, President Giscard invited his three European colleagues to dinner, though he did not ask Mr Jenkins. The summit proper began with breakfast on 28 June and continued in formal session held in the baroque-style Akasaka Palace, under heavy police protection. Reports of the proceedings are unusually confused and contradictory and the account which follows seeks to reconcile several mutually inconsistent stories. The lack of joint preparation on energy matters made for a disorganised meeting, with many uncoordinated bilateral and other contacts.[14]

Macroeconomic policy and other economic issues

The morning session opened with macroeconomic policy, where the oil crisis increased the anxiety of the summit leaders about inflation. This had been creeping up in all summit countries except Japan, reversing the downward trend of the past five years, even before the effect of higher oil prices was felt. The precise impact of these was hard to gauge, because no one knew how much farther oil prices would rise and much would depend on the policy response.[15] But it was clear that there would be an early, powerful effect on inflation, followed after some delay by a depressive impact on economic activity. A preparatory paper for the summit drawn up in late May by Mr Charles Schultze, with the help of his colleagues on the OECD's Economic Policy Committee, had focused attention on inflation.[16] The OECD Ministerial meeting on 13–14 June had stressed that governments should not 'accommodate' the oil price increase, which would make matters worse, but should prevent it being passed on into the overall structure of wages and prices. At the Tokyo summit the leaders strongly endorsed this message and gave it their high-level authority: 'Attempts to compensate for the damage by matching income increases,' said the Declaration, 'would simply add to inflation.' This outcome on macroeconomic policy was simpler and more unanimous than at any previous summit. President

Carter maintained his commitment, from the previous year's summit, to give priority to fighting inflation. In Germany there had been a strong reaction against the growth strategy accepted at Bonn, which had put the German economy in a vulnerable condition as the second oil crisis arrived, in contrast to its solid position after the first. Mrs Thatcher thus found an unexpectedly firm consensus in favour of the austere monetary policies which she favoured.

The summit was meant to tackle monetary, trade, and other economic issues on the second day, but in fact the preoccupation with energy left no time for this. On trade, there was little need for summit attention. The MTN agreements had at last been initialled on 19 April 1979. Mr Ohira had earlier feared attacks at the summit on Japan's large external surplus, aggressive export strategy, and impermeable market.[17] But by the time the summit arrived, by a temporary coincidence of factors, the Japanese current account had moved into substantial deficit. This was partly because of the increased cost of oil imports, partly because of movements in the value of the yen. So Mr Ohira was able to escape all criticism.

The monetary scene was also calm, though this was deceptive. The EMS had come into effect in March, though the United Kingdom remained outside the exchange rate mechanism. The support measures of November 1978 had helped to steady the dollar against the EMS currencies. But the oil price increase had already caused the pound to rise sharply and the yen to go into a long decline, reflecting the United Kingdom's self-sufficiency in oil and Japan's heavy import dependence. By the time of the summit the scale of the US oil import bill was starting to unsettle the dollar again.

The neglect of relations with developing countries was more serious. The summit followed immediately after UNCTAD V, held in Manila during May. There, for the first time since 1974, serious cracks appeared in the unity of the South, as the non-oil developing countries tried to raise energy issues but the OPEC countries refused. But in practice the summit leaders were unable to take advantage of this opportunity to gain the initiative in North–South relations, finding it hard enough to deal with the strains in their own economies. They could do no more at Tokyo than call on OPEC to repair the damage it had caused to the developing countries and to encourage the World Bank's work in lending for energy projects and in agricultural research.

Political issues
The leaders considered refugees over lunch on the first day, the only non-economic subject they had agreed to discuss. The issue did not arise spontaneously, like hijacking at Bonn, as President Carter had said in advance that he wanted to discuss it. A Western summit,

particularly one held in Asia, could not ignore the huge scale of the refugee problem and the human suffering involved. At the time of the summit, more than 300,000 Indochinese refugees were awaiting re-settlement and 3000 'boat people' were leaving Vietnam every day, half of them to be lost at sea. In a separate declaration the summit leaders pledged to admit more refugees to their countries and to make more funds available to help them. President Carter announced from Tokyo that the United States would double the numbers it would receive; and the summit discussion moved other countries, including the United Kingdom, to do more.

Energy

The leaders began to discuss energy over lunch, where they stayed till 4 pm, and continued in the formal session for the rest of the day. The discussion was confused and acrimonious. The news that OPEC, meet-ing in Geneva the day before, had raised official prices a further 25 per cent was a bitter blow. The leaders were deeply divided over oil import targets – their extent, their duration, and the method of calculation. They had no common prepared texts to work on and Herr Schmidt complained that the sherpas had not done their work properly. The exchanges polarised between President Carter and his Energy Secretary, Mr Schlesinger, on one side, and Chancellor Schmidt and his Economics Minister, Count Lambsdorff, on the other. Each side put its case bluntly, with Herr Schmidt attacking US policy in the Middle East as being the cause of the oil price difficulties. The Euro-peans held to the position they had agreed at Strasbourg, even though President Giscard was already looking for compromise. Mr Ohira, in the Chair, faced extraordinary difficulties. In the traditional Japanese way he tried to head off controversy, but this only added to the frustrations of the others, and the meeting stumbled inconclusively to a halt. President Carter recorded it in his diary as 'one of the worst days of my diplomatic life'.[18]

The sherpas and the energy ministers present worked through the night, with active contacts especially between Schlesinger and Lambs-dorff. Though many other issues were resolved, deadlock still remained on import targets when Presidents Giscard and Carter, Chancellor Schmidt, and Mrs Thatcher met for breakfast next day. President Giscard proposed a way out of the impasse. The Europeans would accept national import targets – despite the Strasbourg agree-ment – and persuade the other Community members to do likewise. The Americans, Japanese, and Canadians would set import targets up to 1985, as the Europeans collectively had already done. President Carter accepted the proposal. Mrs Thatcher, though unconvinced about import targets, raised no objection as the United Kingdom was no longer an oil importer. The Germans, and especially Count Lambs-dorff, had been the most sceptical about import targets. But Chancellor Schmidt did not want the responsibility for seeing the summit fail and reluctantly agreed to the compromise.[19]

When the formal meeting resumed, the breakfast compromise came as a shock to those who had not been there. Mr Jenkins saw the Community position set aside in his absence. Sr Andreotti had to 'dig his heels in' to obtain a footnote to the declaration, which would relate Italy's commitment to the Community's collective target and thus allow their national oil imports to rise with economic growth. Canada, having correctly read the signs, was able to negotiate a 1985 target which would permit rising imports to compensate for falling domestic production. The Japanese had the worst setback. Having believed that President Carter would not accept targets up to 1985, they were dismayed at having to find a figure for Japan at such short notice. A ceiling on oil imports placed a far heavier constraint on economic growth for Japan than for any of the others. Such an abrupt decision went clean against the Japanese practice of gradual consensus-building and produced desperate internal political strains. Right at the end of the proceedings, after a day of agonised internal debate by the Japanese government, Mr Ohira offered a 1985 target which would allow Japan's imports to rise by 3 per cent per year, as against GDP growth forecast at 6 per cent.

The Tokyo summit declaration, more than half devoted to energy, therefore contained quantified oil import targets for 1979–80 and for 1985, covering each participant. While the Europeans would each take the level of their 1978 imports as the ceiling for 1985, the Americans were allowed to take their imports in 1977 or 1979. A group of representatives from summit countries plus the Commission was created, on French initiative, to review the results achieved. In addition, the leaders agreed to set up a register of international oil transactions and to urge oil companies to moderate spot market dealings, matching the relevant conclusion of the European Council. Domestic oil prices should be kept at world market levels or raised to those levels as soon as possible. This was aimed mainly at Canada, where domestic prices were still being held down, but was also to encourage President Carter's commitment to decontrol.

On alternative sources of energy the summit declaration also picked up language from the European Council. There was a commitment to develop nuclear power, subject to proper safety precautions. The summit called for the wider use of coal, to be promoted through the IEA, and for an energy technology group in the OECD to examine the potential for synthetic fuels; the Americans had modified their original ideas for new bodies and new funds. Finally, the OPEC decision to raise prices, which was roundly deplored by the summit, precluded any move towards a dialogue with the oil producers, though the door was left open.[20]

Aftermath and assessment

The summit was followed by arduous negotiations in the Energy Council of the European Community and the Governing Board of the IEA to extend the coverage of national oil import targets. These were not easy, as the untidy discussion at Tokyo had left many loose ends. There was controversy between the Americans and Europeans on how the United Kingdom's North Sea production should be counted. The smaller Community countries resented the way the position on import targets agreed at Strasbourg had been abandoned, even though in several other fields the decisions of the European Council had determined the outcome at Tokyo. But eventually, in December 1979, both the Community and the IEA reached agreement on a complete list of oil import targets for 1980 and goals for 1985, for each of their members.[21]

The outcome of the Tokyo summit in the energy field must be judged against a series of different objectives. First, it was intended to have a unifying effect; in this it largely succeeded. At a time of disarray, near panic, and mutual recrimination, the summit was able to agree on a set of reasonably coherent measures, which provided a common response to the oil crisis among Western consumers.

Second, it was meant to have a demonstrative effect, in that this sign of Western cohesion should induce the oil producers to behave more responsibly. Here the results were short-lived: spot prices rose once more after the summer, surcharges and premiums remained widespread, and official prices were raised again by 33 per cent in December. The markets were still too unsettled and OPEC too disorganised to respond to a simple demonstration. An immediate impact could only have been produced if the summit had decided to act directly in the markets, as the French wished. At the time when the Iran–Iraq war broke out in the autumn of 1980, a combination of drawing down stocks and discouraging spot purchases enabled the IEA countries to survive a similar 5 per cent shortfall of supply. The build-up of stocks by oil companies during 1979 had certainly contributed to the pressure on prices and this was not properly understood at the time. But it is very doubtful whether the tactics which worked in 1980 would have had the same success fifteen months before. In 1980 stocks were high and demand was low, while in 1979 the opposite prevailed.[22]

Third, the summit had an exemplary effect on the policies of the participants. As a result governments gave higher priority to energy matters and were more determined in overcoming domestic resistance to stricter conservation and changes in energy use. For example, the United States tightened its import limits, extended them to 1990, and launched a huge investment programme for synthetic fuels. Japan and Italy were encouraged to reduce their dependence on oil. Mr Clark used the summit decisions to support his policy – adopted largely for domestic reasons – of moving Canadian oil prices up to world levels though this provoked the fall of his government in December 1979.

Fourth, there was a strong stimulatory effect on the work of the IEA and the OECD. The French had intended the summit-based monitoring group to bypass the IEA. But in fact, after one meeting of summit energy ministers in September, the IEA's position was restored and even strengthened by the need to involve all the consumers. The summit gave impulses to work in the IEA not only on oil import targets but also on stock control and on coal, through the Coal Industry Advisory Board, while the international energy technology group began work in the OECD.

Last, and most complex, is the judgment on the performance of the oil import targets for 1980 and 1985, which must be taken together with the IEA and Community commitments to 5 per cent savings in 1979. The 1979 operation was not effective and the summit came too late to influence it. The savings in the Community were less than 1 per cent, with oil consumption reaching 521 million tons. The results in the IEA are harder to measure because the commitment was vaguer. But among the major countries only the United States clearly achieved the 5 per cent saving in 1979, as a result of the first stage of oil price decontrol. In 1980, on the other hand, OECD imports were so far below the targets as to make these irrelevant; they totalled 24 million barrels per day, against the target of 27 million. It would in due course appear that by 1985 the gap would be even wider, with imports forecast to reach 20 million barrels per day in that year, about 70 per cent of the target of 28.5 million.[23]

Two main factors combined to make the Tokyo targets irrelevant. First, the 'prisoner's dilemma' faced every country choosing its national target. Each was tempted to provide a margin for itself, in the hope that others would bear the greater sacrifice. At Tokyo, moreover, the idea of national targets was so new that reliable figures were scarce, especially for 1985. So Japan, Canada, and Italy sought to protect themselves by allowing for import growth up to 1985 and the United States did so by choosing 1977 as its base year. Other IEA members likewise tried to build in a safety margin. The Americans soon perceived that all the figures were too high, adjusted their own, and tried for the rest of 1979 and on into 1980 to persuade others to bring their targets down. But they had only limited success. Second, the targets were intended to check the anticipated rise in demand for imported energy. But in fact demand fell away, first under the delayed deflationary effect of the oil crisis itself and then because of the persistence of restrictive economic policies in the major countries. Thus, the restraining effect of the Tokyo oil import targets was never tested.

Preparations for Venice

At Tokyo the leaders had had to bargain among themselves to produce results, a process which many of them – notably Chancellor Schmidt – disliked and considered inappropriate to the summit. Before Venice, due in late June 1980, the preparations were more extensive than ever before, with a copious input from the Americans. The cycle of advance work was launched by the sherpas in December 1979 and they met again in April, May, and June 1980. Gatherings of specialist officials worked on energy, finance, and food for developing countries – not to speak of the separate preparation required for foreign policy issues. But the crisis atmosphere of 1979 had passed. A rough balance had returned to the oil market as the recession cut into consumer demand and government measures to reduce oil began to take effect. There was widespread agreement on short-term economic policy issues. So the sherpas, in preparing for Venice, looked to more distant horizons, an appropriate perspective for the first summit of the 1980s.

Energy

This remained the most substantial subject, with Venice intended to complete the work begun at Tokyo. In the IEA, the Americans were still seeking to tighten the short-term oil import targets and to extend them into 1981, while efforts continued throughout the year to reduce the IEA's collective goal for 1985, especially after the Iran–Iraq war broke out in September 1980. But for the Venice summit the Americans advocated a long-term approach, basing themselves on projections of a serious energy shortfall by 1990. They promoted a triple strategy: quantified objectives for reducing oil and energy dependence over time; commitments to specific policies – not on a national basis – for saving oil and promoting new energy sources; and special help for non-oil developing countries. The Europeans, for their part, were reluctant to specify the results to be expected from long-term measures as much as the Americans wished, regarding this as unrealistic over a ten-year span. The Germans and British, as before, also argued that the pressure of market forces was as important as government intervention. But there was plenty of common ground.

Reducing energy dependence was also being discussed in the Community and the IEA.[24] The IEA governing board agreed at its meeting on 21–22 May 1980: 'To reduce the ratio between the rate of increase of energy consumption and the rate of economic growth . . . over the coming decade to about 0.6 and the share of oil in total energy demand from 52% at present to about 40% by 1990.' This was carried over to the summit, supplemented by a pledge that oil consumption in 1990 would be significantly below present levels.

General undertakings were prepared on reducing the use of oil in electric power – no new base-load oil-fired generating capacity to be constructed – in industry, in buildings, and in transport. The Americans conceded that the potential savings from these measures need not be quantified, but pressed harder for figures on the development of new energy resources. They wished to specify that coal production and use should be doubled by 1990 and that the extra energy produced from non-oil sources should equal 15–20 million barrels per day of oil by the end of the decade. Though sceptical about both figures, the Europeans accepted them, recognising their importance for the Americans in domestic terms. The potential for increased coal production lay largely in the United States and Canada and the development of synthetic fuels was a key element in President Carter's energy policy.[25] The contribution of nuclear power was stressed even more strongly than at Tokyo. Both the report of the international energy technology group, set up at Tokyo, and the studies produced in the much longer INFCE, launched at the London summit in 1977, were incorporated in the preparations, for endorsement at Venice.

Macroeconomic policy

Inflation generated in OECD by the oil shock peaked around April 1980, with consumer prices having risen at an annual rate of 15 per cent over the past six months. The main concern of the summit governments was still to bring inflation under control, by strict fiscal and monetary policies. This matched the national objectives of Chancellor Schmidt, M. Barre, Mrs Thatcher, and even of President Carter in election year, though he had difficulty in convincing US opinion of his intentions. There was no change in this austere prescription in the latest paper for the summit from Mr Charles Schultze, nor in the communiqué from the OECD meeting on 4 June.

The parallel depressive effect of the oil crisis on demand had arrived more slowly than expected. Growth in 1979 had been buoyant in Japan, Germany, and Italy and surprisingly strong even in the United States till 'publicly and unmistakably decapitated' by Mr Paul Volcker's monetary measures in October.[26] By mid-1980 the recession had definitely arrived, notably in the United States, but still too recently to cause much pain. Furthermore, despite the restrictive stance of policy, the belief prevailed that the recession would be short and 'V-shaped' with recovery beginning, if only gradually, in early 1981.[27] This allowed the sherpas to include some elements of hope – especially welcome to Italy and Canada – in the generally sombre message they sent forward to the summit. It also affected the attitude taken to other subjects for the summit: difficulties were anticipated because of the recession, but they were still largely in the future and were not likely to last too long.

Trade, monetary matters, and relations with developing countries
Trade was given low priority in the preparations. The Community was worried about its growing trade deficit with Japan and its disputes with the United States over steel and artificial fibres, but did not seek to place them on the summit agenda. The Americans brought up two peripheral subjects – the renewal of the export credit consensus and the prohibition of illicit payments – which they had raised at earlier summits.

President Giscard had intended Venice to be a monetary summit, as Tokyo had been an energy one. In November 1979 he said on television that the following spring he would take an initiative, in the summit preparations, for 'reconstructing an organised monetary system among the industrial countries'.[28] He had in mind the setting of target zones for the rates among the dollar, the yen, and the EMS currencies, to serve as the first step back towards a stable exchange rate system, an abiding French objective. But when the spring of 1980 came he could see that conditions were not auspicious. The oil price increases were still distorting the exchange markets. The new US domestic monetary policy was producing wild fluctuations in the dollar. Negotiations in the IMF for a substitution account, to replace dollars held in official reserves by an asset based on the Special Drawing Right (SDR) issued by the Fund, collapsed in May 1980 when the Americans withdrew their support. In the absence of any French proposal, summit preparations focused on the recycling of OPEC surpluses, swollen again since the latest oil price increases. Most of the participants foresaw financing difficulties for vulnerable developing countries and a reluctance by commercial banks to lend as freely as before. But they did not anticipate a threat to the system itself and looked to a larger role for the IMF to keep matters under control.

To help oil-importing developing countries, the Americans proposed setting up a special affiliate in the World Bank to finance energy investment. The affiliate would benefit from the high reputation and experience of the World Bank; but it should have a separate capital and voting structure, so as to attract OPEC subscribers. France supported the idea, though favouring a wholly separate organisation, based in Europe. The United Kingdom and Germany were more doubtful, preferring to use existing bodies rather than create new ones. They doubted also whether President Carter would secure funds from Congress for a US subscription. The Europeans were already worried about the President's difficulties with Congress over finance for the World Bank and the International Development Association (IDA). They suggested that a general undertaking at the summit that all should provide their full contributions to these bodies might be helpful to the Administration. All agreed to promote food production in developing countries – a sector where Congress was traditionally sympathetic to aid activity.

The summit would also have to respond to proposals from others on North–South relations, particularly from the Brandt Commission. The Commission's report, published in February 1980, argued eloquently that it was in the mutual interest of North and South to find solutions to the severe problems facing developing countries.[29] It recommended a comprehensive set of policy measures and reforms of the international economic system – including a proposal for a North–South summit meeting. The report attracted much public attention, especially in the United Kingdom. Mr Edward Heath, the former UK Prime Minister and an active member of the Commission, sent a memorandum to each participant shortly before the summit, to focus attention on the issues.[30] But the response of most summit governments was guarded. While recognising the mutual interest, they found most of the measures proposed to be too costly and doubted the wisdom of the reforms.

The extensive preparatory work for Venice and the pressure from the United States for specific and quantified commitments produced a draft declaration of unusual length, worked out in advance down to the last detail. The wide measure of agreement on most economic issues left few matters to be resolved among the summit leaders themselves.

Political issues

The harmony prevailing on economic subjects was in contrast to the differences over foreign policy, in an environment which had become much worse since the Tokyo summit.

In the last days of 1979 Soviet troops occupied Afghanistan, the first such foreign occupation since they moved into Czechoslovakia eleven years before. The Americans moved rapidly not only to condemn the occupation but also to take demonstrative punitive action against the Soviet Union, including an embargo on grain sales. They looked for equivalent action from their allies, to produce a collective Western response. But the European reaction was both slower and less clear cut. Germany and France, in particular, sought to distinguish between Soviet actions in Afghanistan – which they condemned – and the pursuit of détente in Europe – which they sought to preserve. President Giscard was not inhibited from meeting Mr Brezhnev in Warsaw in early June 1980 and Chancellor Schmidt prepared to travel to Moscow at the end of the month.

In Iran the US Embassy had been occupied in November 1979 and its occupants taken hostage. The Americans introduced a wide range of financial and commercial sanctions against Iran and made impassioned appeals to the Europeans and Japanese to do likewise. But again the European reaction fell short of US hopes, partly through legal difficulties, partly through a judgment that economic measures might do more harm than good.

Two further sources of friction emerged just before the summit met in late June 1980. The first was a misunderstanding between President Carter and Chancellor Schmidt over missiles in Europe. President Carter feared that Herr Schmidt, under the pressure of his current election campaign, was wavering in his support for the two-track NATO decision of December 1979. A personal message expressing his concern was leaked to the press and was strongly resented by the Chancellor. The second was on policy towards the Arab–Israel dispute. With the main elements of the Camp David agreements in place by May 1980, the Europeans, and especially the French, wanted to assert a distinctive Community position. The European Council on 12–13 June issued a declaration on the Middle East which stated that the Palestine Liberation Organisation would have to be associated with negotiations for a peace settlement – a role for them which the Americans had always refused.

The idea of using the summit as an occasion to resolve differences among the allies went back to the beginning of the year. President Carter had tried without success to convene a meeting of the foreign ministers of the summit countries in early February 1980 to discuss Afghanistan.[31] But Mrs Thatcher and Chancellor Schmidt, meeting later in the month, agreed that the summit itself in June would provide an opportunity, which should not be missed, to assert a common Western position on this issue. The idea of dividing the summit between a political day and an economic day quickly found support, even from the Japanese, since Afghanistan and Iran were Asian problems affecting them just as much as the members of the Atlantic Alliance. Only President Giscard resisted the proposal for a long time. In the end he too gave way, recognising its merits and thinking that his visit to Warsaw would put him in a position of advantage.

Separate preparation of political subjects was needed, as several of the sherpas had competence only for economic matters. So a group of senior foreign ministry officials met in Rome in mid-June 1980 to draw up a political agenda and a draft statement for consideration at the summit, concentrating on Afghanistan. Meanwhile other officials of the seven countries had been meeting to consider a follow-up statement to the Bonn declaration on hijacking. On US initiative, they drew up a parallel statement condemning the taking of hostages and attacks on diplomatic and consular premises, manifestly aimed at Iran. Finally, yet another draft was prepared on refugees, not only those from

Indochina but Afghan refugees in Pakistan, the sudden exodus from Cuba, and the millions of refugees in Africa.

The Venice summit, 22–23 June 1980

The summit took place at a time of great electoral uncertainty for most of the participants, recalling in this respect Puerto Rico four years before. Elections were due in Japan on the very day of the summit and Mr Ohira himself had died of a heart attack eleven days before; so the Japanese were without a Prime Minister. Chancellor Schmidt faced elections in October, President Carter in November, and President Giscard in May 1981. The position of Sr Cossiga, the host, also looked insecure and in fact his government fell in late September 1980.

The night before the summit Chancellor Schmidt and President Carter thrashed out their misunderstanding over missiles in Europe in a stormy meeting. President Carter later described it as 'the most unpleasant personal exchange I ever had with a foreign leader.' But it served to clear the air; next day 'Helmut was very friendly, as though nothing had happened'.[32] This illustrates the value of the multilateral summits in providing the occasion for bilateral contacts between the leaders. With the antipathy between Carter and Schmidt, meetings between them were always unpredictable, but this time the face-to-face exchange seemed to dispel misunderstandings that had festered at a distance.

The summit opened on the morning of 22 June in a former monastery on the Isola San Giorgio, with the delegations arriving by water. The splendid setting of Venice had attracted the media. Although the leaders were insulated from the outside world while the meetings lasted, they could not escape the journalists once they left the island. All the participants had added energy ministers to their normal delegations. The proceedings began with a round of general economic statements. But the leaders then moved on to political questions, which occupied the rest of the day.

Political discussions

On the previous day Mr Brezhnev had sent a message to President Giscard to say that some Soviet troops would withdraw from Afghanistan – a message later confirmed by Tass. The Soviet motives were transparent: to deter the leaders at Venice from outright condemnation of the Soviet presence in Afghanistan; and to sow discord between President Giscard – whose recent visit to Warsaw had disturbed the Americans – and President Carter. But this clumsy intervention misfired badly. It focused discussion on the offensive presence of the Soviet troops rather than on measures to be adopted against the Russians, on which a consensus might have been hard to achieve. President Giscard, President Carter, and the others found no difficulty in agreeing that the partial withdrawal of Soviet troops – if confirmed – would only be useful if it was the first stage of a total and permanent withdrawal. They issued a strong statement condemning the Soviet occupation as unacceptable and undermining peace in the region and the world at large. The entire political discussion was in fact devoted to Afghanistan and to East–West relations in the context of Chancellor Schmidt's forthcoming visit to Moscow. In addition, the leaders endorsed and issued the drafts prepared by officials on hostage-taking, hijacking, and refugees. The awkward subject of the Arab–Israel dispute, despite expectations, was not discussed.[33]

Economic discussions

On 23 June the leaders returned to traditional economic subjects. But having spent much of the previous day on foreign policy, they now had to move straight into discussion of the long and detailed declaration, amended overnight by the sherpas in the light of discussion among finance and energy ministers.

This left little room for the personal contribution of the leaders. In economic policy and energy they confirmed the main thrust of the preparatory work: top priority to fighting inflation and a long-term programme to break the link between economic growth and oil consumption. Mr Trudeau, however, weakened the commitment to raise domestic oil prices to the level of world prices. His predecessor's government had fallen on this issue and he had yet to announce his own policy. President Carter, in his concern to ensure follow-up for the energy measures, backed President Giscard's suggestion for a new high-level group of summit representatives to review the results achieved. This was all that survived from more extensive French proposals to concentrate energy discussion in the seven-power framework rather than the IEA.

There was no multilateral treatment of trade issues. But Mr Jenkins had a useful bilateral meeting with President Carter on steel and textiles – an indication of the advantage derived by the Commission from taking part in the summit.

There was wider discussion among the leaders of relations with developing countries, with more personal views expressed. Chancellor Schmidt was deeply concerned at the trend of international bank lending. He foresaw developing countries overwhelmed by their debts, leading to trouble for the banks themselves, and commended the idea of a 'safety net' for bank deposits.[34] But he did not convince his colleagues. Herr Schmidt also supported a North–South summit meeting as suggested by the Brandt Commission. President Carter, however, thought this was premature and Mrs Thatcher was silent; and so no agreement was reached.[35]

But the dominant feeling among the leaders was frustration with OPEC, who had ruined the non-oil developing countries, reduced the Western world's capacity to help them, and contrived that the West got all the blame. The West could not bear all the burden of aiding the Third World; OPEC must do more. Herr Schmidt argued, as he had since London in 1977, that the communist countries also should do more. President Giscard agreed, though Mrs Thatcher doubted the wisdom of this. In the end all supported President Giscard's proposal that the sherpas should carry out a review of aid and other policies towards developing countries in this context and report to the next summit to be held in Canada in 1981.

Assessment and conclusion

The immediate political success of the Venice summit, especially over Afghanistan, was confirmed over the following months. The United States and its allies had closed their ranks and ended their earlier disarray. Though some differences of assessment remained over both Afghanistan and Iran, neither issue provoked serious tension among the allies thereafter. German anxieties about missiles in Europe also eased after Herr Schmidt's visit to Moscow at the end of June and the Russians' agreement to open arms control talks later in 1980, which they had refused since NATO's two-track decision of December 1979.

In macroeconomic policy the summit governments faithfully maintained the fight against inflation; President Reagan, on taking office in January 1981, declared this to be his prime objective. With prices still rising 10 per cent per year on average at the end of 1980, they would not contemplate any relaxation of restrictive policies. But the OECD Secretariat began to express concern at the effects of these policies adopted simultaneously in so many countries:

While a single country can retard imported inflation by tight policy, such as tight monetary policy, which tends to raise interest rates and hence the exchange rate, there is a risk that if this were attempted by too many countries, monetary conditions would be tighter than generally warranted by purely domestic considerations.

It noted that unemployment in the OECD area had reached 22 million and forecast that it might go as high as 25.5 million in two years time.[36]

In relations with developing countries, the proposal for a World Bank energy affiliate soon ran into trouble in Congress, as expected. Then the Reagan Administration brought in a critical review of all multilateral aid and finance, which affected not only the energy affiliate but also funds for the World Bank and IDA. In this context, the 'aid study', originally bred of the leaders' discontent at OPEC's influence on North–South relations, became seen as a means of influencing the new and sceptical US Administration.

The energy undertakings were the most important result of the Venice summit and, as after Tokyo, have to be judged against several objectives. There is no doubt that they prolonged and strengthened the exemplary impact on the energy policies of the Western consumers and the stimulatory impact on the work of the IEA, OECD, and European Community that had been begun at Tokyo. Without nationally defined objectives, there was no direct constraint on individual countries. But, in contrast with the difficult negotiations after Tokyo, all the under-takings from Venice fitted neatly into the work of the IEA and other bodies and could be followed up effectively without dispute.

The Venice summit undertakings, however, like those of Tokyo, were based on the expectation that oil prices would continue to rise in real terms throughout the decade and that supplies would remain tight. But in fact the demand for oil in the non-communist world fell by 20 per cent over the next two years; and OPEC was forced to lower official prices in March 1983, with the pricing system undermined not by surcharges, as in 1979, but by rebates. In these conditions perform-ance against the Venice commitments was looking uneven and some-times misleading after three years of the decade had past.

Because of low demand, the outlook for oil savings was very promis-ing. The IEA's revised scenarios in 1983 were suggesting that oil would provide 40 per cent or less of total energy in 1990, while total oil consumption would be well below the 1980 level.[37] But with low consumer demand and falling oil prices the development of alternatives to oil was taking place much more slowly than expected. With surplus generating capacity, no country was wanting to build new oil-fired power stations. But nuclear programmes were not reaching their poten-tial either and the resistance to them, on safety and environmental grounds, was still strong. Coal production might grow by as little as 20 per cent by 1990, against the aspiration of doubling. Synthetic fuels were no longer offering commercial returns and firms would not under-take the heavy investment required. A further influence here was the early decision of the Reagan Administration to cut back sharply Presi-dent Carter's 'synfuels' investment programme. In other respects, however, the new US Administration accelerated progress towards the goals agreed at Venice and earlier summits, decontrolling oil prices at once, in January 1981, and making a start with gas prices. In contrast, Mr Trudeau made full use of the margin he obtained at Venice. His energy programme, announced in October 1980, was only intended to bring domestic oil prices up to 75 per cent of world prices by 1985 – though in practice the drop in OPEC prices in March 1983 would close the gap much faster.

The ratio between the growth of energy use and GNP growth was distorted by the recession, as energy use contracted in 1980–82 while GNP rose, if only marginally. But by 1983 the IEA was becoming concerned that the ratio might climb back to 0.75 or more by 1990, since conditions then prevailing were discouraging conservation and investment programmes. In this context, the long-term programme agreed in Venice, though it had not begun according to plan, was continuing to serve a useful purpose. The goals and ratios set for 1990 were still regarded as valid objectives and were of use to the IEA and the European Commission in their efforts to prevent member governments from becoming too complacent.

Venice involved complex and meticulous preparations and produced the longest and most detailed of all the summit declarations – partly in reaction against the disorder at Tokyo. But this itself led to controversy. The Americans always argued that summit conclusions would not carry weight unless they were specific. The intensive preparations required fitted Henry Owen's exclusive role as President Carter's sherpa, but were laborious for his European colleagues, all of whom had other responsibilities. This approach also suited President Carter's own style of operation and the Japanese wish for predictability. But other heads of government – Mrs Thatcher, President Giscard, and Mr Trudeau – found the format unsatisfactory. They wanted more direct and informal exchanges and disliked having to endorse a massive declaration which did not reflect what they had said among themselves.

The summits were acquiring more and more bureaucratic, institutional attributes. Other ministers were being brought in. The annual timetable had become established. The five-point economic agenda was now also standard. The preparations gave less attention to the links between these topics and became more involved with finding something to say under each heading. Here the Americans actively sought out new subjects for summit treatment, while the Europeans wanted each summit to focus on a few selected topics. The work of the sherpas expanded – more preparatory meetings, a regular review, and now a special assignment, the Venice aid study. This institutional growth worried other established organisations – as the next chapter will show – and attracted adverse public comment. A critical report was published in April 1980 by the Atlantic Council, whose 1977 paper had seen an influential role for summitry, and a much stronger attack appeared later in *Foreign Policy*.[38] The leaders themselves still regarded the summits as useful, on balance. But just as they were ready for a change when President Carter arrived in 1977, promising more orderly and focused discussion, now, as he left office, most of them yearned for a return to more personal and uncluttered exchanges.

9 The Summits and International Organisations

From the beginning it was clear that the summits could not operate in a vacuum. Just as the participants had to deal with other countries which were not invited, so the summits were bound to interact with other international organisations, which provided essential continuity to whatever consensus the leaders reached among themselves.

The founding fathers saw the summits rather as a catalyst, in the chemical sense: as exerting a powerful influence for change, but remaining unaffected themselves by what went on elsewhere. This was in line with the anti-bureaucratic bias of the early summits. These were born of the Library Group, which in turn stemmed from a certain impatience with the large, formal meetings of international organisations. The heads of government were deeply concerned with international economic issues; but they were not directly involved with the organisations which handled them. They did not take part in meetings of the IMF, the OECD, or the GATT, in contrast to the participation of the European leaders in the work of the Community. Indeed, the leaders' occasional contact with these organisations might be disagreeable – for example, Mr Callaghan's struggles with the IMF in 1976. The summit process, however, served to make the heads of government regularly aware of the work of these bodies, with the foreign and finance ministers present at the summits, as well as the sherpas, compensating for the absence of first-hand involvement by the leaders.

The Trilateralists, as one might expect, formulated a more systematic view of the summits' links with international organisations. A Trilateral Commission report on 'The Reform of International Institutions', published in 1976, envisaged 'a series of concentric circles of decision-making'. This would have a 'core group' of a small number of key countries, which could decide on common action through informal discussions. It would work outwards to 'the existing (and newly created) institutions where all relevant countries would become involved'.[1] In their operation over the years, the seven-power summits might be regarded as the core of such a concentric system.

These two approaches continued side by side and were never wholly reconciled. Though the idea of an orderly, concentric system was influential during President Carter's Administration, the earlier concept of the summit being detached from the system continued to have strong supporters. The result was that the summit leaders normally treated their relations with other organisations in an *ad hoc*, not a systematic way and – unlike outside commentators[2] – gave little attention to the summits' place in the overall structure. Unlike the summits' relations with non-participating countries (including those in the European Community), which were defined in the early years, the varying impact of the summits on other organisations only became clear gradually, partly through experience over several years, partly by seeing what happened as a result of the intervention of heads of government in other international contexts.

Comparisons with other types of summits

It is instructive to compare the seven-power summits with the various other multilateral meetings of heads of governments which became prevalent from the mid-1970s onwards. In total these became very numerous, but the comparison can reasonably be limited to those meetings attended by at least two out of the Western summit seven. This confines the list to three recurrent series – NATO summits, Commonwealth heads of government meetings, and the European Council – plus three single events – the Helsinki Final Act ceremony of 1975, the Guadeloupe four-power meeting of 1979, and the Cancun North–South summit of 1981.

NATO summits were held over this period in 1974, 1975, 1977 and 1978; another would take place in 1982. Their purpose was always to give supreme approval to major policy decisions, which had been worked out in advance to the last detail by officials, foreign ministers, and the NATO Secretariat. The summit meetings themselves were formal, even ritual, consisting of a round of set speeches and the issue of a declaration agreed verbatim beforehand. The aim of this careful programming was to avoid unwelcome last-minute surprises which could undermine Allied solidarity on sensitive issues. But the personal element in these meetings would thus be limited to bilateral and other contacts on the side.

Commonwealth heads of government meetings took place every second year, over a period of about ten days. Despite advance preparation by the Commonwealth Secretariat and senior officials, there was a long tradition of frank and spontaneous debate around the table – helped by a common language and, for many participants, a common educational, legal, and parliamentary tradition. The Commonwealth tried to maintain this informality, for example by the weekend 'retreat' for leaders only, but inevitably the tradition became eroded as the numbers present rose. A long declaration was issued, though only parts of this reflected what the leaders said among themselves. The basic aim of the meetings was better mutual information and improved understanding, rather than common policies on wider issues, which would be hard to achieve in such a large and diverse group. The heads of government would also endorse the programme of activities for the years ahead and occasionally reach agreements on matters of central importance to the Commonwealth, such as Rhodesia in 1977.

The European Council met three times every year from 1975, replacing the less frequent Community summits inaugurated by President Pompidou in 1969. President Giscard, who invented it, initially intended the European Council to be apart from the main structure of the Community, to allow the heads of government to consider informally the key issues which faced them. The format reflected this, with heads of government and foreign ministers meeting alone, without officials, and spending part of their time on informal exchanges. The final public statement was made by the country holding the presidency, without necessarily agreeing all of it verbatim with the others. But over time the main business of the European Council became collective negotiation of issues which, because of their intrinsic difficulty, their political sensitivity, or their combination of various topics, could not be resolved at lower levels in the community.

Of the single events, the 1975 Helsinki ceremony was as precisely programmed in advance as the NATO summits. The multilateral part, which endorsed agreements reached during the prolonged Conference on Security and Cooperation in Europe, was pure ritual, though it provided the occasion for many informal exchanges on the side. The 1979 Guadeloupe meeting was quite different, as chapter 7 showed. It was very small, had little advance preparation, and issued no final statement; all the focus was on the personal contacts between the leaders present. The 1981 Cancun North–South summit would be very similar. The participation would be highly selective, to allow for informal debate, and the final declaration would be issued on the authority of the two co-chairmen, with only one short paragraph being agreed with the other participants. Both Guadeloupe and Cancun were regarded as successful by those who took part – especially the former – but both proved isolated events and there were no successor meetings.

Despite the differences among them, it is clear that none of the recurrent heads of government meetings discussed above had the same function as the seven-power summits. The NATO, Commonwealth, and Community summit meetings each represented the apex of the pyramid of an established organisation. None could be regarded as a 'core group', as all members of the organisation could take part as of right. Each was concerned – at least in part – in endorsing or ruling on matters prepared by its subordinate bodies and secretariat (or the European Commission).

The Guadeloupe and Cancun meetings provide more instructive

comparisons. Like the seven-power summits, they were selective but intended their conclusions to spread to a wider circle. The results of Guadeloupe were felt through NATO and, as regards aid for Turkey, the OECD. Cancun would be intended to influence matters in the UN. But since they were only single events, it is hard to draw general lessons from them.

The seven-power summits are therefore without parallel in many respects. They covered a wide range of subjects, which were also handled by a variety of other international organisations. But because of their selective format, their membership was not identical with any of these; and they had the capacity, which few other organisations shared, of relating different sets of issues to one another. As a result, there were no organic links between the summits and bodies like the OECD, the IMF, and the GATT; and the summits played a variety of roles in their dealings with them.

Roles for the seven-power summits

The summits played four distinct roles with regard to other international organisations. Three of them were normally beneficial, each being more ambitious than the last. These were: endorsing their objectives; stimulating their activities; and exercising leadership. A fourth role was less positive, when the summits came to circumvent the organisations and duplicate their work.

Endorsement, the first role, was essentially passive. The summit declarations would often contain passages reaffirming the general or particular objectives of the OECD, the IMF, or the GATT, for example, without adding to them. Authoritative support from the summit could give encouragement to the organisations, even though the statements did not always reflect what the leaders actually said among themselves. The hidden purpose of these statements might be to encourage reluctant summit countries to live up to the objectives in question. But often the statements would be so broadly phrased or so qualified as to provide an inadequate incentive to action.

The summits would exercise their second, more active role when they gave a high-level stimulus to the activities of international bodies. Here it was not always necessary for the summits to go deeply into the technical issues involved. The heads of government, by virtue of their wider political perspective or their ability to integrate a range of different problems, could generate movement in negotiations or overcome outstanding difficulties, particularly when these arose among the summit countries themselves. Once the stimulus was given, further treatment would continue in the organisation concerned, so that the non-summit members and the staff were involved in a cooperative effort.

Leadership by the summit – the third role – would go beyond giving political stimulus to an existing direction of an organisation's work. It meant imparting a new direction, which the organisation and its members were then in practice obliged to follow, whether they agreed with it or not. Collective leadership was the key role seen for the summits by early commentators like the Atlantic Council of the United States.[3] They often envisaged more organic links between the summits and the bodies concerned, so as to facilitate such leadership – for example, inviting the Secretary-General of the OECD, the Managing Director of the IMF, and the Director-General of the GATT to take part in the summits. The summit leaders resisted such practices, which they saw as diluting the personal quality of the meetings. In the absence of organic links, clear examples of the summits 'giving a lead' to other organisations would usually be controversial, even though they might be justified by the results.

Leadership still involved the other organisations and their members in the process, if only as 'followers'. But in their fourth, less helpful role, the summits could on occasion bypass the organisations altogether and limit follow-up activities to the circle of the seven countries and the Commission. The most conspicuous evidence of this was the creation of their own groups of officials, or even ministers, from the seven summit countries and the Community to conduct follow-up work. This might occasionally be useful as a transition to wider international discussion. But in general, it would demoralise the other organisations concerned and generate a sense of exclusion among both non-summit members of these bodies and the professional staff.

It is worth noting a fifth possible role which the summits have never played; they have not tried to promote reform of the system. There was a moment, right at the beginning, when it looked as though they might attempt this. Mr Wilson gave his colleagues at Rambouillet a list of no less than 38 different international bodies concerned with the economic subjects they were discussing.[4] His aim was to demonstrate that the system was too cluttered and needed an overhaul. But though this raised some positive echoes, it was not considered further. The subject was on the agenda for Puerto Rico, but was never reached. The heads of government would not return to the question of reform – at least until the run-up to Williamsburg in 1983, when President Mitterrand would raise the idea of a 'new Bretton Woods' to reform the monetary system and the Americans would propose new machinery for treating trade and financial issues together. Instead of reform, the summits generally aimed to protect the existing system and to make it work better. In this, their preference was for flexible adjustment and discretionary management, rather than for precise rules or contractual arrangements.

It is now necessary to look more closely at the interaction of the summits with the specific organisations at issue: the OECD and the IEA; the IMF and the World Bank; the GATT; and the United Nations.

The OECD and the IEA

The OECD was involved with all the economic subjects considered at the summits and had the same capacity to treat them in relation to one another. It sought to influence policy in a variety of ways: by supplying its members with comprehensive high-quality data and careful analysis of policy issues; and by mutual persuasion and argument, conducted mainly among national officials and the Secretariat, with foreign and finance ministers meeting only once a year. In principle, the summits and the OECD ought to dovetail together neatly, with the former providing occasional, high-level political impulses to move forward the continuous, highly professional work of the latter. In practice, however, the relationship would prove to be uneasy. The OECD faced a difficult choice: to seek close links with the summits, at the risk of losing its independence; or to remain detached, at the risk of being bypassed.

If the summits had limited themselves to giving political impulses, that would have been easier for the OECD and its Secretary-General to accept. But the summits soon moved on to adopt precise commitments, notably in economic policy, with direct consequences for the OECD and sometimes moving in directions with which it disagreed. Such an approach – close to a leadership role – might justify a more organic link between the two, for example with the Secretary-General attending the summits and summit country representatives forming a nucleus at the OECD. But in practice neither side moved in this direction. The summit leaders wanted a compact, personal format and did not consider inviting Mr van Lennep, though this placed him and the OECD at a disadvantage in relation to the Commission when they admitted Mr Jenkins. The OECD, for its part, found it hard to accommodate new committees or groups which were not open to the entire membership.[5]

In these conditions looser procedures were needed to keep the summits and the OECD together. The most visible of these was the practice, in regular operation from 1976, of holding the OECD's annual ministerial meeting shortly before the summit, so that the other members had the chance to put across their concerns to the summit countries. More informal arrangements prevailed for a time in the preparation for the summits. From 1977 the representatives of the seven summit countries in the OECD's Economic Policy Committee (EPC) began to meet for the express purpose of preparing the economic policy part of the summit's discussion.[6] The chairman of this group – from 1978 the Chairman of the US Council of Economic Advisors –

would send forward a report to the sherpas. Even so, the OECD Secretariat was not actually present at the meeting of the seven officials (and the Commission) devoted to summit preparation. It still had to exercise its influence at one remove, through providing economic forecasts and assessments and through its frequent contact with the EPC members.

This osmotic arrangement worked best when there was consensus between the summit countries and the OECD Secretariat on the direction of economic policy. After Rambouillet and Puerto Rico there had been some disagreement about economic prospects. The London summit in 1977 produced a result in line with OECD objectives but was followed by sharp disputes at OECD meetings, especially over German policies.[7] But the Bonn summit provided the keystone to the OECD's 'concerted action' strategy of 1978 and during the period of 'non-accommodating' policies in 1979–80 the summits and the OECD were able to reinforce each other effectively.

Thereafter, however, the policy prescriptions began to diverge, while neither President Reagan nor Mrs Thatcher were as well disposed to the OECD as their predecessors. The summit countries (except France, for a time) continued with restrictive policies, giving absolute priority to fighting inflation; the OECD Secretariat began to worry about the effect of these policies on the severity of the recession. The informal collaboration over summit preparations could not survive this strain. The group formed of EPC members ceased to handle preparations for the summit after 1981. The summit countries, instead of operating in a context close to the OECD, prefered to do the work by themselves or turn to the IMF. This aggravated another problem: although the OECD's involvement before the summits had been fairly well defined, follow-up procedures were always haphazard. The sherpa from the host country would give an early report of the meeting to the OECD, but there were no more precise arrangements for associating it with the consequences of the summits. Thus other OECD countries and the Secretariat came to feel that they were being starved of information and that summit proceedings had become furtive, ambiguous, and obscure.

In the central field of macroeconomic policy, therefore, the summits gradually took the limelight from the OECD, possibly thereby weakening it. In technology, too, the Versailles summit of 1982 bypassed the OECD's capacity and created its own special group. But in other areas the relationship has worked better. The early summits gave helpful endorsement to the OECD's 'trade pledge' against import restrictions. The skilful work done in the OECD (and IEA) on aspects of East–West economic relations helped greatly to repair the damage done by the Versailles summit.

In the energy field, the link proved beneficial; the summits served to invigorate the IEA and OECD, despite the continued absence of France from the Agency. The Tokyo summit of 1979 clearly sought to exercise leadership through the fixing of oil import targets for each participating country and other commitments. The French contrived that the results of the summit should be followed up by a special monitoring group composed of the summit countries and the European Commission. But although their intention had been to bypass the IEA, in practice only the combined Energy Staff of the IEA and the OECD had the technical expertise required to carry forward the work. Dr Ulf Lantzke, the Agency's executive director, was admitted to the monitoring group, on a personal basis, and the French acquiesced in this. This established a direct, if still informal, link between the Agency and the summits, and meant that the Energy Staff became much more closely involved in the summit process than their colleagues who dealt with economic policy. The monitoring group was renewed after the Venice summit in 1980, though after the easing of the second oil crisis its regular meetings would cease. The Bonn summit of 1978 also stimulated work in the OECD on new and renewable sources of energy and Tokyo did the same with energy technology.

The 'leadership' decisions taken at Tokyo were highly controversial. Dr Lantzke and his staff doubted whether national import targets were in fact the best answer to the oil crisis because of the severe difficulty of negotiating them. But they welcomed them because they obliged member governments to concentrate on using less oil and opened the way for IEA work not only on targets but also on other issues, such as stock-building policy. The Venice summit, on the other hand, gave a strong impetus to the work on energy-saving measures and alternatives to oil which was already in hand in the IEA and the OECD. The follow-up work therefore proceeded much more smoothly than after Tokyo.[8]

The IMF and the World Bank

The summits had an easier relationship with the Bretton Woods institutions than with the OECD, for two principal reasons. First, the degree of ministerial involvement and the tolerance of limited groups were much higher in these institutions. An informal transmission mechanism linked the summits to the Fund and Bank, via the Group of Five (whose members were always at the summits), the Group of Ten, and the Interim and Development Committees, all meeting several times a year at ministerial level. Second, the Fund and Bank had distinct functions which the summits could not duplicate; in short, they had money to lend, while the summits did not. So there was not the same fear that the summits would steal the limelight from the Bretton Woods institutions.

The Rambouillet summit of 1975 exerted a very strong stimulus to the closing stages of the reform negotiations in the IMF. It also tried to set up separate collaborative arrangements on exchange rates, which might well have clashed with the Fund's own responsibilities, had the new arrangements endured. But thereafter for many years the summits did no more than endorse the current objectives of the Fund. They had little or no influence on the debates concerning quota increases, the substitution account or new issues of SDRs. The leaders only returned to exchange rates in 1982 and to monetary reform in 1983, both times with some reluctance, under strong pressure from France.

There was also a mutually reinforcing effect between the summits and the IMF in the field of economic policies. This gained in importance from 1981, as the summit countries came to be more in sympathy with the traditional concerns of the Fund, which stressed control of budget deficits and money supply, than with the prescriptions of the OECD. This trend led to the idea of 'multilateral surveillance', first introduced at Versailles in 1982, which brought the Managing Director of the Fund into meetings of the five finance ministers. His role was to advise on how their economic and monetary policies could best fit together so as to promote exchange rate stability, rather than to act as a bridge between the summits and the IMF. This gave M. de Larosière a privileged position close to the summit process, comparable to that achieved by Dr Lantzke in energy matters; but it could also lead to tension between his involvement in this select group and his broader responsibilities to the IMF and all its members.

The summits began to concern themselves with the World Bank from 1977 onwards. President Carter and Henry Owen used the summits both to stimulate new activities in the Bank, often in consultation with its president, Mr McNamara, and, with European co-operation, to overcome Congressional resistance to appropriating funds for US contributions. After 1980, the Europeans continued to try through the summits to keep up pressure on the Reagan Administration, which seemed at times as reluctant to provide new money as Congress. At all times the summits' interventions were welcome to the Bank, but they seldom seemed decisive, even where the objective was attained, such as the capital increase for the Bank in 1977–8. With other issues, such as the energy affiliate proposed in 1980 and the replenishment of IDA in 1981–3, summit endorsement of the objective, often qualified, proved clearly inadequate to remove the obstacles on the US side.

The GATT

The work of the GATT was highly technical, pursued essentially by officials and the Secretariat, with meetings of ministers exceedingly rare. But the GATT depended on the underlying political commitment of its members to uphold the open, non-discriminatory trading system. It could therefore benefit greatly from the sort of external stimulus which the summits could give, especially from the heads of government, who were directly exposed to the political pressures for trade protection.

The summits applied their stimulus to the GATT Multilateral Trade Negotiations (MTNs) over several years from 1975 to 1978. The leaders themselves never examined in detail the issues involved. But they insisted that the agreements should be wide-ranging and kept up the pressure for their conclusion by setting a series of deadlines. Difficult disputes were resolved through the influence of the 1978 Bonn summit, and even on the margins of the summit itself. The results of the MTNs may be criticised for falling short of expectations. But without the strong political push from the summits they might well have run into the sand or settled for much less.

The Ottawa summit of 1981 led the GATT in a new direction by its powerful promotion of the idea of a GATT ministerial meeting. This was a more controversial move. Because of the persistence of the recession, the ministerial meeting, held in November 1982, took place when protectionist pressures were at their fiercest. In the event, the meeting served to show the ministers present how fragile the open trading system had become. 'The ministers went to the edge of the abyss, looked into it, and drew back.'[9] But it might well have weakened the GATT rather than strengthening it, without the timely appearance of economic recovery in early 1983.

Alongside these specific impulses to the work of the GATT, the summits regularly endorsed the general aim of preserving the open trading system. These authoritative statements of principle, together with the pressure to complete the MTNs, helped to keep protectionist demands at bay in the 1970s after the first oil crisis. But from 1979 onwards these repeated statements from the summit began to wear very thin. Protectionist measures made visible headway, especially in sectors like textiles, steel, and cars, and the summit countries disputed among themselves. The European countries, after unsuccessful attempts to use the summits to put pressure on Japan, increased their trade restrictions on Japanese exports. The Americans, though they were always the most active in promoting GATT activities through the summits, introduced new restrictive measures on steel imports very soon after the summits in 1982 and again in 1983, despite undertakings at those meetings to work towards the future opening of markets and to dismantle trade barriers.

The United Nations

The summits and the UN stood at opposite extremes. The summit found its virtue in being a select group of influential countries, the United Nations in being universal and comprehensive. Both were concerned with economic relations between developed and developing countries. But the North–South dialogue as conducted at the UN, through formal exchanges between group spokesmen, was hard to relate to the frank, personal discussions at the summits. It was not surprising that direct interaction was slight. Specific references to the UN at the summits were rare. For their part, the developing countries felt too remote from the summits to want to use the UN as a channel for influencing them.

The summits made general statements of approval and encouragement about UN activities, but with no visible impact; Williamsburg, in 1983, for example, did this about the forthcoming UNCTAD VI in Belgrade. The summits also, on occasion, gave some political stimulus at critical points in the North–South dialogue. This was done in 1977 in the closing stages of the Conference on International Economic Co-operation; and in 1978 for the negotiations for the Common Fund for commodities. The Ottawa summit of 1981 did the same before the Cancun North–South summit; and Versailles in 1982, in relation to the UN 'global negotiations'. In every case the momentum proved inadequate to produce lasting improvement. North–South relations, in the UN context, would remain an area where the summits had yet to make their mark.

Summary assessment

The summits were originally intended to have a catalytic effect on other international organisations, exerting a powerful influence while remaining themselves aloof and detached. The idea of the summits as the hub of a concentric system, with international institutions on the rim, was superimposed on this earlier concept. The two approaches were not entirely compatible and each generated its own set of problems.

One factor limiting the impact of the summits was that the heads of government, meeting occasionally, were not subject to the same pressures for continuity which applied to the other organisations. They usually focused on immediate policy issues, working through 'administrative discretion in collective management', in preference to 'tightening the rules governing international economic relations and increasing the power load on the machinery for their enforcement'.[10] This was only natural for a brief two-day meeting and natural too in a turbulent, rapidly changing world. But it meant that the summits' influence on other bodies like the GATT and the IMF would be in the direction of flexible adaptation to circumstances rather than working out new rules and contractual arrangements. The danger here, if adaptation was pursued indefinitely, lay in seeing the existing rules, which largely survived from the postwar period, become obscured by exceptions and qualifications.

The summits had important successes, when the impulses they imparted to other institutions were decisive in producing results which could not have been achieved within the institutions themselves. The IMF's monetary reform negotiations would not have been so satisfactorily concluded without the intervention of Rambouillet, nor the MTNs in the GATT without the pressure from the London and Bonn summits. The OECD benefited when the Bonn summit rounded off its macroeconomic strategy, as did the IEA when the Tokyo and Venice summits focused attention on energy policy.

But even while the summits were invigorating these other organisations, they were building up their own parallel apparatus. In particular, as explained in chapter 7, the practice developed of creating special summit-based groups on specific issues – hijacking after Bonn, energy monitoring at Tokyo and again at Venice. From 1981 there was something of a reaction against detailed and specific commitments at the summits, which thus became more detached from the work of international organisations. But the special groups expanded unchecked: a group on trade (the 'Quadrilateral'), from Ottawa in 1981; three groups, on technology, exchange market intervention, and surveillance of economic policies, from Versailles in 1982; and a remit to finance ministers on improving the international monetary system, from Williamsburg in 1983. The summit began to look like a rival to the other organisations, instead of a catalyst or a source of strength; not so much, perhaps, to the Fund and Bank, which had distinct operational roles, but certainly to a body like the OECD concerned with policy coordination and cooperation. The examples of successful stimulus to other organisations grew less frequent, raising the question whether the law of diminishing returns was beginning to apply – a question to which chapter 13 will return.

Studying summits is in one respect like climbing them: it is easier to interpret the terrain some distance back than that recently traversed or just ahead. From our present vantage point the patterns in the successive summits of the 1980s cannot be so reliably deciphered as those of the 1970s. Nevertheless, in several important respects these most recent summits are plainly marked off from their predecessors.

Actors and agendas in the early 1980s

Five of the eight summiteers who gathered in Montebello, just outside Ottawa, in July 1981, were newcomers, the highest rate of turnover at any summit so far. Gaston Thorn had succeeded Roy Jenkins as President of the European Commission. The Italians were led by Giovanni Spadolini, the first non-Christian Democrat to rule Italy in three and a half decades. Japan was represented by Zenko Suzuki, a rather provincial figure, adept in the quiet consensus-mongering of Japanese politics, but hardly equipped to assume the more active role on the world scene that Japan's economic power seemed to justify.

The remaining newcomers, President Ronald Reagan and President François Mitterrand, had more sharply etched political profiles. Both had been borne into office on landslides of popular discontent with past economic policies, and both were inclined to be tougher on East–West security matters than were their respective predecessors. But in virtually all other respects the affable conservative homilist and the contemplative Socialist intellectual were poles apart. The dialectic between them would dominate the summits of the early 1980s, just as the summits of the late 1970s had been structured by the force field between Jimmy Carter and Helmut Schmidt.

Ronald Reagan was the most conservative president the United States had elected in more than half a century. He had a popular mandate for a more militant foreign and defence policy.[1] His supply-side economic policy called for massive cuts in taxes, balanced by cuts in domestic social programmes. Publicly, at least, the Administration claimed that this package would generate enough growth to fund their arms build-up and still balance the Federal budget. The President quickly established his dominance over Congress, aided by the neo-conservative mood in the country. To carry out his programme, he staffed the Treasury, the Pentagon, and the White House with men of adamantine conviction, who believed in the magic of the free market, anti-communist vigilance, and global US leadership. Just as Jimmy Carter's agenda had provided the grist for previous summits, the doctrines of the Reaganites would powerfully affect the agenda of summitry in the years ahead.

Barely two months before the Ottawa summit François Mitterrand captured the French presidency, at the head of the most leftist coalition to govern France since 1936. The new government immediately increased spending for welfare and employment, boosted the minimum wage, and announced a far-reaching nationalisation programme. The Socialists in the Elysée recognised that this package, more Keynesian than Marxist, was out of phase with international economic trends, but they counted on France's substantial reserves to tide them over until the Western recovery that was expected by the end of the year. As one of them recounted ruefully later, they hoped to ride the wave of recovery like a successful surfer.

By 1981, the issues that had preoccupied the summits of the Carter–Schmidt years – the weak dollar, German and Japanese reflation, even energy – had virtually vanished. In their place appeared a new set of issues that would dominate the Reagan–Mitterrand era – US interest rates and the strong dollar, East–West trade, and the East–West military balance. To a remarkable extent, the arguments and alignments that would preoccupy summiteers at least through Williamsburg were manifested in the weeks leading up to Ottawa.

During the first half of 1981 the European economies were stagnant, but the US economy rebounded sharply from the V-shaped recession of 1980, and the Administration expressed optimism for continued growth. But the Americans' expansive touch on the fiscal accelerator was more than offset by their heavy tread on the monetary brakes. Consequently, US interest rates soared. The prime rate shot from a low of 11 per cent in mid-1980 to 21 per cent at year's end, oscillated in the high teens and low twenties throughout 1981, and was still at 16 per cent in the spring of 1982. Since the underlying inflation rate was dropping from double digits to below 6 per cent over this same period, the 'real' rate of interest remained unprecedentedly high.

The dollar followed US interest rates up and down, but mostly up. 'In the twelve months from August 1980 to August 1981 the average value of the dollar in terms of the currencies of the ten major industrial countries (as measured by the Federal Reserve) rose by 30 per cent; in relation to the currencies of the European Monetary System, the increase was more than 40 per cent.'[2] The dollar's rise, along with the high interest rates, exerted a deflationary effect on the US economy, pushing inflation down and unemployment up, presumably a tradeoff that the Administration found acceptable, if regrettable.

Reaganomics put other governments in an unwelcome dilemma, especially, but not only, the expansion-minded French Socialists. If they allowed their currencies to fall, inflation would be given a powerful fillip, particularly since oil and many other imports were priced in dollars. On the other hand, if they tightened monetary policy to defend their currencies, they would add further to the deflationary pressures on their own economies. For the most part, the major governments split the difference and suffered both depreciating currencies and tight money.

Throughout the next three years, the non-American summit participants would be virtually unanimous in complaining about US interest rates and the strength of the dollar. But there was a good deal less unanimity about causes and cures. The simplest remedy would be for the Americans to loosen their monetary policy. This recommendation was particularly appealing to those economists who argued that uncoordinated monetary stringency could lead to a deflationary effect greater than any single country intended.[3] However, most of the governments were politically committed to the path of monetary rectitude embarked upon after the second oil shock, and they were uneasy about recommending any other course to the Americans. If the issue was simply the strong dollar and US interest rates, then the Americans were isolated, but if the issue became monetarism versus Keynesianism, then the British and probably the Germans and Japanese, too, would desert the French.

A second approach would be for the Americans to change their mix of fiscal and monetary policy, by reining in the budget deficit, which was presumably causing lenders to demand an 'inflation risk premium' that padded the real interest rate.[4] This approach had no disadvantages for the foreigners, unless they happened to be concerned about maintaining the pace of US rearmament. It might seem inappropriate for the French or Italians to preach fiscal austerity to the Americans, but the Germans and the British urged this course with growing insistence. Cutting the budget deficit received widespread verbal support in the United States too, but it encountered severe political obstacles. The Administration gave higher priority to defence spending than to budget balancing, and after the initial round of domestic spending cuts in 1981, further cutbacks in that sector proved increasingly difficult, particularly after the Democrats' Congressional gains in November 1982. A tax increase might resolve the dilemma, but this would fly directly in the face of the central tenets of Reaganomics. From Ottawa to Williamsburg, the Americans assured their partners that they too wanted to get the US budget deficit down, but the red ink flowed unstanched.

Intervention in currency markets was advocated by some as an approach that might provide at least symptomatic relief from the strong dollar. As we shall see, this alternative was discussed extensively in connection with the Versailles and Williamsburg summits. American Under-Secretary of the Treasury Beryl Sprinkel, a passionate free-marketeer, had announced shortly after the Reagan Administration took office that the Americans would henceforth adopt a hands-off approach to currency markets, but elsewhere there was a broad consensus that coordinated intervention might usefully reduce the day-to-day volatility of exchange rates. On the other hand, there was an even broader consensus in support of the view, traditionally defended by the Americans and supported by the Bundesbank and others, that such intervention could have no sustained impact on the dollar's strength, since currency values were determined by 'the fundamentals' of relative economic performance and prospects. As the divergence between French and US inflation rates widened, stabilising exchange rates by intervention became less and less plausible.

Since none of the three primary alternatives was both technically and politically feasible, only interlocutory solutions to the conflict could be found.[5] No doubt the force of the attacks on the Americans was reduced by the absence of consensus among the others about just what they wanted done, but there is no evidence in any event that the Americans were prepared to bend their principles in response to international pressure. The President told the Annual Meeting of the World Bank and IMF on 29 September 1981, 'The most important contribution any country can make to world development is to pursue sound economic policies at home.' Thus, as we shall see, the Americans mostly temporised. 'Wait a while', was their message in Ottawa; 'Let's study it', the approach in Versailles; and 'Our boom will solve it', the line in Williamsburg. The Americans often added, with considerable justification, that some Europeans were using the strong dollar and US interest rates as a convenient excuse for home-grown policy failures.

The second set of issues that was to buffet the summits of the early 1980s involved East–West relations. US public scepticism of détente had begun to mount as early as 1974, and in the aftermath of Afghanistan the gap between US and European opinion had grown alarmingly. Under the Carter Administration, differences with Europe over East–West relations were sharp, but mainly tactical. However, many in the Reagan Administration had a fundamentally different assessment of Soviet policy from most Europeans, an image of the Soviet Union at once more threatening (militarily) and more vulnerable (economically). In his first news conference as President, Reagan indicated that he was in no hurry to begin arms control talks until the United States could negotiate from a position of strength. This was a position that many Europeans, and particularly many Germans, found deeply disquieting, particularly in light of the 1979 NATO 'double-track' decision that coupled deployments of new intermediate-range US missiles with Soviet–US negotiations that might make the missiles unnecessary.

Traditionally, Americans had been readier than Europeans to employ economic sanctions. This issue had been a source of tension under the Carter Administration in connection with both the Afghanistan and Iranian crises. Carter and his predecessors had invoked economic sanctions in part for symbolic reasons and in part as 'leverage' to seek specific concessions. To these justifications, the Reagan Administration added two more. The first, which many Europeans found persuasive, was that the Soviets had gained specific military advantages from leakages of Western technology. The second, however, was much more worrisome: some influential Reagan advisors believed that by waging economic warfare, the West could undermine the Soviets' ability to pursue their militarist and expansionist policies, forcing them to spend more on butter and leaving less for guns. This thesis was expounded most insistently by Defence Secretary Caspar Weinberger and by the President's National Security Advisor, William Clark, who announced that it was Administration policy to 'force our principal adversary, the Soviet Union, to bear the brunt of its economic shortcomings'.[6]

For historical and geographical reasons, East–West trade was more important economically to Europe than to the United States, but many Europeans were willing to concede the economic senselessness of subsidising that trade. They were much less open to political arguments against East–West trade, however, particularly since the Reagan Administration had withdrawn Carter's embargo on US grain sales to the Russians. Moreover, even the most anti-communist of Europeans, like Prime Minister Thatcher, were offended when the Americans proposed to abrogate contracts that had already been signed and (still worse) sought to extend this policy to foreign subsidiaries of US firms.

Precisely these questions of retroactivity and extraterritoriality were raised by the Americans' offensive against the proposed trans-Siberian gas pipeline. This massive project would be built with Western technology and Western credits of about $15 billion. It would nearly triple European gas imports from the Soviet Union to a total of approximately one-fifth of European gas consumption (or one-twentieth of total energy consumption).[7] Among a panoply of arguments against this deal, the Reagan Administration stressed that it could expose Europe to Soviet energy blackmail and boost Soviet hard currency earnings, but few Europeans were convinced.

France's position on these East–West issues was nuanced. On questions of military security, such as the Euromissiles, Mitterrand was a staunch supporter of the US position, having regard both to the East–West military balance and to the risks of renascent German neutralism.

On the other hand, on East–West trade, Mitterrand fully shared his European colleagues' hostility to retroactivity, extraterritoriality, and economic warfare. Calculating that the Reagan Administration valued French solidarity on security issues, the new French Administration sought to strike an implicit bargain. At his first OECD meeting, Finance Minister Jacques Delors referred to 'a linkage' between reliable security partnership and 'our mutual economic interests', and President Mitterrand observed that 'one cannot hope for more political and military cohesion in the Atlantic Alliance and be content with an every-man-for-himself attitude in economics'.[8]

This cross-issue linkage was implicit from Ottawa to Williamsburg, as we shall see, but as the French themselves ultimately recognised, it was not fundamentally credible. Since the French position on East–West security was manifestly rooted in a hard-nosed assessment of French national interests, it was not credible that they would deviate from that position simply to retaliate against Reaganomics. The Reagan Administration's deafness to French pleas on economics suggests that the Americans understood the weakness of the French position. On East–West economic issues, on the other hand, some bargaining was possible, but a prolonged and acrimonious controversy would ensue before it was clear whether the minimal demands of the two sides overlapped at all.

Prologue at Montebello, 19–21 July 1981

Schmidt, Thatcher, and Trudeau, the only veterans at Ottawa, were all in political difficulty at home, primarily because of the continuing economic strains of the recession. Reagan and Mitterrand, however, were in the first flush of victory. The ideological polarisation around the table would clearly be greater than at any previous summit, and the newcomers were hardly likely to modify their newly minted policies, whatever the international discordance. Thus, Trudeau was reconciled to a 'getting to know you' summit, 'consciously putting aside the hard issues', as one of his top aides said later. Hoping to set the proper tone, Trudeau hosted the summit at Le Château Montebello, an isolated hunting resort 50 miles outside Ottawa. His approach was consistent with the widely shared desire among this generation of summiteers to avoid 'decisional' summits.

The sherpas held the by now standard four preparatory meetings, and by their final session in July they had drafted a long, almost encyclopaedic communiqué. However, the French and US Administrations were too new to have well-articulated positions on many topics. Indeed, the official French sherpa did not join the preparations until June. The US sherpa, lacking detailed guidance from the White House except to avoid commitments that would cut across domestic priorities, insisted that 'there will be no concrete conclusion, no numbers in the communiqué, no specific policy agreements'.[9] Even more than Jimmy Carter's first summit in London, this was to be a summit of preliminary sparring, in which arguments were rehearsed, but little resolved, at least on the most fundamental issues.

The meeting opened with a dinner discussion of political issues. Schmidt laid out his argument for balance and stability in East–West relations, and Mitterrand sought to establish his bona fides with the Americans by pledging to honour French commitments to the Atlantic Alliance. Reagan followed with a vintage declamation on the Soviet military threat, Soviet economic failings, and the need to link political and economic relations and to give priority to rearmament, not arms control. Schmidt brusquely retorted that the Western convoy could not be expected to shift course merely because one of the ships had a new captain. Mitterrand agreed with the firm anti-Soviet stance of Reagan and Thatcher, particularly on strategic questions. Even German commentators concluded that the tough language on East–West relations in the final 'chairman's summary on political issues' reflected essentially Reagan's line.[10]

Two other political issues were touched on at Ottawa. During the conference itself Israeli planes bombed targets in Lebanon, angering all the leaders, particularly the Americans, who had been seeking an anti-Soviet 'strategic consensus' that would bridge the Arab–Israeli dispute. In the joint political declaration read by Prime Minister Trudeau, the leaders deplored the continuing violence and called for restraint on all sides. A separate statement recalled the Bonn declaration on hijacking and proposed to apply sanctions in a recent case involving Afghanistan. Perhaps most notable about the political pronouncements, however, was the widespread acceptance that (as Prime Minister Suzuki said later) 'it was natural for leaders at such summits to exchange views on political problems'.[11]

The original demands of Reagan's most hawkish advisors that East–West trade be substantially curtailed had been toned down on the eve of the summit, in response to Secretary of State Alexander Haig's concern that Alliance solidarity should not be risked over this issue. (Two years later French officials privately would regret that this slightly softer line misled them about the depth of the President's commitment on the matter.) Nevertheless, both in the plenary session and in an inconclusive bilateral talk with Schmidt, the President expressed his unhappiness about East–West trade and technology transfer, and especially about the pipeline. However, the Europeans, led by Schmidt and Mitterrand, held their ground, and the outcome was a stand-off. Apart from an agreement to intensify consultation in COCOM (the standing joint committee charged with controlling exports of strategic goods to the Soviet bloc), the communiqué merely noted blandly that 'consultations and, where appropriate, coordination are necessary to ensure that, in the field of East–West relations, our economic policies *continue to be* compatible with our political and security objectives'.[12] The Americans found virtually no audience for their complaints about the pipeline, but their vexation persisted.

The essentially unyielding European response on East–West economics was matched by the US attitude on macroeconomic and monetary affairs. In what one aide later described as a 'gloves-off' exchange, Schmidt, Trudeau, Spadolini, and Mitterrand all sharply criticised high US interest rates, Schmidt claiming that they had brought Germany 'the highest real interest rates since the birth of Christ'. Mitterrand said that it would be 'intolerable' if US interest rates were to remain high past the end of the year. Only Margaret Thatcher rose in defence of Reagan's policies, though in that pre-Falklands summer of 1981 her position was weakened by urban riots and low polls at home. Reagan gave a vigorous defence of his economic programme; and after railing against Carter's weak dollar and inflationary policies, the Europeans could hardly criticise Reagan's avowed objectives. US spokesmen, such as Treasury Secretary Donald Regan, expected that interest rates would drop within six months, but gave no guarantees. In short, all agreed reluctantly to return home and wait a while for Reaganomics to work.

The language of the communiqué gave unemployment the same priority as inflation, and foresaw 'a prospect of moderate economic growth in the coming year'. In terms of policies, however, the meeting endorsed a generally austere, monetarist line quite congenial to the Anglo-American conservatives. The communiqué lauded 'low and stable monetary growth', stressed the need 'urgently to reduce public borrowing', and called for educating electorates to lower their expectations. Prime Minister Thatcher enthused: 'They think at home that I am out on a limb, but frankly I am right in the middle of the road as far as summitry is concerned.'[13] Chancellor Schmidt, too, exploited the summit results domestically, citing them as justification for German belt-tightening. Since the German budget cuts had been in the cards, whatever the outcome of the summit, the argument was, as one of Schmidt's aides later put it, 'not intellectually valid, but politically useful'.

Prime Minister Trudeau hoped to make North–South relations the centrepiece of his summit, and the new French government and the European Community were strong supporters of this emphasis.[14] This group wanted the summit to send a signal of openmindedness to the upcoming North–South summit in Cancun, Mexico. In that context, the immediate demand of the developing countries, represented by the

Group of 77, was that 'global negotiations', linked to the UN, be launched to address their economic concerns. Predictably, the greatest scepticism was voiced by Reagan and Thatcher. The US Treasury and the White House were deeply suspicious of the Group of 77 proposal – 'another global jamboree', they labelled it derisively – and the new Administration had disavowed the Carter initiative at Venice for a World Bank energy affiliate.

However, some US officials took advantage of the summit preparations to focus the President's attention on these issues and to try to push Administration thinking beyond conservative homilies about self-help and wasted aid. At the summit itself, the President agreed to compromise language on global negotiations, official development assistance, and the energy affiliate. The Canadians and other supporters of a more generous stance hailed the agreement as 'a major breakthrough'.[15] The accord did allow the West to approach Cancun in a constructive spirit. However, progress on this front would continue to encounter stiff resistance within the Reagan Administration, and would be measured in fractional shifts in the language of successive communiqués.

Trade was the final subject to receive notable treatment in 1981.[16] Two cross-cutting alignments were apparent during the preparations, and were to recur in subsequent years. On the one hand, US and European resentment at Japanese trading practices was mounting. The Reagan Administration had already negotiated a 'voluntary' import ceiling on Japanese automobiles. Europe's trade deficit with Japan had doubled to $10 billion in 1980, and rose another 56 per cent in the first half of 1981, triggering a demand by the European Council in May that Japan exercise restraint on 'sensitive' imports and provide better access for European exports.[17] The European Community sought to include a critical phrase aimed at Japan in the summit communiqué, but they did not win the support that they had expected from the Americans. Japanese spokesmen reported afterwards that no particular policy steps were required of Japan by the summit.[18]

Beyond the 'Japanese problem', the Americans and Germans renewed their traditional battle against protectionism, in face of the equally traditional passive resistance of the Italians, the British, and (less passively) the French. The summit preparers had agreed that a new GATT conference should be held at the ministerial level in 1982, and this proposal was duly fed through the GATT machinery and 'welcomed' by the summiteers. The Americans hoped to use this venue to press for further liberalisation of investment rules and of trade in agriculture, services (banking, insurance, and so on), and high-technology products. The Europeans were generally sceptical of these US initiatives; they hoped instead to use the GATT meeting (and a 'Quadrilateral' group of trade ministers from the United States, the

European Community, Japan, and Canada, founded at Ottawa) to maintain pressure on the Japanese. In a final example of the summit's familiar role as an 'energiser' of ongoing negotiations in other forums, the summit endorsed OECD discussions of the thorny problem of export credit subsidies.

Like the introduction of a symphonic sonata, the Ottawa summit contained an exposition of virtually all the themes that would be developed in subsequent summits. Presidents Mitterrand and Reagan had kind words for one another following the summit, aware that they would meet across the same table at least three more times. Yet the tension between their regimes had provided the summit's primary polarity on issues ranging from interest rates to agricultural subsidies and from East–West credits to North–South aid. (Reagan was comforted by support from Mrs Thatcher, and Mitterrand had tried to assure himself of backing from Schmidt in a Franco-German summit just before Ottawa.)

Discord at the summit itself was minimised by its 'non-decisional' character. Virtually every participant returned home to announce that no changes were required in his or her policies as a result of the summit – 'no change in direction', said Regan; 'not one line', averred Mitterrand.[19] In a world without interdependencies, this sort of congenial 'live and let live' anarchy could ensure international comity. However, summitry had emerged precisely because the modern world is not so simple as that. Before they next met in Versailles, each leader would be reminded that achieving his own purposes required cooperation from the others, cooperation that would prove elusive.

The road to Versailles

By autumn, it was clear that (along with many other observers) both the Reagan and the Mitterrand administrations had been excessively optimistic about the economic outlook. Instead of the steady growth that Secretary Regan had predicted at Montebello, the US economy lapsed into what would be the longest and deepest recession since the Great Depression. The Socialists' expansionary measures left France exposed in the face of continued stringency elsewhere, and in October 1981 they were forced to their first devaluation of the franc.

When the US budget in January 1982 projected mounting deficits, both the real interest rate and the dollar climbed sharply. European complaints rose several decibels, and not just in Paris. Chancellor Howe told the House of Commons that 'it is important that our country and other countries help to make plain to the United States our concern about the level of their prospective budget deficit and its implications for interest rates around the world', and a senior German official grumbled that 'we have simply never before seen an American Administration that displayed this degree of indifference to the effects of its actions on its allies'.[20] For the ninth year in a row, unemployment in the European Community continued to climb.

Symptomatic of allied discontent with Reagan's 'ideologies', the sherpas' paper on macroeconomic issues, traditionally a US responsibility, was assigned instead to the British. The analysis broadly reflected an international consensus. France and Italy were chided for lax fiscal discipline, but more crucial for monetary and trade relations were the criticisms of US and Japanese policy mixes. Fiscal policy in the United States was said to be too loose and monetary policy too tight, inducing a strong dollar and international deflation. The Japanese were accused of precisely the reverse, excessive budgetary restraint and low interest rates, leading to slow domestic growth and an undervalued, export-boosting yen.

The international criticism evoked little apparent resonance within the Reagan Administration, which somewhat disingenuously pointed a finger at the Congressional impasse over the budget. The situation in Tokyo was rather different. Although it was not widely recognised abroad, powerful currents within the Japanese government, including MITI, some business groups, and several key LDP leaders, favoured a more expansionary fiscal stance. This coalition faced firm opposition from the Ministry of Finance and some senior figures in the business community, but as late as April 1982 many of these opponents privately expected that, just as in 1977–8, domestic and international pressures would combine to produce a significant stimulus package around summit time.

That nothing of the sort happened is instructive of how summitry in the 1980s is different from summitry in the 1970s. Like Fukuda in 1977–8, Suzuki was personally committed to fiscal orthodoxy, but unlike Fukuda he did not feel obliged to respond to international complaints, primarily because those complaints were muted by the monetarist mood of the 1980s. In particular, US representatives refused to countenance criticism of Japanese macroeconomic policy, despite the likely negative impact of that policy on United States–Japanese trade relations. In May, the OECD suggested discreetly that the deepening crisis justified more German and Japanese stimulus, along with looser US monetary policy (once the Congressional budget impasse was overcome), but these suggestions, too, fell on deaf ears. The ill repute of the 'locomotive' experiment continued to burden international economic policy coordination.

Meanwhile, within the circle of the sherpas an unusually sharp debate raged about US monetary policy, both domestic and international. Treasury Under-Secretary Sprinkel was regarded as almost irresponsibly dogmatic by a number of his foreign counterparts, and back in Washington he was urged by his US colleagues to seek some means of reconciling his differences with the Europeans. There had been internal proposals as early as January 1982 that the Administration should strive for international coordination of medium-term economic performance, and both the State Department and the Federal Reserve argued privately that some intervention in currency markets might have a stabilising effect.[21]

The international dispute reached a climax at the preparatory meeting held at Rambouillet on 24–25 April 1982. To general astonishment, after a heated debate Sprinkel and his French counterpart Michel Camdessus reached a procedural accommodation. This agreement was committed to writing and confirmed by the Group of Five finance ministers, meeting on the margins of the Interim Committee in Helsinki three weeks later. Slightly elaborated, the compromise struck at Rambouillet in April became the monetary accord unveiled at Versailles in June.

The dispute between Sprinkel and Camdessus directly paralleled the disagreement between the Americans and the French prior to the Rambouillet summit seven years earlier. Defending floating exchange rates, the Americans argued that monetary instability could be avoided only by policy convergence among the major economies. The French, whose long-term goal was a less flexible monetary system based on the Japanese and European currencies as well as the dollar, stressed the utility of coordinated intervention by central banks to offset 'erratic fluctuations'. The agreement sketched at Rambouillet in 1982 resolved this 'convergence versus intervention' debate only in a procedural sense. On the one hand, to address the French concerns, it was agreed that a collaborative study would be undertaken on the effectiveness of past interventions aimed at stabilising exchange rates. On the other hand, in line with the US position, the Group of Five finance ministers, joined by the Managing Director of the IMF, would meet periodically to conduct 'mutual surveillance' of their respective economic policies with an eye to encouraging policy convergence and exchange rate stability.

The very essence of this double-barrelled compromise, like the Rambouillet accord of 1975, was that it enabled the two sides to agree on procedures, while continuing to disagree about where those procedures were likely to lead. The US Treasury was convinced that careful inquiry would demonstrate the futility of intervention in currency markets, whereas the French saw the joint study as a first step towards collective management of exchange rates. The Americans believed that, given the broad monetarist consensus internationally, the mutual surveillance exercise would lead to convergence 'downward', that is, in a disinflationary direction; the involvement of the IMF was intended to seal this commitment to financial orthodoxy. The French recognised this danger, but they no doubt recalled the unanimous criticism that US policy had encountered at the previous meeting of the Group of Five in January,[22] and they were pleased at any recognition by the Americans that their policies had international implications. 'If anyone had said several months ago that we would be able to get the United States to consider a medium-term convergence of economic policies,' said one French official, 'no one would have believed it.'[23]

The other Europeans were happy with any agreement that might moderate the extreme positions of the Americans and the French and perhaps reduce exchange rate volatility, although both the British and the Germans felt, sceptically, that there was less to the agreement than met the eye. The Japanese were noncommittal. Canada, Italy, and the European Community were somewhat disconcerted at having been left out of the mutual surveillance exercise, but consoled themselves that nothing much could come from it, given the divergences among the Five.

If the Europeans were *demandeurs* on monetary issues, it was the Americans who wanted joint action on East–West economics, the second leitmotif of the Versailles pageant. Already controversial at Ottawa, this issue had become even thornier after the declaration of martial law in Poland in December 1981. On 29 December President Reagan retaliated with a series of economic sanctions against the Soviet Union, including an embargo on energy-related equipment and technology. This embargo caused difficulties for European firms with existing contracts for work on the gas pipeline, particularly because the President left open the possibility of extending his action to cover foreign subsidiaries and licensees of US firms. The reaction of the Europeans, especially the Germans, to events in Poland was much more measured. When Chancellor Schmidt referred to martial law as a regrettable 'necessity', teeth gnashed in the White House. Western foreign ministries feared a revival of conflict within the Alliance like that after the Afghanistan invasion.

Secretary of State Haig sought to steer the international discussion away from the obvious risks of a renewed debate about the pipeline. In an effort to divert pressure by hard-liners in the Pentagon and White House, a mission headed by Under-Secretary of State James Buckley was dispatched to the other Western capitals in early March 1982, seeking agreement to curb credits to the Soviet bloc. This seemed a promising alternative, given the ongoing OECD discussions aimed at limiting subsidised export credits, coupled with growing concern about the creditworthiness of Eastern Europe. However, the Europeans remained deeply suspicious that the Americans wished to embark on an economic war against the Soviet Union, a war that would be fought largely at European expense, since US cash sales of grain to the Soviets would be unaffected by credit curbs.

In the face of European resistance, the Buckley mission dragged into a series of very difficult meetings in Paris among representatives of the summit countries. Although the French continued to insist that East–West trade was not on the agenda for Versailles, the Americans emphasised that this was a high priority for the Administration and that the President's action on the pending pipeline sanctions would depend on summit action on East–West economic relations. Since French (and Italian) export competitiveness traditionally relied heavily on subsidised official credit, they felt particularly threatened by the US demands. The Germans claimed that they already abstained from export credit subsidies, but they were even more worried than the French about the political implications, both domestic and international, of interrupting East–West trade, for this trade had been the basis of the government's *Ostpolitik* and was also the object of the vociferous 'East-trade lobby'. The more the US demands became politically freighted, the more distressed the German government became. The UK government, cross-pressured by the Prime Minister's ideological sympathy for President Reagan, political solidarity with its European partners, and commercial interest in East European markets, was ambivalent about the US request.

Meeting in Paris right up to the eve of the summit, the Buckley group succeeded in clarifying the technical complexities created by diverse national export credit arrangements, but the basic political divergences remained. The foreign ministries of France, Germany, and the United States each sought language that could narrow the differences, but resistance to compromise remained strong in the Elysée, the Chancellery, and the White House. Meanwhile, parallel negotiations continued in the OECD about renewal of the broader agreement covering export credits in all markets. In the third ring of the Paris circus, the Ottawa-initiated discussions aimed at strengthening COCOM's controls on technology transfer went forward, amid European concern that the Americans wanted to define the proscribed categories too broadly.

The third broad topic debated during the preparations for Versailles was trade. As in 1981, this rubric covered several overlapping controversies. First, the Americans, supported by the Germans, pressed for preliminary agreement on the issues to be discussed in the GATT ministerial meeting scheduled for November 1982. There was general agreement to address several issues left over from the Tokyo Round, particularly the question of safeguards, but as the Americans had already indicated at Ottawa, they wished to extend the GATT to liberalise trade in services, high technology, and foreign investment. In the background rumbled the continuing transatlantic disputes about agriculture and steel, the latter made more urgent by a 10 June 1982 deadline for resolving an anti-dumping complaint by the US steel industry. On most of these issues, opposition to the Americans was led by the French, who argued that a precondition for trade liberalisation was economic recovery.

For most participants an even more urgent trade issue was the 'Japanese problem', both Japanese penetration of Western markets and barriers to the Japanese home market. The Americans preferred to deal with this problem bilaterally, so as not to isolate Japan, but the Europeans hoped, on the contrary, to use the summit to put Japan on the spot. As in previous years, the Japanese sought to defuse the conflict by offering a placatory package of liberalisation measures. For the more internationalist forces within Japan, including (by now) MITI and some of its business constituents, the summit's advent provided a propitious moment to try to overcome domestic resistance to trade liberalisation. In Tokyo's consensus-bound policy process, the inexorable international deadline and the threat that, without action, the Prime Minister might lose face in the eyes of the world, provided the leverage necessary for forcing agreement. One week before the summit, the Japanese government announced a list of concessions on tariffs and other import restrictions, the second such package in four months.

The first 'failed' summit: Versailles, 4–6 June 1982

For the first time since 1978, virtually the same cast of characters gathered in Paris as had met the previous year.[24] Hosting the summit was meant to be the most important foreign policy initiative of the year-old French government. Preparations, both substantive and logistic, were tightly centralised at the Elysée under the direction of Jacques Attali, Mitterand's chief of staff. The decision to hold the summit in the re-gilded splendour of Versailles, however incongruous for a Socialist government battling record unemployment, reflected this high-profile approach.

Technological progress was the upbeat theme of the French preparations, exemplified both in the high-tech gadgetry put at the disposal of the various delegations and in Mitterrand's 90-minute introductory presentation to the plenary session. Drawing on ideas from his Socialist intellectual advisors, the French President called for international collaboration in developing the economic potential of new technologies in such fields as energy, telecommunications, robotics, artificial intelligence, and biotechnology. The more conservative summiteers disagreed with the *dirigiste* flavour of the French proposals, but all reluctantly agreed to a follow-up study of the issue, including possible joint projects. Proud of their technology initiative, the French hoped that it would allow a positive outcome to a difficult summit, but their hopes were to be disappointed.

To begin with, Versailles was overshadowed by distant wars in the Falklands and in Lebanon. For two months the UK government had been wholly preoccupied by the battle in the South Atlantic, and Prime Minister Thatcher's primary objective at the summit was to gather support for the UK cause. During private meetings and over dinner on Friday the others urged a restrained and 'magnanimous' UK stance.[25] Allied solidarity with the British was disrupted that same evening by an embarrassing series of US (and Japanese) muddles over a UN vote. Nevertheless, the Prime Minister declared herself fully satisfied by post-summit declarations of support from Presidents Mitterrand and Reagan.

For the second year in succession, the summit was confronted with an Israeli attack in Lebanon, this time a massive invasion. The frustrated summiteers endorsed a Security Council call for a ceasefire, but the episode suggested less decisiveness than disarray. The steady trend, from Bonn to Ottawa, towards ever more extensive and more formal treatment of political issues at the summit was interrupted at Versailles.

Macroeconomics was discussed surprisingly little. The summiteers had little hope of mutual accommodation on this terrain and little confidence in a coordinated approach. President Mitterrand, the natural advocate of economic stimulus, knew privately that within days he would be forced to shift to a restrictive stance. The leaders continued to stress 'prudent monetary policies' and 'greater control of budgetary deficits', as a means to fight inflation and bring down 'unacceptably high' interest rates. At a time of the highest unemployment in decades, the absence of any call for additional stimulus was a stark reminder of how the political environment had changed in barely four years. Prime Minister Thatcher observed with considerable satisfaction, 'I've never known such unanimity on economic and financial policies . . . the sort of policies Britain has been following.'[26]

Trade issues among Western countries played only a marginal role at Versailles. The GATT ministerial meetings were blessed, but without agreement on agenda items. The Franco-American dispute was swathed in the woolly observation that trade would restore growth and vice versa. The steel dispute was touched on only inconclusively in a bilateral meeting between Reagan and Thorn. To the dismay of Thorn and other European officials who had hoped for some 'finger-pointing', the other summiteers, preoccupied with other issues, once again backed away from confronting their Japanese colleague.

The summit agenda on North–South issues focused on a revised proposal for global negotiations that had been offered by the Group of 77 early in the year. The Reagan Administration, particularly the US

Treasury, continued to worry about such a conference getting out of hand and interfering with the independence of the existing international bodies, such as the IMF and the World Bank. By now, however, the Americans were isolated. Intensive negotiations had ensued between the Americans and the Commission, representing the Europeans. In the last few days before the summit, Henry Nau of the National Security Council staff finally had got clearance in Washington for compromise language acceptable to the Europeans. At the summit, the others agreed in return not to depart from that text in negotiations with the Group of 77 without US concurrence at the highest levels. The episode provided another example of how summitry can serve an action-forcing function within governments, strengthening the hand of the more 'internationalist' forces. Among Western development experts, there was hope that this agreement might finally clear the way for progress in the North–South dialogue, although in the end, the hard-liners in the Group of 77 would reject the Versailles offer, and the negotiations would remain stalled.

As expected, centre court at Versailles was occupied by the Franco-American clash over monetary policy and East–West trade. Talk of a 'package deal' was in the air, and on the eve of the summit, President Thorn had limned the most prominent possibility, somewhat indiscreetly:

All Europeans are ready to recognise the principle that we ought to harmonise our approaches to East–West trade, and growing doubt about some East European countries' ability to pay already is making us more cautious in this area. [In exchange], there must first be a gesture [from the United States] to say, 'We're also going to make a contribution to Western economic solidarity in the form of an effort to correct the malfunctioning of the monetary system.'[27]

Unlike the comparable stage of the 1978 summit, however, there was far from universal agreement on the contours of the possible package. For the Germans, who saw little of interest in the monetary compromise but cared deeply about East–West trade, the proposal seemed all cost and no benefit. Neither the US nor the French government had yet made up its mind about the tradeoff, and in any event the elements of the deal were still ambiguous.

The essentials of the monetary accord had been set since the Rambouillet meeting in April 1982. This agreement was endorsed at Versailles, but interpretations of it rapidly became contradictory. Speaking to the press after the first meeting of finance ministers in Versailles, Delors referred to 'tripolar monetary concertation' and 'returning to the spirit of Bretton Woods', and at the close of the conference, Mitterrand hailed the agreement as initiating 'reform of the international monetary system'.[28] Secretary Regan, on the other hand, suggested that the French President 'didn't read the fine print', and described the US position as 'far from changed'.[29]

Whatever its ambiguities, the monetary agreement had at least been hammered out ahead of time, but there had been no similar prior accommodation on East–West trade and credit. After some initial sparring among the heads of government on Saturday, over Sunday breakfast Secretary Haig and his counterparts reached a tentative agreement on language limiting credits.[30] When this language was reported to the heads, however, President Mitterrand rejected it, and a nerve-wracking bargaining session lasting more than three hours ensued. Thatcher supported the US demands, while Schmidt, Trudeau, and Mitterrand argued for a softer line. Seeking additional leverage, President Reagan withheld final approval of the agreed text on North–South issues, which the French wanted, until agreement was reached on the East–West credit issue. Unable to achieve a meeting of minds on strategic objectives and policy instruments, the summiteers were reduced to debating phraseology – 'limit export credits in the light of commercial prudence' versus 'the need for commercial prudence in limiting export credits' – and linguistic nuances – did 'limit' have the same (ambiguous) meaning in French and English?

Despite the confusion, some US officials initially thought the outcome was satisfactory, even though President Reagan had not won the quantitative limits on credits and credit subsidies that he had sought. In addition to 'commercial prudence in limiting export credits', improvements in COCOM controls were promised; information on East–West economics would be exchanged within the OECD and monitored by officials from the summit countries; and the renewed export credit consensus was expected to tighten the terms for credit to the Eastern bloc.

However, the bitter bargaining had left nerves raw on all sides, and as French Trade Minister Jobert observed about the Versailles compromises, 'each delegation can interpret the new agreement as it wishes'.[31] In one sense, of course, this was the attraction of the agreement, but it had risks. Ominously, the summiteers broke their tradition of a joint news conference, apparently in a misguided effort to avoid directly contradicting one another.

The fragile compromise rapidly unravelled. German Finance Minister Lahnstein returned home to proclaim that 'we will continue to work with East European countries and the Soviet Union as usual', and *Die Zeit* reported that 'the Federal Chancellor even proudly declared that the whole passage [on East–West trade] hardly touched us'.[32] A week after the summit, still angered at Secretary Regan's apparent denigration of the monetary accord, President Mitterrand told reporters that France continued to reject efforts by the Reagan Administration to enlist Europe in economic warfare against the Soviet Union. He added that France was already charging appropriate interest rates on East–West credit, and denied that the summit declaration had any further implications for French policy.[33]

The impression that the Europeans were reneging gave invaluable ammunition to the hard-liners in the White House and on the National Security Council staff, who had been convinced all along that the President, badly advised by Secretary Haig, had been bamboozled. Over the opposition of the State Department, the Treasury, and the Commerce Department, the President's counsellors, led by National Security Advisor William Clark, convinced him that his credibility with the Soviets, with the allies, and with domestic opinion required a rough response.[34] On 18 June 1982 the White House, far from relaxing the US pipeline sanctions as the Europeans had hoped, announced that they were being extended to cover US subsidiaries and licensees abroad. Not incidentally, this move signalled the demise of Secretary Haig, and on 25 June he resigned and was replaced by George Shultz.

A firestorm of protest swept Europe, as the pipeline decision followed on the heels of the acrimonious collapse of the steel negotiations and the unilateral imposition of countervailing duties by the Americans. The German government expressed 'dismay' at what it termed 'a contradiction to what was agreed and discussed at the world economic summit'. Speaking after a meeting of the European Council, President Mitterrand said, 'We wonder what concept the United States has of summit meetings when it becomes a matter of agreements made and not respected.' Privately, he reportedly told one visitor that after long efforts to establish rapport with Reagan, he had concluded that there was not a single issue on which he could trust the US President.[35] Even Prime Minister Thatcher was incensed at the retroactivity and extraterritoriality of the pipeline sanctions; she told the House that 'it is wrong [for] one very powerful nation' to try to prevent the fulfilment of 'existing contracts'. The Reagan Administration threatened to escalate the conflict, as Under-Secretary of Commerce Olmer warned that the United States would blacklist foreign firms that violated the sanctions. EC trade negotiator Sir Roy Denman observed that 'our trade relations with the United States are the worst that I have seen since the end of the war', and the usually sober *Financial Times* concluded that 'the components of the Western Alliance are coming apart'.[36]

Summitry had clearly exacerbated the conflict, not restrained it. What had gone wrong?

First, the issue of East–West economics had been unsatisfactorily prepared for the summit. Partly because of French reluctance to accept this item on the summit agenda, and partly because of US bureaucratic rivalries, the Buckley negotiations were kept separate from the sherpa process, which meant that questions of technical practicality were divorced from questions of political necessity. Robert Hormats, the US sherpa, made clear to his colleagues that this was an issue of great importance to the President, but Hormats did not have sufficient access to the President to know the President's bottom line.[37] Indeed, given the unresolved differences within the US government, it is not clear that anyone really knew what the President would settle for. In April 1982, while still a private citizen, George Shultz had visited the other summiteers on behalf of the President, but by all accounts these encounters were too abstracted from the ongoing summit preparations to be useful in practical terms. Neither during the preparations nor at the summit itself did anyone on the US side actually have both the technical competence and the political clout to say 'It's a deal', and make it stick.

In a classic failure of diplomacy, neither side fully understood the depth of feeling on the other side. One French official, for example, said later,

it would have been helpful to know how far your President and the three or four people around him were ready to go on this East–West question. Buckley could convey Reagan's real thinking, but he wasn't part of the regular summit preparations, so we couldn't get the message completely, and when you've got parts of a message, you don't have the substance.

There was much selective perception, as officials tended to overlook messages that were inconsistent with their own hopes. Consequently, both sides arrived at the summit expressing unfounded optimism about the outcome.[38] In effect, it was a game of 'chicken' in which both sides were blindfolded.[39]

The sherpa process had been invented precisely to prevent this from happening. Significantly, the principal foreign ministries had recognised the risks of conflict and within each capital pressed for more conciliatory policies. However, each of the presidents disavowed efforts by his own foreign minister to reach a compromise, Mitterrand during the summit itself and Reagan two weeks later. This lack of presidential self-restraint, probably based in each case on excessive optimism about his own negotiating position and an underestimate of the other's intractability, was a crucial part of the explanation for the failure of Versailles. Not until they actually had to confront the costs of their failure would they begin to moderate their expectations. The direct involvement of the heads of government in these negotiations almost certainly complicated the resolution of the issue – a powerful indictment of summitry.

A further serious mistake at Versailles, shared again by both sides, was the failure to recognise that both the monetary agreement and the accord on East–West trade could endure only so long as their essential ambiguities were left unchallenged. Each was an agreement on procedural first steps, leaving unresolved the disagreements about ultimate destinations. When US and European officials began to make claims about goals and likely outcomes, those claims were bound to diverge. This point had been understood perfectly well at Rambouillet in 1975, when Edwin Yeo and Jacques de Larosière had so carefully swaddled their newly born monetary accord. They went to extreme lengths to ensure that neither the heads of government nor the other sherpas knew precisely what had been agreed. Yeo had rejected requests from his foreign counterparts that they at least be allowed to see the joint memorandum, saying that the agreement must be allowed to 'settle' and needed 'tender loving care'.[40] The most that could be hoped for at Versailles was the beginning of a slow process of mutual adjustment. That process was interrupted by the escalating sequence of divergent briefings.

But what if these procedural errors – before, during, and after the conference – had been avoided or minimised? In principle, was an agreement between the Europeans and the Americans possible? There was a certain formal analogy between the deal done at Bonn and the package that Thorn, for example, proposed for Versailles. However, the underlying political situation at Versailles was much less promising.

To begin with, cross-issue deals are easiest to achieve when intensities differ, that is, when one side cares most about issue A and the other cares most about issue B. Under those circumstances, each is more willing to make concessions on the issue that is the top priority for the other side. At Versailles, however, both sides had intense preferences about both issues. Second, the United Kingdom had helped to broker the 1978 deal, and Prime Minister Thatcher was well placed in 1982 to mediate between her fellow Europeans and her fellow conservatives, but the Falklands crisis pre-empted her government's attention.

Most fundamentally, foreign and domestic forces in 1982 were not pushing in the same direction, as they had been in 1978.[41] Virtually no one in the Reagan Administration (at least in 1982) favoured international monetary reform, and virtually no one in power in Bonn or Paris wanted to use economic leverage against the Soviets.[42] Indeed, the dominant domestic pressures encouraged the leaders' own obstinate instincts. Before the summit, for example, Republican hawks in the US Senate (probably encouraged by forces within the Administration) demanded that Reagan use all tools at his disposal, including extension of the US embargo to foreign firms, in order to block the pipeline.[43] At the same time, fearful that the foreign ministry might bend to US pressure, the German Chamber of Trade and Industry demanded that the Chancellor not concede limits on East–West trade and credit, while

SPD strategists privately advised Schmidt that standing up to Reagan would be good domestic politics.[44] In neither case was there in fact much danger that the chief executive would yield, given his private convictions. Even the inclination of the various foreign ministries to seek a compromise reflected not intellectual persuasion of the merits of the opposing case, but rather concern about the international consequences of failure to reach an accommodation.

On the other hand, the summit confrontation and its bitter summer sequel obscured the areas of agreement that had in fact been achieved during the summit process. The monetary accord represented a certain accommodation between the French and US views, and in fact this compromise itself survived the post-summit polemics. On East–West trade, during the immediate aftermath it was not clear, even to people closely involved in the summit, whether the minimal positions of the two sides overlapped enough to sustain any genuine accord. Yet the preliminary discussions had produced latent agreement on certain points.

- East–West trade was a legitimate collective concern of the Alliance and had to be viewed in the context of broader allied political and security interests.
- East–West trade and technology transfer that contributed to the military or strategic advantage of the Soviet Union should be halted.
- East–West trade, which was falling off anyway for economic and financial reasons, should not be artificially subsidised.
- East–West economic warfare was not desirable.

While hardly novel, these principles were not trivial, for they ruled out certain of the more extreme positions in the continuing debate. If temperatures could be lowered through the familiar device of further joint study, this preliminary consensus might be consolidated.

In effect, although the twin agreements on monetary issues and East–West trade reached at Versailles were overturned two weeks later, these agreements represented a point of equilibrium among the contending forces. In the end, this fact would be recognised by all participants. As we shall see in the following chapter, by the time of Williamsburg the Alliance would have returned to the Versailles accords. In short, Versailles would prove to be a substantive success, if a procedural failure.

The changing summit process

The seven-power summit was an established practice when the current generation of Western leaders ascended to power. If the institution had not already existed, these people would probably not have invented it. For them, unlike the founding generation, summitry was a routine they encountered, not something moulded to fit their own backgrounds and interests and personalities. Unlike their predecessors, the new leaders were not specialists in macroeconomic and international finance. Moreover, as a group they were generally less internationalist in outlook, more insular and domestically oriented, than their predecessors, a change that probably in part reflected the politics of economic adversity.[1] In terms of substance, as opposed to appearance, they tended to take summitry less seriously. As we noted in chapter 4, for example, the role of the personal representative gradually became less personal. Finally, as we have seen, international policy concertation was ideologically uncongenial to the more conservative of the newcomers. Summitry was part of the problem, not part of the solution. As the German business daily *Handelsblatt* said on the eve of Versailles:

Mistaken decisions of heads of government in the context of their annual summit meetings are partially responsible for today's global economic crisis. The internationalisation of economic problems fostered by the economic summits all too often can exempt governments and politicians from the duty of putting their own house in order more decisively.[2]

This transformation of the summiteers' attitudes to the institution of summitry was widespread, but it was most marked in the case of the United States. As we have seen, Jimmy Carter's Trilateralists had had a very expansive view of summitry, but the Reaganites were wary that summits might ensnare the President in international commitments that would contravene his domestic responsibilities. In their view, the summit should be more an encounter than an institution, more for exchanging ideas than for changing policies. 'You don't go to the summits for the purpose of changing your mind or making policy deals,' explained one of Reagan's aides. 'Nobody in that group has any political accountability except to his people back home.'

The question of the proper nature of summitry comprised two issues, logically distinct, but empirically related. First, the *scope* of summitry: What kinds of issues and problems should be within the jurisdiction of summitry? What should be handled through other channels and other institutions, or left to domestic decision-making? Second, the *process* of summitry: How should summiteers and their aides go about the business of summitry? How elaborate and 'bureaucratic' should the preparations be?

The Library Group image of summitry aimed to combine breadth of scope with simplicity of process, but at the level of heads of government that combination, as we have seen, proved unworkable almost from the start. The Trilateralists instituted a more complex process to fit their ambitious objectives. However, as chapter 8 showed, by the end of the Carter years there was already widespread discontent with what was seen as the bureaucratic degeneration of summitry – the lengthy and detailed planning by the sherpas, the proliferation of preparatory groups, the bloated, prenegotiated communiqués. As an aide to one of the second-generation summiteers said privately,

All this preparatory and follow-up business puts politics more and more in the hands of civil servants. You send your president or prime minister to the summit with a songsheet and let him sing what civil servants think ought to be the policies, and he listens to the songs of all the others, one after another, like a song contest.

From 1981 on, there was a broad, if not universal, consensus that the process of summitry should be simplified. However, success proved elusive. In reaction to the Venice experience, a serious effort was made to keep communiqué-drafting from overwhelming the Ottawa summit, but in the event the preparatory process produced mountains of paper, and the summit became (as one German participant put it) 'a hurdles-race to the communiqué'.[3] The communiqué itself was more than twice as long as the Rambouillet statement of 1975 had been. Prime Minister Trudeau's desire to hold several heads-only, hair-down sessions at Montebello was vetoed by the Americans, with support from the Japanese, apparently fearing that the newcomers were ill equipped for that kind of summit.

In preparing for Versailles, the hosts attached great importance to 'debureaucratising' the summit process. The communiqué was not to be drafted ahead of time nor to constrain the discussion among the summiteers, and the preparatory process was to be tightly centralised. In fact, the size of the sherpa meetings was successfully restricted, and the communiqué was considerably shorter. However, as we saw in the previous chapter, the communiqué was prenegotiated in detail, both among the sherpas and in other forums. Moreover, the crux of the summit itself became once again the bargaining among the heads over the precise language of the communiqué.

Why had it proved so difficult to accomplish the simplification that nearly everyone said was desirable?

First, organisational inertia: like any small group with well-established traditions, the summit preparers shared clear norms about how things were done. Moreover, as one disaffected participant pointed out, there was a kind of Gresham's law at work, in the sense that any country that tried to opt out of the preparatory process would find itself at a substantial disadvantage.

Second, persisting ambitions about the scope of the summitry: even though the high tide of Trilateralist summitry had passed, summit participants still hoped to use the process to accomplish important substantive objectives, such as changing US monetary policy or curbing East–West trade. Despite talk of returning to the roots of summitry, breadth of scope and simplicity of process proved incompatible, and scope determined process.

The Versailles fiasco altered all this. The risks of a failed summit were no longer hypothetical. A few officials began to talk seriously about ending the summits, and most agreed that (as one sherpa put it), 'We cannot have a rerun of Versailles. If we do, we could well see the collapse of the whole institution.' Expectations would have to be lowered, both in terms of public relations and in terms of governments' own objectives.

Rightly or wrongly, the failure at Versailles was attributed, particularly by the heads themselves, to a 'summitocracy' that had escaped from political control. Both the Americans and the French were determined to streamline the preparations. In October 1982 President Mitterrand proposed that the summit meetings be transformed into small seminars, closed to all but the heads themselves.[4] The advent of an alumnus of the Library Group as the new US Secretary of State gave additional impetus to the idea of a summit as a fireside chat with no agenda and perhaps even no communiqué. In February 1983 Secretary Shultz reported that soundings with the other summiteers had shown that all of them wanted 'to avoid a super-structured kind of agenda that would interrupt the free flow of conversation'. A 'top-down' summit, rather than one that was elaborately prepared by officials, was what the Americans now proposed. 'In a sense, you can see this as a contest between the heads of state on the one hand, and the bureaucracies in government and the press on the other. We'll see which ones get their way.'[5]

As we shall see shortly, this approach was also encouraged by the advent of new governments in Germany and Japan, each inclined to favour a less structured sort of summit. Chancellor Schmidt had always criticised bureaucratisation of the summits, of course, but under his regime the Germans had been enthusiastic participants in the preparatory process, whereas the new administration consisted of strong advocates of lowering expectations, scaling down preparations, avoiding decisions, and eliminating follow-up. In the Japanese case, the new Prime Minister was personally more comfortable in spontaneous give-and-take than his predecessors.[6]

It was not the first time that aspirations for less structure had been expressed, but they were more nearly realised in 1983. Compared to prior summits, preparations for Williamsburg began later and focused less on substance and more on logistics, protocol, and relations with the media.[7] The personal representatives themselves were less central to the preparations in 1983. Reflecting a feeling in the White House that the sherpas had been responsible for the troubles at Versailles, and hoping to engage the heads themselves more directly in the preparations, the Americans relied to an unprecedented degree on written communications between the chief executives.[8]

The most obvious innovation in the 1983 preparations was the absence of any draft communiqué, as well as of the papers on substantive issues that previously had been prepared and debated by the sherpas. An aversion to prenegotiated communiqués was widely shared among the summiteers themselves, and indeed had been so for some time. Their officials had always been acutely sensitive to the risks of an unprepared discussion, but Versailles had shown that calamity could occur even with extensive prenegotiation. President Reagan strongly insisted to his own sherpas that no joint drafting of a communiqué should begin before Williamsburg.

However, as one old hand at summitry observed, 'Not preparing a communiqué and not preparing a summit are two different things.'[9] In the absence of the framework that had previously been provided by the draft communiqué, the sherpas agreed to work with a 'themes paper' drafted by the Americans. Described variously as 'a laundry list' or 'an algebraic summation', this paper catalogued the national positions on various issues, with little attempt to reconcile divergent views. The other participants thought that this effort was done fairly, and unlike the earlier sherpas' paperwork, it was submitted to all the heads as a kind of joint briefing paper. Controversy about wording in this document was reduced by the Americans' insistence that it was not to be considered a draft communiqué. In the event, however, it did serve as a basis for the communiqué-drafting proper when that began mid-way through the summit itself. Afterwards, US participants reflected that this technique for forestalling controversy over language probably would work only once.

This simplified preparation was possible because ambitions about the scope of summitry were trimmed to fit aspirations about the process. First, no one expected the summiteers to deal with questions of practical policy. As one American observed,

A consensus had emerged that summits were not the right place or the right vehicle for working out details. Summits should be used as an opportunity for the heads to review what their finance ministers, their trade ministers, their foreign ministers, are doing and to lay out general directions for the future, but they should avoid getting into details on energy, trade, domestic economics, and so forth.

Lowered expectations allowed lighter preparation.

Second, as we shall see in more detail later, negotiations on many of the issues in the background to the summit were decentralised to other forums. East–West economic questions were addressed in the OECD, the IEA, COCOM, and elsewhere. Monetary and macroeconomic issues were argued out among finance ministers, and trade issues among trade ministers.[10] In short, despite public denigration of 'bureaucratic' preparations, much of what was proclaimed at Williamsburg had been carefully elaborated by officals beforehand. The summit itself had been 'debureaucratised', to some extent, but the treatment of the issues had not.

This decentralised approach had several advantages. In principle, it allowed a better integration between the summit process and the existing international institutions. Moreover, it relieved the summiteers of as much technical controversy as possible, delegating those issues to the bureaucracies to resolve. On the other hand, it posed the risk that necessary progress in the decentralised bureaucratic forums might not be completed when expected, or that the technical work might not be linked adequately with the political needs and perspectives of one or more of the summiteers. Indeed, a case in point had been the handling of the East–West economic issue by the Buckley group in 1982. As we shall see, there were intensive behind-the-scenes efforts in 1983 to provide careful political tending of this explosive issue.

The problem of the news media
In the aftermath of Versailles, special attention was devoted, as well, to the problem of media coverage of the summits.[11] Following the Library Group precedents, the original summiteers had not even intended to hold a news conference following the Rambouillet summit, but as they became aware of the intense press interest and of the risks of independent national briefings, they had improvised a joint session with the media. Thereafter, press coverage of the summit grew, stimulated particularly by the special attention that is focused on the US President, both by the US press corps and by the international media. By 1982, for example, President Reagan, whose attendance at Versailles was part of his first official trip to Europe, was escorted by 800 journalists and media technicians.

Through most of the first round of summits, the participants were able to convey an impression of common purpose, and relations with the press were not problematic. Gradually, however, even as the press became more sceptical about the efficacy of the summits, government publicists became more concerned to present their own principals in a favourable light. Official press 'agentry' increasingly presented the summit as a kind of international jousting match, and the summiteer as a national paladin, vigorously (and usually victoriously) defending national interests against obtuse and even malevolent foreigners. By 1981, for example, a leading international newspaper offered 'An Ottawa Scorecard' to help the reader 'to see who is scoring which points against whom', and a US spokesman concluded that President Reagan 'walked away with most of the prizes'.[12]

Prime Minister Trudeau had hoped to recreate the Rambouillet atmosphere by holding the 1981 summit in an isolated setting 50 miles from the press headquarters in Ottawa. However, the US Administration, eager to present the new President in a favourable light on his maiden foreign voyage, mounted a media 'blitz', with Secretary of State Haig and other senior officials helicoptering back to Ottawa periodically to brief reporters, thirsty for reportable news. The other summit participants were resentful at what they felt to be a violation of the rules of the game, particularly since one consequence of the US actions was that the world saw the summit largely through US eyes.[13]

At Versailles a year later, the others were prepared to match the US efforts. In particular, the French hosts went to great efforts to provide both technical facilities and extensive briefings for the gathered reporters, who (together with technicians and cameramen) were estimated to number as many as 3000, compared to roughly 1500 at Ottawa. The magnificent gardens, the fireworks, and the splendour of the Sun King's palace, spotlighted at night for the benefit of television, created a vivid sense of the summit, not as retreat nor as work site, but as spectacle.

In earlier summits, the practice had developed of independent background briefings by each summiteer for his or her own national press. Indeed, interventions in the plenary sessions of the summit itself were said to be increasingly designed as much for their domestic impact, via careful leaking, as for the other summiteers. The deleterious impact of media relations reached a peak at Versailles, however, for (as we saw in the previous chapter) divergent briefings by national spokesmen contributed crucially to the failure of the summit. In the 'global village', rhetoric intended primarily for internal consumption can bring international complications.

Press coverage of the summits, as it had developed through the years, had several advantages. Summit publicity provided a kind of international education for the broader public, especially in countries like the United States and Japan, who provided the largest press contingents. Moreover, favourable publicity associated with the summit was a political bonus for the summiteers, and that encouraged them to seek international compromises that could be presented as evidence of successful personal diplomacy. Press coverage also enhanced the 'action-forcing' function of summitry.

On the other hand, press coverage tended to raise public expectations unrealistically. 'Just like Moses, the leaders are expected to hand down stone tablets on their return from the summit,' said one sherpa. Like the problem of divergent national briefings, the issue of excessive expectations had been highlighted by the Versailles experience.

Therefore, in the preparations for Williamsburg a concerted effort was made to reduce the risks of press coverage. Much time in the sherpa meetings was devoted to working out explicit ground rules, covering such things as the timetables for national briefings and the nature of off-the-record accounts of the summit. In the event, divergent briefings were minimised, partly because participants were less dissatisfied with the results of the summit itself, partly because of the better discipline that the sherpas had imposed.[14] Similarly, efforts were made by all governments to play down expectations. Secretary Shultz, for example, suggested that the United States was aiming for a dull summit instead of 'a razzle-dazzle media event'.[15] The picturesque setting assured numerous photo opportunities, to be sure, and the number of media personnel reportedly jumped to an all-time record. However, the media problems that had helped to torpedo the Versailles conference were successfully avoided.

The scene transformed: from Versailles to Williamsburg
More than one summit participant observed that from some points of view Versailles had come too soon. One finance minister confidentially regretted later that the agreements were plucked prematurely; 'these issues have to ripen, to mature'. Moreover, within weeks of the summit, both the Americans and the French had shifted course economically, and the agenda of global economic concerns had been transformed. Noted one French Socialist privately, 'We knew that we were on the verge of changing our policies, though we could not say so beforehand, and we thought (correctly, as it turned out) that the Americans might be, too. A summit held after each of us had made our mid-course corrections might have been more productive.'

The French switch, apparently decided a month before the Versailles summit, came less than a week afterwards. On 11 June 1982 the franc was devalued, wages and prices were frozen for four months, and a deflationary package of higher taxes and cuts in social spending was introduced. Another devaluation (Mitterrand's third in two years) and a second, stronger dose of fiscal austerity were administered in March 1983. The Socialist government had conceded defeat in its attempt to force-feed the French economy, but at the same time, it was resisting the temptation to retreat to a more autarkic, 'proletarian' line.

The US switch just after Versailles had even more profound effects. At its regular closed meeting in July 1982, the 'Open Market Committee' of the Federal Reserve relaxed its tight money policy, setting off a general decline in interest rates that would continue for nearly a year. The key 'Federal funds rate', which had been above 14 per cent almost continuously from November 1980 through June 1982, plunged four points in July alone and by January 1983 was less than 9 per cent, where it would remain until just before the Williamsburg summit.[16] The Federal Reserve's three-year experiment with strict monetarist targeting was over.

The Reagan Administration welcomed this relaxation of monetary policy. Easier money, combined with the fiscal stimulus of the budget deficit, triggered a powerful US recovery from the recession of 1981–2, though the strength of this rebound would not become apparent until mid-summer 1983. Also during the last half of 1982, the Administration and Congress reached agreement on tax increases and spending cuts that would reduce somewhat the looming 'structural' budget deficit.

Both the French and the US shifts were influenced by international conditions, but in different ways. In the French case, restrictive policies elsewhere had doomed what the *Guardian* called 'this bold, if ill-fated attempt to have Socialism in one country'.[17] The OECD noted later, 'For reasons that begin with the balance of payments and end with inflation, countries have little scope, in the great majority of cases, to allow their domestic demand to grow significantly faster than that of their trading partners.'[18]

In the US case, lower interest rates, reduced deficits, and economic revival were what other summiteers had been demanding for two years, but there is no evidence that this foreign criticism had any impact at all on US policy. Apparently the primary factors in the Federal Reserve's July 1982 decision were mounting worries about the domestic recession and, in particular, the rising risks of failures in the banking system. When the relaxation was confirmed in August, international factors were reportedly more important. However, it was not Paris, Brussels, or Bonn that the Americans were watching, but rather Mexico City, Brasília, and Buenos Aires. The threat of a massive default by Mexico and other major Third World debtors, triggering a collapse of the world financial system, helped persuade US policy-makers of the need to increase world liquidity.[19]

The debt crisis monopolised the attention of monetary officials throughout the fall of 1982. International monetary crisis management worked surprisingly well. In particular, the Group of Five deputies met repeatedly, both to coordinate rescue operations and to prepare the ground for agreement on a substantial increase in IMF resources, finally announced in February 1983. In retrospect, however, it is striking that the impending crisis had been virtually undiscussed during the 1982 summit process, even though people like Helmut Schmidt had been concerned about Third World debt since Venice, and even though outside observers had warned of the gravity of the problem on the eve of Versailles.[20] As one official said later, 'Our record of crisis management is not bad, but our record of crisis prevention is very poor.'[21]

Meanwhile, efforts had begun to clear the rubble left by the collapse of the Versailles agreement on East–West economics. On 30 June 1982 the European Community finally agreed to raise interest rates on export credits to the Soviet Union, as part of a new OECD export credit consensus. The escalation of Atlantic trade tensions throughout June and July worried US foreign policy officials and the US business community, and by the beginning of August even Republican Congressmen were describing the pipeline ban as 'a failed policy'.[22] On 23 July the President created a new top-level committee on international economic policy, amid signals from the new Secretary of State to his old Library Group colleague, Helmut Schmidt, that the Americans wanted to resolve the row amicably.

In early October 1982, NATO foreign ministers met privately in Canada to explore approaches to the problem of East–West trade. Several weeks later the ambassadors of the summit countries to Washington met with US officials to search for a way down from the rhetorical peaks rashly scaled the previous summer. Finally, on 12 November 1982 the President withdrew his attempt to extend the US pipeline sanctions to the allies, having been convinced by Shultz that they had agreed to 'stronger and more effective measures'. In fact, the new agreement simply called for an interrelated series of joint studies, in most cases building on work that was already under way in various international organisations. Export credits and the future of East–West trade would be considered in the OECD; problems of technology transfer, in COCOM; Western energy dependence, in the IEA; and the linkage between East–West economics and security relations, in NATO.

Prime Minister Thatcher and the other Europeans correctly insisted that they had made no 'fresh commitments' beyond those made at Versailles, but they were obviously pleased that the Americans had found a way to climb down. However, even this reconciliation occasioned another Franco-American contretemps, when the Elysée loudly objected to Reagan's claim that France was a party to the 'new agreement'. Relations between the White House and the French Presidency reached a new low. Special efforts would be needed to prevent these tensions from disrupting the Williamsburg summit.

The Americans kept up pressure on the issue throughout the spring of 1983, and many observers, including some officials close to the preparations, feared a repetition at Williamsburg of the Versailles fiasco on East–West economics.[23] To forestall this, efforts were made within the US Administration, beginning in February, to ensure that those who had prompted the veto of the Versailles accord were coopted into discussions of the so-called 'Shultz studies', in order to avoid last-minute second-guessing. Moreover, the Administration privately reviewed the benefits and costs of an all-out offensive on the East–West economics issues, and settled instead on a more modest demand for 'satisfactory progress'.

Meanwhile, internationally, the two main protagonists were working towards what one insider later called 'a well-implemented non-aggression pact'. In December 1982, Secretary Shultz and Foreign Minister Cheysson had jointly buried the Franco-American misunder-standing of the previous month. By April 1983, the French and US sherpas agreed privately that neither side had an interest in exacer-bating this two-year-old conflict at Williamsburg. A fragile agreement not to push the conflict past the breaking-point was then confirmed in top-secret messages between the White House and the Elysée. At the same time, Reagan's men were using both bilateral and multilateral channels to clarify the President's minimum requirements for 'success' in the Shultz studies. During a mid-April visit to Washington, the new German Chancellor, Helmut Kohl, got the impression that President Reagan would not push for a written agreement on East–West credit, but given the previous year's experience, the Germans were not certain that this position would hold. Hard bargaining followed over the details in the OECD, IEA, and COCOM; as one official said, 'it was as if [the lower-level officials] had been told, "There will be a ceasefire at the beginning of May, so shoot all you can now." '

By early May, the results of the Shultz studies were becoming clear.[24] Energy ministers, meeting at the IEA on 8 May 1983, approved a report cautioning against 'undue dependence' on any single source of natural gas, but the Americans retreated from an earlier demand that 'undue' be defined in quantitative terms (more than 30 per cent), which might have reopened the pipeline issue. An OECD report painted a grim picture of Soviet economic prospects and concluded that East–West trade was relatively small and declining in importance. Secretary Shultz and his opposite numbers worked out language for the OECD com-muniqué, issued on 10 May, that satisfied the White House. The non-summit countries, particularly the neutrals, were not entirely happy at the way this technique involved the IEA and the OECD in politically loaded discussions, but they did not block the agreements. The COCOM discussions encountered problems in defining proscribed technologies, but the Americans were pleased by new provisions for tighter enforcement, and they were willing to let the discussions spill beyond Williamsburg. A similarly benevolent stance was taken on the continuing talks about renewal of the OECD export credit consensus.

A week before the summit, President Reagan declared that there was now 'peace among us [the allies] on East–West trade'.[25] Given the events surrounding Versailles, the other delegations were still not sure what to expect, but at Williamsburg only a few minutes were needed to confirm the convergence of views. The combination of technical studies and political prudence had worked.[26]

In key respects, the ideological climate in Williamsburg was predetermined by developments in Bonn and Tokyo the previous autumn. On 2 October 1982 Helmut Schmidt, last of the founders of Western summitry, was succeeded as Chancellor by Helmut Kohl. Kohl's CDU-CSU-FDP coalition adopted a distinctly more conservative stance, proposing to trim state spending, encourage private investment, and improve relations with the United States. On 6 March 1983, following a heated campaign focused on economic policy and the Euromissiles, the Kohl coalition won a decisive electoral mandate.

Meanwhile, on 26 November 1982 Prime Minister Suzuki was succeeded by Yasuhiro Nakasone. More articulate and more activist than his predecessor, particularly on security issues, Nakasone immediately confirmed his intention to adopt an unusually high profile internationally. His inaugural statement called for Japan to strengthen its military position in order to 'uphold unity and cooperation with the United States and the free nations of Europe'.[27]

Coupled with the political resurgence of Prime Minister Thatcher, as she moved towards her widely expected victory in the General Election to be held ten days after Williamsburg, the new recruits to the summiteers' club intensified its conservative ideological cast.[28] Indeed, the first half of 1983 would see conservative parties, each committed to austerity and a strong defence, soundly defeat expansionist, détente-minded challengers in national elections in the United Kingdom, Germany, and Japan. Despite the longest recession in half a century, the conservative wave continued to sweep across the West. As one of Reagan's aides put it later, 'the President went to this summit convinced that the political realities abroad were moving in his direction'. These victors shared a belief that the top priority economically was for government to get out of the way and let a reinvigorated private sector lead the recovery, rather than worrying about international policy coordination.

By contrast, President Mitterrand's economic setbacks had seriously weakened his standing, both domestically and internationally. The opposition made impressive gains in local elections in March 1983. Although Mitterrand's own mandate had five long years to run, polls on the eve of his departure for Williamsburg reported his popularity the lowest ever recorded for a President of the Fifth Republic. Streets in Paris and elsewhere were blocked by demonstrating students, doctors, farmers, shopkeepers, and rightist rowdies. The still plummeting franc had never been so weak vis-à-vis the dollar. The leftist daily *Liberation* observed that to pound on the table you need a fist, and 'France doesn't have one'.[29]

The French government was acutely conscious of its ideological isolation in the summit arena. President Mitterrand, said one aide, 'really wondered what is the use in going there if he would just face leaders interested only in getting international endorsement for their monetarist approach. That is not his approach. He is a bit of a black sheep in that assembly.' French isolation was most complete within the Group of Five and only slightly less so within the summit context, where the Canadians, the Italians, and the European Community provided some moral support. Tactically, therefore, the French sought to widen the arena of international economic policy discussions to include potential allies among the smaller countries. Finance Minister Delors suggested that the mutual surveillance exercise be enlarged from the Group of Five to the Group of Ten, and that the role of the even larger OECD forum be enhanced.[30] Ten days before the summit, President Mitterrand hosted a meeting of five European socialist premiers to underline his critique of monetarism. Nevertheless, the march to Williamsburg proceeded under the banner of the new conservative orthodoxy.[31]

Outside the circle of the Seven, the winter and spring of 1982–3 witnessed a lively discussion of the possibilities of an internationally coordinated recovery programme. As unemployment within the OECD rose to a postwar record of 32 million, while inflation dropped to levels not seen since the first oil shock, many observers concluded that the West now had scope for reflation. In a statement reminiscent of the 1977 Brookings report that laid the groundwork for the 'locomotive' debate, in December 1982 a group of 26 economists from 14 countries called for Japan, Germany, and the United Kingdom to take expansionary measures and for the United States to relax monetary policy and reduce its structural budget deficit.[32]

During the ensuing months similar recommendations came from many sides, including Henry Kissinger, Helmut Schmidt (now favourably recalling the locomotive episode, following several years in which he had publicly condemned it), Robert Hormats (Reagan's 1982 sherpa), the 'Group of Thirty' (a prestigious committee of international bankers, businessmen, and economists, chaired by ex-IMF Managing Director Witteven), and even – astonishingly, but abortively – Beryl Sprinkel, who announced on 17 January 1983 that it was 'critically important' that the United Kingdom, Germany, and Japan join the United States in taking steps to ensure 'a credible economic expansion'.[33] (Sprinkel's colleagues in Washington promptly denied that the Administration was changing its monetarist tune, and CEA Chairman Martin Feldstein opined that 'the only thing that could have happened to Beryl on the road to Damascus is that he discovered the international monetary crisis'.) Under the slogan of 'margins for maneuver', an analogous 'differentiated approach' to recovery was suggested by the OECD staff in January and appeared in a diluted form at the OECD ministerial meeting in May.

All suggestions that they stimulate their economies were sternly rejected by the Americans, the British, the Germans, and the Japanese. Chancellor Howe and Economics Minister Lambsdorff, for example, both argued that this approach would simply reignite inflation.[34] So firm was the hold of these four conservative governments on the preparations for Williamsburg that proposals for coordinated reflation were reportedly not even raised during the sherpas' meetings. The main debate in that forum pitted the United States, the United Kingdom, Germany, and Japan, who argued that recovery was already under way and should be sustained by continuing to lean against inflation, against the others, who were more pessimistic about global trends. For the first time since the accession of the monetarists to power, the optimists turned out to be right, at least in the short term, for as the summit approached, it became clear that the US recovery was proceeding faster than even the Reagan Administration had predicted. (US growth in the second quarter of 1983 would turn out to be nearly 10 per cent on an annual basis.)

The conservative coalition was divided, however, on the issue of US fiscal policy. By now it was almost universally agreed that the US structural budget deficit was responsible for continued high interest rates. Pressuring the Americans to adjust their policy mix was a top priority for each of the other summit participants. These foreign criticisms were increasingly echoed within the US government, particularly by Paul Volcker, Chairman of the Federal Reserve, and Martin Feldstein, Chairman of the Council of Economic Advisors, along with much of the US business community. Ten days before the summit, Congress passed a bipartisan budget resolution that envisaged higher taxes and lower military spending. However, the Administration, while calling for additional cuts in domestic programmes, continued to reject criticism of its fiscal policy. On the eve of the summit, the *Washington Post* reported that 'some Reagan economic advisors, although they can't say so publicly, hope that Mitterrand and the other heads of governments will hit the issue hard, perhaps impressing the President during this summit weekend with the political danger of record American deficits'.[35]

International monetary issues received much attention, too, during the preparations for Williamsburg. At the end of April 1983 the seven finance ministers released the study of currency intervention that had been commissioned at Versailles. Representing a moderate consensus, the report concluded that intervention, particularly if internationally coordinated, could be an 'effective tool' against short-term volatility, but that exchange rate stability over longer periods required convergent monetary policies. The ministers endorsed coordinated intervention 'in instances where it is agreed that such intervention would be helpful'. Despite yet another Franco-American dispute afterwards about whether this vague formula implied any change in US policy, it represented the highest common denominator that could be achieved, and it would be repeated verbatim in the Williamsburg communiqué.

However, US officials were increasingly concerned about both volatility and misalignment. Deputy Secretary of State Kenneth Dam noted, for example, that the yen had depreciated from 230 yen to the dollar to 276 between May and November 1982 and then rebounded to 230 by the end of that year.[36] Moreover, the prospect of ballooning US trade deficits, as the US economy recovered, focused the attention of US businessmen on the overvalued dollar.[37] Throughout the winter and spring there was growing talk, both in the United States and elsewhere, about the possibility of international monetary reforms that would move towards some sort of more managed exchange rate regime, perhaps via a system of 'target zones' or 'warning zones' for currency values.[38] In April 1983 Chairman Volcker expressed support for currency intervention 'when exchange rates seem clearly wrong'.[39]

Most striking was the suggestion from Secretary Regan himself in early December 1982 that the United States might favour some sort of 'new Bretton Woods' conference, aiming to achieve greater 'viscosity' in exchange rates.[40] This statement was quickly reinterpreted in less dramatic tones, but at the end of March 1983 Regan returned to the subject, saying

I admit that it would be a much easier world if exchange rates would not fluctuate as much as they have over the last four or five years. But how to achieve that stability still eludes us. [A new Bretton Woods agreement to achieve more currency stability] is entirely possible. I am not forecasting or promising another Bretton Woods, but I do think that nations of the world have got to talk more about their currencies.[41]

The Administration's concerns were clearly focused more on the debt crisis than on currency instability per se, and in any event no consensus on specific proposals for reform had yet emerged. In general, however, the mood was more hospitable to a reassessment of international monetary arrangements than at any time since 1975. As the *New York Times* editorialised, 'A recovery and better coordination of economic policies could reduce the swings [of currencies], but it's also time for a fundamental review of the rules.'[42]

Nevertheless, when on 9 May 1983 President Mitterrand called for 'a new Bretton Woods' conference on international monetary reform, his proposal was greeted with widespread scepticism. Secretary Regan said, 'We are not prepared for a new Bretton Woods summit.' Chancellor Howe described the proposal as 'premature'. Prime Minister Nakasone said that to abandon the current floating regime was wholly unrealistic. Economics Minister Lambsdorff declared himself 'very sceptical', adding that France's monetary problems were due to a 'lack of discipline'. Even the Italians, Sancho Panza to Mitterrand's Quixote for most of 1983, privately expressed the view that his statement must have been intended for domestic consumption.

In fact, the statement, which had been drafted without the involvement of the Ministry of Finance, was quite free of detailed reform proposals, although it clearly reflected traditional French interest in a fixed rate regime.[43] The proposal seemed designed to stimulate further discussion, to establish the French position in the avant-garde of monetary reform, and perhaps to reinforce President Mitterrand's nationalist credentials, rather than to press for any immediate changes. As the summit approached, the French softened their initiative to an evocation of 'the spirit' of Bretton Woods.

The second half of the Versailles monetary compromise, the Group of Five mutual surveillance exercise, was a reasonably successful innovation. The five finance ministers continued their established practice of regular meetings, with their deputies conferring personally at least monthly. Beyond this, however, the ministers met twice between Versailles and Williamsburg with the IMF Managing Director to discuss the international implications of their domestic policies on the basis of a paper prepared by the Managing Director. 'Mutual surveillance' proved to be the political counterpart of the market's tendency to induce 'deviant' governments back toward the international policy median. During 1982–3, for example, the group sharply criticised French and US fiscal laxity. The present mutual surveillance guidelines, worked out among the deputies and codified in the Annex to the Williamsburg communiqué, enshrine 'the current orthodoxy of monetary and fiscal discipline'.[44]

The Americans made trade liberalisation a top priority in the preliminary discussions for Williamsburg. The GATT ministerial talks in

November 1982 had coincided with the very bottom of the recession, a most inauspicious moment for trade liberalisation, and had achieved only agreements to 'study' agriculture, safeguards, and trade in services. As a result of the recession and the debt crisis, world trade in 1982 had contracted for the first time since 1975, and trade disputes metastasised throughout the West. The Americans sought endorsement for a new GATT round that might focus on North–South trade liberalisation, arguing that only through increased exports could the developing countries repay their debts. The US proposal for a joint meeting of Western trade and finance ministers was also intended to highlight this linkage. The US call for 'standstill' and 'rollback' of protectionist measures, which had not been accepted at the GATT meetings in the autumn, was endorsed at the OECD ministerial meetings in May 1983 and would be blessed at Williamsburg as well.[45] Finally, US attacks on European agricultural export subsidies continued. As usual, most of these proposals elicited quiet sympathy from the Germans and Japanese and scepticism from the others. Once again, the Japanese sought to defuse trade tensions by announcing liberalisation packages ahead of time, but the issue seemed less heated this year, probably because restrictions on Japanese exports throughout the West had helped check the growth of the Japanese trade surplus.

The Europeans were particularly incensed at the Reagan Administration's new proposals for strengthening the US Export Administration Act, aimed at extending the extraterritorial reach of US export controls. In late April the dispute became increasingly bitter. One hawkish US official threatened that if the Europeans proved uncooperative, the United States might 'reconsider [its] military commitments to Western Europe'.[46] The European Community replied that the Administration's proposals were 'unacceptable in the context of relations with friendly states' and 'contrary to international law and comity'. The issue would be raised by the British and Germans at the summit, but without result.

Mustering at Williamsburg, 28–30 May 1982

The 1983 summit site, a reconstructed colonial village, was meant to suggest US simplicity and informality, by contrast with the roughly coeval Palace of Versailles. Compared to previous summits, more time was spent in private discussion among the summiteers themselves. The Americans and Japanese, who had objected to Trudeau's initiative along these lines for Ottawa, were now more comfortable with the idea, and most participants were pleased by the more spontaneous exchanges that this innovation allowed.[47]

Economically, the Williamsburg deliberations were inconclusive.[48] The US budget deficit and high interest rates were the target of virtually universal criticism, both in bilateral meetings with President Reagan and in the plenary session. Chancellor Kohl later reported that US interest rates 'were clearly opposed by everyone, from the Japanese to the Canadians to us Europeans'.

Despite these attacks from their ideological allies in the United Kingdom, Germany, and Japan, as well as from the others, President Reagan and Secretary Regan remained unmoved. One US aide said privately later, 'That issue has been hammered at so much, I don't think anybody really hears it any more.' Besides pointing with pride at the recovery under way and with censure at budget-busters in Congress, the Americans argued – to the consternation of their interlocutors – that there was no evidence that high interest rates and the overvalued dollar were caused by budget deficits. Despite the widely acknowledged linkages between trade and monetary problems, the Americans were generally unconcerned about the massive US trade deficit that was almost certain to result from the combination of US domestic expansion and the overvalued dollar.[49] There had been a debate within the Administration about whether the prospective trade deficit posed unacceptable domestic political risks, but as one participant observed, 'Since the Commerce Department was not involved in the summit preparations, the trade deficit was not an issue as far as we were concerned.' Indeed, Secretary Regan stressed that this deficit would help to pull Europe out of the recession, with the United States serving in effect as a kind of locomotive for world recovery.

Buoyed by their own unmistakable recovery, the Americans sought to celebrate their optimism in a 'message of hope' from the summit. However, the French reportedly feared that such 'a hymn to the re-election of Reagan and Thatcher' could be politically embarrassing, should Mitterrand later be forced to introduce additional austerity measures. The final communiqué said 'we now clearly see signs of recovery', but the operative recommendation for fiscal and monetary policy was 'discipline'. It was a prescription for 'more of the same'.[50]

Two days after the summit, CEA Chairman Feldstein wrote plaintively that 'perhaps Williamsburg has made a contribution toward . . . raising everyone's awareness of the importance of the dollar's high value and of the role the anticipated budget deficits are playing in creating this problem'.[51] However, Feldstein had not sought actively to mobilise international pressure in support of his view, and in any event, he was isolated within the Administration, which seemed increasingly aligned behind Secretary Regan's benign view of the deficit.[52] None of the other summiteers was prepared to push President Reagan to increase taxes, if necessary, to cut the deficit, and he was satisfied with communiqué language that stressed the need to restrain spending. Nevertheless, the others returned home dismayed at the lack of US responsiveness. Chancellor Kohl, for example, told the Bundestag that it was 'unsatisfactory for us all' that the Reagan Administration was 'not yet ready to consider extensive, practical steps to ease the monetary and financial situation of its partners'. Privately, he complained about the Americans' 'selfish attitude' on the budget issue.[53]

Both the Americans and the French had to be satisfied with minimal results for their efforts on trade and monetary issues, respectively. In the summit communiqué, the US initiatives were watered down to generic agreements to 'give impetus to resolving current trade problems' and 'to continue consultations on proposals' for a new GATT round. This language was no more binding than the counterpart phraseology (for which it was directly traded in the final session of the summit) on the French-proposed monetary conference. The communiqué invited 'Ministers of Finance, in consultation with the Managing Director of the IMF, to define the conditions for improving the international monetary system and to consider the part which might, in due course, be played in this process by a high-level international monetary conference'. Both commitments were obviously much hedged. On the other hand, both international trade negotiations and international monetary reform are prime examples of issues with a long gestation period. Perhaps some years from now, the Williamsburg summit will be seen to have been a significant step on the path towards a freer trading system and a more stable exchange rate regime.[54]

By far the most striking achievement of Williamsburg was the political statement released mid-way through the conference. The fact of the statement, and its signatories, were more notable than its content, which repeated well-established Western positions on defence, arms control, and the Euromissiles. Agreement on these basic and controversial security matters by the Seven – including France and Japan, neither of whom is a member of NATO's military command – was symbolically quite important. The statement was traceable to several mutually reinforcing factors.

First, as we have already seen, politics had played an increasingly important role in successive summits. By 1983, resistance to the notion that the Seven should issue political statements was confined to France, and even the French reluctance was no longer absolute.

Second, 1983 was destined to be 'the year of the missile' in Europe. Ever since 300,000 Germans had demonstrated in Bonn in October 1981 against the deployment of the Pershing II and cruise missiles, this issue had posed a formidable political threat to those European governments that were scheduled to receive the new missiles. During the first half of 1983, parties favourable to the NATO double-track decision won re-election in the United Kingdom, Germany, and Italy, but even those governments felt a need for collective international support as they girded for the actual deployment. So strongly did President Mitterrand feel about the issue that he had spoken to the Bundestag on the eve of the German election campaign, exhorting Germans to be prepared to deploy the missiles, if necessary, and warning against those who would divide the United States and Europe.

The missile issue posed compound dangers to Alliance unity. As US policy-makers had seen with foreboding even before the 1979 NATO decision, the Euromissiles potentially divided the Western powers in at least three ways. Ominously, the Soviet negotiating position highlighted each of these three fault lines.

1. The United States vs. Europe: while the United States was responsible for the Western negotiating position in Geneva, the missiles were to be deployed in Europe. Many in Europe, particularly in Germany, were concerned that the Reagan Administration would not be sufficiently forthcoming in the arms talks. In effect, the Americans were negotiating as much with European opinion as with the Soviet Union. Even Chancellor Kohl, while reassuring the Americans of his readiness to deploy the missiles, added that 'we are not eager to have these missiles, not at all. . . . [We] want these negotiations to succeed'.[55] At Williamsburg, the Americans sought endorsement of their negotiating position, while others argued for greater US flexibility and urgency in the Geneva talks.

2. The nuclear vs. the non-nuclear allies: the Andropov proposals of December 1982, linking SS-20 deployments to the UK and French independent deterrents, raised the awkward question of whether those forces should be treated as part of 'Western' forces. The UK and French governments strongly resisted any inclusion of their forces in the Geneva intermediate range missile talks, even implicitly, but some officials, particularly in the non-nuclear countries, found that position untenable. At Williamsburg, Prime Minister Trudeau argued strongly, but unsuccessfully, that the West had to be prepared to compromise on this point.

3. Europe vs. Japan: Soviet negotiators had asserted the right to transfer to Soviet Asia any SS-20s removed from Europe as a result of the Geneva talks. Secretary Shultz visited Tokyo in January 1983 to reassure Prime Minister Nakasone that no deal would be made at Japan's expense. Nevertheless, the Japanese remained understandably uneasy. This dilemma was even more complex than that involving the UK and French deterrents, since Japan was not a member of the Atlantic Alliance. From the US point of view the two problems were analogous: how to avoid one ally being pitted against another. Alluding directly to this issue, the Williamsburg communiqué affirmed that 'the security of our countries is indivisible and must be approached on a global basis'.

Only at the Western summit were all of the key countries implicated in these multiple cleavages represented.

Finally, under Prime Minister Nakasone Japan was coming of age in international politics. The Japanese public and especially Japanese elites had reacted sharply and negatively to signs of Soviet aggressiveness in Afghanistan and elsewhere in Asia, and there had been increasing indications that the subject of security was no longer taboo in Japanese politics. From his first statement as Prime Minister in November 1982, Nakasone's goal had been to associate Japan more actively with the Europeans and the United States in terms of security. In January 1983 Foreign Minister Abe had secretly suggested to the Europeans that an informal 'consultation mechanism' be established to link Japan with NATO, but (to the Americans' regret) the French had objected.[56] That same month, Nakasone's high profile on security issues was reinforced by his description of Japan as an 'unsinkable aircraft carrier' available to the Americans against the Soviets. As Nakasone left for Williamsburg, the SS-20s were at the top of his agenda. He would later state publicly that Japan could not tolerate a solution to the Euromissile problem that would 'make Asia a dumping ground for Soviet missiles'.[57]

Nakasone's aides had expressed concern that his assertive stance on security matters would be costly in domestic politics, and some Japanese summit participants were surprised at his forthright stand.[58] However, despite press criticism of Japan's association with the Williamsburg statement, Nakasone's standing in opinion polls rose sharply thereafter. In the two national elections later in 1983, foreign and defence policy seemed to be a favourable element for Nakasone, although it was offset in the December campaign by domestic issues, including charges of LDP corruption.

The notion of a joint statement on security had been broached at the preparatory meeting of political directors two weeks before Williamsburg, but the French had expressed reservations. Therefore, unlike the political statements for Venice and Ottawa, no joint draft was prepared for Williamsburg, and on the eve of the summit the Americans were apparently still undecided about whether to force the issue. On the other hand, pressure for such a declaration was intensified by a Soviet statement on 27 May 1983, warning against deployment of the Western missiles. Like the Soviet statement on Afghanistan just before the Venice summit, this clumsy intervention backfired.

Discussions on the security issue began over dinner on the first evening at Williamsburg and occupied most of the next day. Few summit debates have been so heated. President Mitterrand was initially reluctant to endorse any public statement at all. The US draft, which referred explicitly to NATO decisions, violated long-standing French sensitivities, and moreover, France was unhappy about appearing to extend the geographical scope of the Alliance. ('Discussing these problems with Japan is like discussing them with the whole world,' Foreign Minister Cheysson reportedly said.[59]) Finally, for tactical reasons, France wanted to withhold its consent to the political statement until the economic and monetary issues had been resolved. On the other hand, as Cheysson later conceded, Mitterrand could hardly block the conference from saying essentially what he himself had said to the Bundestag in January.[60] Nevertheless, when President Reagan alluded to press reports of the impending statement and demanded that it be issued without delay, Mitterrand was left embittered by what he apparently felt approached blackmail, tactically speaking.

While France had objections to the form of the statement, other summiteers disagreed about the substance. Prime Minister Thatcher, supported by President Reagan, wanted a resolute tone, partly to induce a more compliant Soviet negotiating position, partly to underline international support for her tough policies on the eve of the UK elections, in which she faced a Labour opposition that could be cast as out of tune with the rest of the West's leaders. On the other side, Pierre Trudeau sought to stress the allies' interest in arms control, once again for both international and domestic political reasons. Chancellor Kohl was eager for international solidarity as the difficult moment of deployment approached, but he was concerned that full weight be given to the possibility of an arms control agreement, a concern that precipitated a difficult clash with his fellow conservative from the United Kingdom. Prime Minister Nakasone stalwartly supported a firm statement, particularly one that recognised Japan's special interests, however indirectly. After hours of debate, the group finally settled on a balance that did not differ significantly from previous Western pronouncements. On the other hand, the reference to the 'indivisibility' of the security of the participants was an important symbolic step.

Agreement on the statement was widely seen as a personal success for President Reagan.[61] Several sherpas described the process as 'nail-biting', calling the absence of preparation 'a gamble' that worked this time. Whatever the statement's short-term impact on the Euromissile controversy, it may be even more important in historical perspective as a landmark in the involvement of Japan in Western security discussions. Despite some European uneasiness about extending NATO's reach, more than one US observer concluded that 'Japan is increasingly moving into the status of a de facto member of the Western military system'.[62]

Conclusions

After the Versailles miscarriage, all the participants at Williamsburg had recognised that another visible failure might doom the whole summit enterprise. Consequently, 1983 saw a kind of conspiracy to avoid catastrophe, a joint effort to lower public expectations and muffle controversy. In effect, on the two major issues that had troubled the summits since 1981, the Americans resigned themselves to minimal results on East–West economics, while the others left empty-handed with respect to US economic policy. Measured against lowered expectations, Williamsburg was a success.

The world's economic problems, however, were essentially untouched by summitry in 1983. Robert Hormats observed on the eve of Williamsburg that 'there is a possibility of missed opportunities for substantive agreement on a strategy for increasing growth and employment, helping developing countries to overcome their economic problems, and improving the international trading system. . . . As they attempt to avoid the Versailles mistake of trying to do too much, it is important that they not make another mistake – of trying to do too little.' Measured against this more ambitious standard, Williamsburg was less successful.

Economics has been an unusually dismal science in the early 1980s, and political relations among the allies have been stormy. However, the measure of summitry's effectiveness cannot simply be growth rates and allied comity. Rather, we must ask whether the summits made things better or worse, a tougher, more conjectural test.

In the macroeconomic field, there is reason to argue that absence of coordination among the major governments after the second oil shock led to competitive deflation and a steeper decline than any single government anticipated.[63] Despite discussions about their common objectives, the governments did not adjust their own policies in the light of the policies (or the problems) of the others. In short, policies were independently set, but not added up.

Economic instabilities were exacerbated by the divergent approaches of the Mitterrand and Reagan administrations. To be sure, by the end of the summer of 1982, French and US macroeconomic policy had begun to converge. As one White House official said privately, 'Both regimes have obviously been schooled by the realities of the last couple of years.' However, this convergence was driven primarily by international financial linkages (and to some extent, domestic considerations), not by international policy coordination.

It would probably have been wiser and less costly, both politically and economically, if these adjustments had been made somewhat earlier.[64] However, given the powerful domestic forces that had sustained the initial policies of Presidents Reagan and Mitterrand, and their own strong convictions, it would have been very difficult for international exchanges, such as summitry, to have eased this transition. In particular, of course, the greater size and lesser openness of the US economy meant that at least in the short term the Americans could more easily decline to follow the foreign advice or foreign examples than could the French. Though its postwar hegemony was long past, the United States was not merely 'an ordinary country'.

By the time of Williamsburg, disagreement within the Reagan Administration on economic policy was publicly apparent. This debate concerned precisely the issue raised by foreign critics, namely, US interest rates and the budget deficit. Strikingly, however, the internal debate was virtually unaffected by the international pressure, unlike the entangling, transnational alliances of the summits of 1977–8. In 1983, the dissidents were less sensitive to the possibility of exploiting international pressures, and even more important, unlike their German and US counterparts in 1977–8, they did not have the ear of the chief executive.

Officials in the Reagan White House were determined from the start not to let summitry interfere with domestic economic policy-making, and they succeeded. In this endeavour to restrict the policy impact of summits they found ready support from the present generation of summiteers. President Reagan could have been speaking of all three of his summits, not just Williamsburg, when he concluded that none of the participants' views had changed 'in any major way' as a result of the summit discussions. Asked if he had changed any of his own views as a result of Williamsburg, he replied with disarming candour, 'Not really.'[65] The interdependence–autonomy dilemma remained intractable.

On the other hand, some accommodation of divergent national policies did take place during this period, on both East–West trade and international monetary issues. The US sherpa for 1983, Allen Wallis, summarised the Administration assessment of the East–West trade issue in a speech three weeks after Williamsburg.[66] He repeated that the United States did not seek to wage economic warfare against the Soviet Union, and indeed said that the collapse of the Soviet economy would be a dangerous development, an assessment at some variance with earlier pronouncements of Administration spokesmen. He concluded, 'The United States and its partners have agreed to conduct their economic relations with the Soviets in a way that does not give preferential treatment to the Soviets or benefit their military position.' Naturally, he did not add that this relatively modest formulation did not differ in substance from the Versailles accord later rejected by the Administration. As one German official concluded, 'Things worked out the way they should have from the beginning.'

What had been achieved by the 1981–3 struggle? The tightening of COCOM rules governing exports of strategic technologies was the most important practical change that could be attributed to the US initiative, though it must be added that throughout the period this was the theme least contested by Europeans. European trade and credits to the Soviet bloc declined over this period, though those trends owed more to purely commercial factors, such as the shaky credit ratings of East European countries and the worldwide energy glut, than to US-induced policy changes. Administration spokesmen claimed that theirs had been a successful exercise in 'consciousness-raising': the issue was manifestly being taken more seriously in Europe than before, and 'we regard this shift as a consequence of the pressure we have applied in the last year'.[67] Some European officials privately agreed with that assessment, although atmospherics are hard to measure. On balance, however, the marginal gains to Western security from the summit-linked discussions of East–West trade seem in retrospect outweighed by the damage to Western political solidarity caused by the post-Versailles travail.

Institutionally, the most portentous development of this period was the mutual surveillance mechanism involving the Group of Five and the IMF. The Group of Five is, of course, the direct descendant of the original Library Group. Information about its activities is tightly held but, according to most accounts, it is still an exceptionally close-knit and effective forum, often acting as a kind of steering committee for the IMF and other broader organisations. Like the Library Group, it offers an occasion for unusually frank, serious, and wide-ranging discussions, not only of monetary issues, but also of macroeconomics, trade, and even North–South issues. During the 1982–3 debt crisis, the Group of Five proved to be, as one member said, 'an effective world fire brigade'. Even the French, ideologically isolated in this group, reported privately that 'this is a place and a framework where people do serious work. It's a good basis, rather pragmatic, for working together.'

One of the original advocates of mutual surveillance within the Reagan Administration has argued that

The multilateral surveillance initiative . . . is the one means by which we can keep our economies from again moving off in radically different directions in terms of basic domestic policies and performance. It's the one way in which we can avoid in the future what happened in 1981 – the United States moving in a highly disinflationary direction and the French economy moving off in a sharply inflationary direction.[68]

Given the current political constellation, this institution has tended to reinforce the austere line favoured by Reagan, Thatcher, Kohl, and Nakasone. However, there is nothing intrinsically deflationary about this mechanism itself. Rather, it tends to discourage policies that deviate from the international average, and in a different ideological environment it might well propagate more expansionary policies.[69]

'Mutual surveillance' was, in one sense, one original purpose of Western summitry. As summiteers themselves have focused less and less on the links between domestic and international economics, the role of the Group of Five in this field has expanded. Historically speaking, this tendency may mark the reversal of the process by which Western summitry was originally instituted. First, the growing importance of the Group of Five implies a partial reversal of the 1975–7 decisions that added Italy, Canada, and the European Community to the charmed circle. Second, the enhancement of the Group of Five represents the reconquest by finance ministries of some of the turf that summitry had forced them to relinquish to chief executives, foreign ministries, and other economic agencies. These trends, coupled with the increasing willingness of summiteers to concentrate on political topics, mark an important institutional transformation, the most significant since Jimmy Carter's Trilateralists appropriated the Library Group.

Defenders of the Library Group image of summitry argued that face-to-face discussions among leaders can build mutual confidence and ease international tensions. Although there is much truth to this claim as a general rule, it is not clear that it applied to relations between the Reagan and Mitterrand administrations in 1982 and 1983. France and the United States clashed about nearly every aspect of the Williamsburg summit, not merely the substance of issues, but even such matters as the time and place of the summit. During the conference itself, Mitterrand reportedly complained to French reporters that they were making him seem 'too conciliatory'. Afterwards, he was even more bitter:

I have doubts about the usefulness of such meetings, at least in their present form. The personal relations between the participants were seriously altered by the astonishing diplomacy of everyone beating his own drum, and by public posturing that has taken precedence over everything else and prevents useful negotiation. I do not believe that this is a good development, and I do not wish to see French policy associated with it further, unless the methods are radically changed.[70]

Nevertheless, the French President subsequently agreed to attend the summit in 1984, illustrating once again the magnetic power of this remarkable institution.

12   Consequences of the Summits

Any student of the Western economic summits is bound to ask 'So what?' Have the summits played a significant role in the international political economy, or have they been evanescent public relations spectaculars? Have the summits helped to reduce tensions among the allies, or have they made things worse? Have the summits actually influenced national policy-making in any way? This chapter addresses these questions, reviewing the historical account presented in previous chapters.

Assessing the consequences of summitry is frustrating for three reasons. First, as history is not an experimental science, we cannot be sure how the attitudes of leaders and the policies of governments would have evolved in the absence of summitry. We must be content with conjectural, 'what if' comparisons.

Second, as a summit is merely one event in a continuing stream of multilateral and bilateral exchanges, its specific effects are hard to disentangle from the effects of other international contacts. Moreover, the delayed effects of a summit may be quite different from its immediate consequences. As we have seen, several summits – London and Versailles, for instance – were declared, prematurely, to have accomplished nothing.

Third, as governments are national governments and summiteers national politicians, the effects of international discussions on policy decisions are usually secondary to domestic pressures. The summit should not be seen as a sort of supranational institution, and the summit communiqué should not be read as a kind of treaty to be implemented. Summits have seldom witnessed definitive decisions on fundamental issues of trade, energy, macroeconomics, and so on. Those seeking realistically to understand the consequences of summitry must look primarily for indirect effects of the summit process, especially within the domestic arena.

Bearing these qualifications in mind, we review in this chapter the consequences of summitry in each of the three contexts outlined in chapter 1. In the light of the experience from Rambouillet through Williamsburg, we discuss the implications of summitry for:

- political leadership and the processes of government;
- international policy coordination and collective management of the Western economy; and
- interdependence and the entanglements of domestic and international affairs.

Summits and political leadership

Personal acquaintance with their fellow leaders is the effect of summitry most often stressed by summiteers and their closest aides. Unlike bureaucrats (and academics), who are typically 'paper-readers', politicians are typically 'people-readers', for whom face-to-face exchanges are important. One former chief executive says,

The summits were for *us* – for the people who went. I got an understanding of you and what your real problem was – as distinct from what your State Department said to the foreign ministry – and what domestic troubles you had in formulating an agreement. Heads of government share a certain sense of the loneliness of our position, and in some ways we could talk to each other more frankly than to our colleagues at home.

Such personal ties can lubricate international relations. Many sherpas and summiteers note the utility of 'being able to pick up the phone' and talk to a well-placed friend and colleague in another capital. Occasionally, personal rapport can have real significance for policy. For example, some Labour aides believe that Helmut Schmidt, through his personal relations with James Callaghan, influenced the last Labour government's economic policies in the direction of somewhat greater stringency.[1] Prime Minister Fukuda's impressive personal performance at the London summit apparently forestalled planned complaints by others about Japanese trade practices. Moreover, as the leaders trade stories about their domestic political woes, they understand better their mutual constraints and how to adjust to those constraints. At Bonn, Jimmy Carter's frank discussion of the domestic politics of energy helped pave the way for the international bargain.

Summiteers note that personal amity – and the knowledge that one would have to face one's colleagues again next year – can have a 'shaming' effect, inhibiting unilateral national policies. Said one UK minister, 'You would think twice about taking actions against a friend.' 'It is like a schoolboys' club,' noted one of his French counterparts, 'and you would not like to violate the rules of the game.' When Germany failed to meet the growth targets agreed at the London summit, Helmut Schmidt is said to have been personally chagrined. Fear of having their Prime Minister put in 'the pillory' or 'the prisoner's dock' has induced the Japanese to make anticipatory trade concessions just prior to several summits. In discussions within the Labour Cabinet about selective protectionist measures, Callaghan's disinclinations towards a protectionist strategy were strengthened by his international contacts, and he used that international pressure with his colleagues to some effect. 'This would embarrass me at the next summit,' he would say; or, 'I've just been talking to Helmut [or Jimmy], and I think we should avoid that sort of thing now.'

It would be a mistake to dismiss such examples as mere sentiment, unimportant in the hard-boiled world of politics. Strategic theorists have shown, as practical politicians have long known, that concern for one's reputation is highly rational, even for an unsentimental egoist, particularly when the players in a game encounter one another fairly frequently.[2] Thus, personal pledges by leaders on such matters as protectionism (recall the incident involving Wilson after Rambouillet) or the supply of nuclear fuel (promised by Carter in London and Bonn) were important even though they were not legally binding.

On the other hand, the moral suasion derived from summit-engendered personal relations can be important only at the margins. It can strengthen prior convictions, but, for example, neither Callaghan nor his protectionist colleagues thought that the internationalist argument would have carried the day in the face of strong contrary currents in domestic politics. In recent years the anti-protectionist pledges at the summit have worn even thinner, their deterrent effect eroding under the grinding frictions of recession-spawned trade disputes. Moreover, as the confrontations between Carter and Schmidt, and especially between Reagan and Mitterrand, sometimes have illustrated, face-to-face encounters at the summit do not always increase mutual trust or ease international tensions. It is perhaps significant that our best illustrations of how personal amity can smooth international relations all derive from the earlier generation of summiteers.

However, even the most recent participants have found that summits can have an educational effect. The prospect of meeting their colleagues forces chief executives to do their homework on foreign economic policy and to focus on the international dimensions of the problems they have been grappling with domestically. Aides can use the advent of the summit to encourage their chiefs to reconsider the international costs and benefits of their policies. Thus, for example, preparation for the London summit eased some rigidities in Carter's non-proliferation policy, and Ottawa provided a rare occasion for Reagan to re-examine his position on North–South issues. Moreover, face-to-face encounters convey the international constraints more vividly than dry diplomatic cables. 'Any meeting of the head of government with his foreign counterparts shows him that it's all more complicated than he thought,' explained one slightly jaded official. A summiteer concluded: 'The main point is to learn how the others see the problems.'

This educational effect is especially important for politicians whose background is more insular, a category that includes a growing number of Western leaders. The Italians have a word for it: well-placed observers there say that the single most important effect of the summits has been to *sprovincializzare* ('de-provincialise') Italian leaders, a phenomenon paralleled in other summit countries. The summits have provided a kind of 'culture-shock' for Japanese politicians; Prime Minister Ohira reportedly said after the Tokyo summit, 'I felt naked – like a little child.' Insiders say that the summits were important in overcoming Prime Minister Thatcher's initial reluctance to focus on international issues. One Reagan aide argues that 'the summits shape the way in which politicans view certain issues over the medium term, which may subsequently influence what they do back home. For example, the qualms that Kohl had on the political statement [about the Euromissiles in 1983] probably did a lot by way of educating the President.' From the perspective of one seasoned European diplomat, 'Summits introduce politicians whose primary experience has been domestic to the long-running serial of international collaboration: "New readers begin here." '

Nor are the benefits of *sprovincializzazione* limited to politicians. Even in France, for example, where preparations for the summit have been most closely held in the Elysée, one senior participant-observer argues that the most enduring effect of summits has been a tendency to internationalise the agendas and the outlooks of domestic officials. 'I remember clearly the Tokyo summit, for example: everybody at the Commissariat du Plan and at the Ministry of Industry was talking about international energy topics. It was quite unlike the provincialism of the French administration between 1972 and 1974.'

Summits engage the prestige and the power of the highest authorities in each country. Consequently, summits energise the policy process, both nationally and internationally. A former US deputy sherpa has written that

the certainty that there is a summit meeting up ahead, where the head of government is going to be confronted with tough questions from peers, compels the internationally oriented section of the bureaucracy to consider domestic needs, exposes the domestic bureaucracy to international factors, and forces the government as a whole to resolve internal splits on the relevant issues.[3]

The summit can enable central executives to overcome bureaucratic and political obstacles that would be more obdurate under normal circumstances. For example, in countries as diverse as the United States, Italy, and Canada, the pressures of summit preparation have been used by some officials to increase the low priority normally attached to North–South issues. An approaching summit has sometimes encouraged the European Community to move more briskly towards common positions on such issues as the Common Fund, international monetary questions, or trade with Japan. By engaging the international and domestic credibility of the heads of government, the summits of London and Bonn reduced the ability of narrower interests to resist concessions that the respective negotiators knew were necessary to complete the Tokyo Round. As discussed in earlier chapters, Rambouillet and Tokyo provided essential impetus to international negotiations on monetary reform and energy policy, respectively.

The energising effect of summits is most marked in Japan, where traditional consensus-building seems interminable. The characteristic reluctance of Japanese leaders to override strongly held differences of opinion and to dictate policy is, in the context of the summit preparations, somewhat offset by the equally characteristic fear that the prime minister may 'lose face' internationally unless a more defensible policy can be agreed upon within the government. For example, during the 1982 summit preparations Chief Cabinet Secretary Miyazawa is said to have demanded with 'un-Japanese' bluntness that the various ministries concerned with trade issues resolve their differences. 'I understand the necessity of discussion,' he told recalcitrant bureaucrats, 'but it is now time to decide.'

Strikingly, in most of the cases we have cited, it was the prospect of the summit rather than the summit discussions themselves that made the crucial difference. The summit's advent created pressure for success because of widespread fear of summit 'failure'. This factor, only latent before 1982, became dramatically evident after Versailles. As we saw in chapter 11, concern about another catastrophe encouraged accommodation on international monetary issues and especially on East–West economics prior to Williamsburg. In short, summits have often been important less for what happened *at* them than for what happened *in anticipation of* them.

As we have seen, the most recurrent procedural issue about the summits has involved preparations. Most of the leaders themselves have seemed to prefer more casual, less 'bureaucratised' summits. However, preliminary negotiations have been crucial to most summit successes, from the Rambouillet monetary accord to the Bonn package, and from the Venice reconciliation of the post-Afghanistan tensions to the battle avoided at Williamsburg over East–West economics. In two important instances, preparatory discussions failed to resolve serious issues – energy for Tokyo and East–West economics for Versailles. In the first case, the leaders were able to cobble together an acceptable outcome, but in the second, they were not. The only major summit initiative successfully consummated without extensive work during the preparatory phase was the Williamsburg statement on security issues. Here, however, the basic position (and even the language) enunciated at the summit had been exhaustively debated among the governments in previous years. What remained, as a US aide noted, was 'the question of political nuance, and that [the summiteers] can probably handle better than the bureaucrats. That's how these guys get elected.' However, the record suggests that when an issue requires more than a deft political touch, success at the summit is powerfully influenced by the adequacy of the preparatory process.

It would be wrong, however, to see in this record, evidence of bureaucratic usurpation. First, officials charged with the preparations are acutely aware of their accountability to their political masters. One participant, recalling an intense debate among the sherpas about possible communiqué language, put the point vividly: 'There's nothing these guys care more about than that. After all, they are responsible for protecting the ass of the number one honcho back home, and they care . . . like I've never seen anyone in my life.'

Moreover, the term 'bureaucrat' is a misleading appellation for most of those most intimately involved in the preparations. Though not elective politicians, neither have they typically been classical, apolitical civil servants. More commonly, they have been hybrid figures, adroit in the borderland between pure politics and pure administration, men (so far all personal representatives have been male) for whom political sensitivity has been as important a credential as substantive expertise.[4]

Ironically, despite demands by the current generation of leaders that the summit process be 'de-bureaucratised', they have in some respects moved the process in the opposite direction. The uneven, but unmistakable trend towards depersonalisation of the role of personal representative has meant that the sherpas of the 1980s have a more bureaucratic cast than their predecessors. Moreover, the recent tendency to decentralise the detailed treatment of erstwhile summit issues to other forums may actually dilute political control. As we have seen, the mutual surveillance exercise inaugurated at Versailles and reinforced at Williamsburg might be interpreted as a resurgence of the role of finance officials in the coordination of national economic policies. If so, it might over time reduce the effectiveness of summitry as a means of asserting comprehensive political leadership.

Summits and policy coordination

Not everyone involved in summitry agrees that summits should address policy differences. One senior financial official, for example, argues that

the role of the summit is to provide visible leadership and stability in a troubled world. Confidence matters to the world economy in quite practical terms. Summits are for stressing common purpose, not debating policy. That's why the group photographs and the bishop-like blessings for the IMF, the GATT, and so on are important. It's not much, but that's what summits can do.

However, most participants, even among the current generation, have a somewhat more ambitious conception of summitry: they see summit meetings as one means of increasing international economic cooperation. As Robert O. Keohane has pointed out (in a slightly different context), 'we need a conception of cooperation that is somewhat tart rather than syrupy-sweet', that is, a conception that reckons with conflict and power, as well as shared interests.[5] In the language of game theory, the summit is a 'mixed motive' game, involving both joint problem-solving and hard-nosed bargaining.

Conflict in the Western political economy arises, as we have seen, because of international inconsistencies among the policies of interdependent countries. In seeking to resolve such conflicts, summit participants have attempted four different types of cooperation, representing successively more ambitious types of policy coordination:

1. Mutual enlightenment, that is, sharing information about national policy directions.
2. Mutual reinforcement, that is, helping one another to pursue desirable policies in the face of domestic resistance.
3. Mutual adjustment, that is, seeking to accommodate or ameliorate policy divergences.
4. Mutual concession, that is, agreeing on a joint package of national policies designed to raise the collective welfare.

Let us consider each in turn.

Information about the policy intentions of other countries can be an important ingredient in national decision-making. A decade's experience has disconfirmed the theory that flexible exchange rates would free national policy-makers from the need to follow international policy fashions. As the cases of the United Kingdom in 1976, the United States in 1978, and France in 1982 show, even the major countries cannot deviate substantially over a sustained period from the international median policy mix. Obviously, the constraints on smaller, more open economies are even more immediate.

The most powerful countries can try to adapt to this 'regression toward the mean' by using the summit process itself to shift the international climate of opinion in the direction of their preferred policy mix. For example, this was in part the strategy of the Carter Administration in 1977–8 and (with a different set of policy preferences) the Reagan Administration in 1981–2. Large countries are in that sense 'policy-makers', just as large suppliers in commodity markets are 'price-makers'.

Smaller countries, on the other hand, are essentially 'policy-takers'. For them, the summit process offers an important opportunity for learning the likely future of the international policy market place. 'When we are deciding on our policies,' said a key Italian economic official, 'we need to know where the others are headed. We cannot simply wait until the exchange markets show us we are out of line. That's why the sherpa meetings and the summit itself are so important for us.' A Canadian participant (and football enthusiast) referred to the importance of 'getting on side' in policy terms.[6]

One experienced participant in summit preparations put the point vividly: 'The lemmings need to get together each year to tell each other where they are going.' A less cynical colleague explained that 'you return from the summit feeling more secure that you know the general drift of the others' policies, so that at least you know where the problems are going to arise'. (In theoretical terms, this phenomenon of 'policy-taking' is the exact opposite of the 'free-rider' problem; perhaps it should be termed the 'forced-rider' problem.)

Although this distinction has been phrased so far as if all countries were either pure policy-makers or pure policy-takers, it would be more accurate to say that countries pursue mixed strategies of policy-making and policy-taking. For instance, even though the Thatcher government has been disinclined to take economic advice from abroad or to engage in international policy coordination, one economic aide noted that the summits provided useful information: 'They focus one's mind on where difficulties will emerge. For example, after Ottawa we recognised that US policies were going to lead to high interest rates, and that had implications for our borrowing policy.'

Aside from sniffing the winds, leaders usually go to summits to get international legitimation for their existing policies. Thus, mutual reinforcement is a second type of international policy cooperation. Much of the communiqué negotiation involves efforts by each participant to obtain as ringing an affirmation of his or her programme as possible. The ideal outcome for any summiteer, particularly on the eve of national elections, was represented by a US newspaper headline following the Puerto Rico summit: 'Summit Leaders Endorse Ford's Economic Policy'.[7]

Both government and opposition politicians in many of these countries believe that international endorsement has real impact in domestic politics. We have seen that Margaret Thatcher, for example, repeatedly cited communiqué language to defend her austere policies, and the Giscard–Barre government found summit language on the dangers of inflation a useful 'cooperative constraint'. Conversely, it is widely believed that a summit declaration contrary to the thrust of a government's current policy could be used profitably by its opponents. Naturally, given the care with which the communiqués are drafted, this hypothesis has rarely been tested. It is noteworthy, however, that immediately after the Bonn summit, Prime Minister Barre came under attack for having endorsed reflation abroad, while continuing to reject expansionary measures at home.[8]

Sometimes the search for 'helpful' language is intended to forestall any weakening of the government's own commitment to a given policy.

Italian officials favouring a stringent economic line are said to relish and occasionally to invite the inclusion of language emphasising the need for austerity. Statements on the importance of nuclear energy have been inserted in successive communiqués at the request of the German and UK governments, seeking international reinforcement for domestically controversial programmes. The focus on energy in the 1978–80 summit deliberations raised the salience of energy conservation in most summit countries. Summit discussions of the dangers of protectionism have helped forestall some (though obviously not all) infringements of free trade principles. Beyond the cases involving the Labour government under Wilson and Callaghan, several Americans cite specific decisions by Carter to forego shoe import quotas and other protectionist devices.[9]

By definition, mutual reinforcement does not involve governments pursuing policies that they would not otherwise wish to conduct, but it can help them to follow policies that would otherwise be more difficult to implement domestically. For example, the Williamsburg statement on security was clearly designed to help sustain the German, British, and Italian governments during the controversial Euromissile deployments. Giscard found the Rambouillet accord useful in fending off critics within his own majority who favoured Gaullist monetary orthodoxy. On the other hand, international legitimation is not necessarily sufficient to save a government that is pursuing internationally desirable, but domestically unpopular policies. Canadian Prime Minister Joe Clark lost office in 1979, in part over his policy of raising oil prices, despite international encouragement of that policy at the Tokyo summit a few months earlier.

If the communiqués were pure 'tossed salad' documents, with no concern whatever for internal consistency, mutual reinforcement would have no impact on international policy coordination. In fact, however, mutual reinforcement has selectively benefited policies near the international median, thus marginally encouraging moderation. As a leading international banker noted, 'It is harder to put forward some lunatic domestic proposition in an international forum, so summits and other such meetings tend to moderate doctrinaire points of view.' Of course, in recent years domestic politics in a number of countries have thrown up unusually ideological governments, probably more than offsetting the moderating impact of summitry. Nevertheless, without such international confrontation of views, the tendency towards divergent national dogmas might have been even more destabilising.

Thus, mutual reinforcement tends to merge at the margins with mutual adjustment of policies, the third type of policy coordination found in the record of summitry. Summits provide an opportunity for reciprocal commentary and even reciprocal criticism of national policies.

Formally speaking, national sovereignty would seem to imply a principle of *liberum veto*, that is, that unanimous consent would be required for any summit deliberation, and any government could remain impassive in the face of criticism. In fact, however, there are numerous instances in which one country has modified its position to avoid isolation. Examples include the British on trade restrictions in 1975, the Americans in 1977 on non-proliferation, the French in 1978 on the Multilateral Trade Negotiations, the Germans (and subsequently the Japanese) on energy in 1979, the Americans on North–South issues in 1981 and 1982, and the French in 1983 on the joint statement on security. Since unilateral policies in these instances might have brought with them blame for the failure of the summit, the costs of a veto could not have been confined to the single issue. In effect, summit participants have often acted as if absolute unanimity were not required for summit action.

In some cases, mutual accommodation reflects simply a political process of 'splitting the difference', but in other instances, accommodation is based on increased understanding of the logic and the objectives of the opposing positions. For example, the 1977–8 period witnessed a gradual convergence in assessments of the macroeconomic situation, and even in the more difficult 1981–3 period, the confrontation over US interest rates tended to become less simplistic as the debate progressed. Similar tendencies were encouraged by the joint studies of nuclear energy in 1977–80 and of exchange rate intervention in 1982–3. None of these instances of mutual accommodation eliminated national divergences completely, but as one ex-summiteer pointed out, 'It is the cumulative effect that counts.' To be sure, mutual adjustment is the bread and butter of everyday diplomacy, but the summit process plays a special role in encouraging movement when (as in many of the instances cited here), the chief executive has been personally identified with the policy in question.

Mutual surveillance of macroeconomic policies is designed to institutionalise this process of adjustment. However, the experience of summitry offers an interesting lesson about the limitations of this method for achieving greater international policy coordination, for the logic of economics and the logic of politics collide here. In economic principle, of course, properly coordinated policies need not be identical policies. Indeed, if all countries adopt similar policies simultaneously, this may lead to collective overshooting – excessive restraint in 1975–6 and 1981–2 and perhaps excessive stimulation in 1978–9. Nevertheless, every government appears to find it politically awkward to press upon its allies a policy line different from its own. Instances in the history of summitry include Carter's reduced ability to demand German and Japanese reflation in 1977, following the withdrawal of his $50 tax rebate; the unwillingness of the British and Germans to urge a looser monetary policy on the Americans in 1981 and 1982, or to urge the Americans to raise taxes in 1983; and the Reagan Administration's reluctance to press for more Japanese domestic expansion in 1982 and 1983.[10] In short, pressures for political and ideological consistency limit the ability of any individual government to press for a differentiated strategy of policy adjustment.

The first three types of policy cooperation we have discussed are consultative but fundamentally unilateral, in the sense that each government determines its own policy in the light of information, reinforcement, and criticism from its summit partners. By contrast, mutual concession represents conditional adjustment, in the sense that each government's actions are conditioned on some counterpart action by other governments – in short, a package deal.[11] Though much discussed in theories of international political economy, this ambitious brand of cooperation has been relatively rare in the practice of summitry. Nevertheless, two important instances in 1978 and 1979 are worth recalling here.

The Bonn package deal was the most elaborate example of policy coordination yet achieved at a Western summit. One salient feature of the accord was that it involved a linkage among different policy sectors – fiscal policy, energy policy, and to some extent trade policy – a linkage that was fundamentally political, so to speak, and not functional. Such 'artificial' linkage is sometimes thought to hamper the resolution of international conflict. However, it can be shown theoretically – and Bonn demonstrated practically – that without cross-issue linkage, important positive-sum international games may never be concluded.[12] At Bonn, for example, there was no possible German concession within the energy field that could have induced the US energy concession.

As we noted earlier, summitry encourages governments to address linkages and priorities among issues traditionally handled by separate networks of specialists. One personal representative explained, 'In working out an agreement, I might say to my fellow sherpas, for example, "I know that's what my development aid specialist said, but there are more important things than that." ' Since, in the modern state, distinct issue areas are normally handled by different bureaucracies and respond to different domestic constituencies, cross-issue deals rarely can be accomplished without the active involvement of the chief executive. Only he or she has the authority to compel one sector to make what is, for it, an uncompensated concession, and only he or she can balance those costs against the benefits that will presumably flow from the counterpart concession by the other party.[13] As a Reagan aide pointing out to an American colleague while they were debating a potential, but unconsummated cross-issue deal in 1983, 'This is what the President is elected to decide. If East–West trade is more important to him than his current policy on exchange markets, then irrespective of all the technical questions, this is politics.' Assuming adequate attention to sectorally relevant detail, the involvement of chief executives and their staffs in international negotiations makes it easier to overcome the centrifugal effects of sectoral 'sub-governments' and to strike mutually beneficial deals. In this respect, summitry can make a valuable contribution to international policy coordination.

The Tokyo agreement on oil import targets illustrated a different form of policy coordination, limited to a single issue, but involving a classic prisoner's dilemma. In the face of the OPEC challenge, it was clear that all Western consumers would benefit if all could reduce their demand for imported oil, but each individual country would be better off if it did not limit consumption, regardless of what the others did. The logic of collective action in such a situation required that the major consuming nations each make a credible, binding commitment to reduce consumption, which was essentially the result achieved at Tokyo.

The summit is a particularly useful venue for addressing such collective good or prisoner's dilemma problems. First, all the major countries whose involvement is necessary are present, and yet their number is sufficiently limited for the responsibility of each to be clear. Second, the visibility and authority of the summiteers make their mutual commitments more credible, for it is costly to renege on a commitment made by the head of state. As a senior IEA official pointed out

We decided at the official level on 1–2 March 1979 that we would all bring down our oil demand by 5 per cent, but real action at the national level was very, very rare. When you have ministers take a commitment to their colleagues, it has a different political weight, and if heads of state engage themselves at the level of the Seven, you have even stronger policy.

Third, credibility is enhanced by the continuity of the summit as an institution, for defectors from an agreement are liable to subsequent retaliation. Game theorists have shown that all three factors – small size, credibility of negotiator, and repeated play – enhance the likelihood of overcoming the prisoner's dilemma.[14]

Nevertheless, as we have seen, the impact of the Tokyo agreement was more symbolic than practical. Given the haze of uncertainty surrounding estimates of future demand, each country sought to minimise its commitment. As a result, the agreed targets were too high to constrain imports effectively, and consequently the collective gains were minimal. The episode illustrates that even when the logic of the prisoner's dilemma is plain and the apparent benefits of cooperation high, the obstacles to successful coordination are imposing.

As we discussed in chapter 1, summitry emerged in part in response to the waning of US hegemony. What does the experience of summitry tell us about the role of US leadership in contemporary management of the Western economy?

The United States has not dominated the summits any more than it can command the Western world, but for better or worse, US policies have been at the centre of most summit controversies. Virtually every major summit initiative was either promoted by or (somewhat less often) aimed at the United States. America was the crucial advocate of the coordinated recovery programme of 1977–8 and the most energetic proponent of monetary restraint in 1981–3. It has provided the primary initiative on both trade and East–West issues throughout the period. Energy was essentially a German-American duet in 1978 and a French-American duet in 1979. The French led the way on monetary issues at Rambouillet, Versailles, and Williamsburg, but the United States was the primary respondent, and in each case the French ended up making the bigger concession. US leadership was necessary, if not sufficient, for decisive summit action in all these fields. Only on North–South issues have the Americans been consistently on the sidelines. Similarly, on questions of procedure the Americans have been the most influential participants. Jimmy Carter's Trilateralists triggered the institutionalisation of summitry, and despite growing discontent, this trend was not really reversed until his successor hosted the summit at Williamsburg.

To be sure, the substance of US policy has often been hotly contested by other summit participants, and the United States has certainly not always won these arguments. Nevertheless, as the *Neue Zürche Zeitung* has observed: 'Two characteristics pervade the history of the summits, in the judgement of summit veterans: on the one hand, the desire on the European side to enlighten and educate the American presidents, and on the other, the European hunger for American leadership.'[15] When US leadership within the summit context has faltered, no other country has been able successfully to pick up the slack. Hegemony is behind us, but the United States is hardly an ordinary country.

Summits and the entanglements of interdependence

Theorists of international relations distinguish two approaches to understanding foreign policy. 'Inside-out' explanations emphasise domestic factors, such as political coalitions, whereas 'outside-in' explanations focus on systemic forces, such as the international power structure.[16] These two perspectives are, of course, not mutually exclusive. Nevertheless, the changing patterns of international cooperation reflected in the history of summitry offer much evidence in support of the 'inside-out' perspective.

The basic structure of international politics and economics has remained relatively stable over the decade reviewed here, but the character and intensity of international cooperation have varied substantially. For example, despite certain macroeconomic similarities between 1977–8 and 1982–3 – as reflected in the parallel reports of economic experts in November 1976 and December 1982 – the summit outcomes were very different indeed. Surely the most crucial explanatory factor lies in the contrast between Carter–Callaghan–Schmidt, on the one hand, and Reagan–Thatcher–Kohl, on the other. The changing mosaic of political and ideological alignments within the summit countries has clearly had a powerful influence on summit outcomes.

Entanglements between domestic and international pressures were most manifest in 1978. As we have seen, agreement was reached in Bonn only because within each of the key governments a powerful faction actually favoured the policy being demanded internationally. Without that domestic resonance, international forces would not have sufficed to produce the accord, no matter how balanced the package of concessions and no matter how attractive it was on purely economic grounds. On the other hand, the international pressures, coupled with the balanced character of the final package, allowed policies to be 'sold' domestically that would not have been feasible otherwise. As one Japanese observer put it, 'For a snowflake, you need not only the right temperature and humidity. You need some particle as a precipitant. Foreign demands can provide that precipitant.'

Divisions within a government are often thought to hamper international cooperation. However, the summit experience suggests that under some circumstances internal divisions can actually facilitate cooperation.[17] Dieter Hiss, the 1978 German sherpa, later wrote that summits are likely to effect changes in national policy 'only insofar as they mobilise and/or change public opinion and the attitude of political groups. . . . Often that is enough, if the balance of opinion is shifted, providing a bare majority for the previously stymied actions of a strong minority.'[18] The reshuffle of alignments at the domestic game board thus achieved permits a deal to be struck at the international table.

Summits have frequently eased international tensions by strengthening the hands domestically of those within a government who favoured an internationally desired policy. Aside from the Bonn package, this pattern was illustrated by the hesitation of the Labour government in 1975–7 to introduce protectionist measures; by the willingness of all governments in 1977–8 to seek a major MTN agreement, rather than the 'mini-package' that important domestic interests wanted; by the US energy initiatives in 1979; by the Japanese trade liberalisation packages in 1981 and 1982; and by the gradual moderation between 1981 and 1983 of the Reagan Administration's initial hostility to North–South negotiations and to monetary cooperation. In all these cases, the internal cleavage was a necessary, though not sufficient condition for international accommodation.

Most governments are internally divided in some degree, of course, but not necessarily in a way that allows international pressure to be decisive. Other potential summit packages failed, as we have seen, because of the absence of the appropriate domestic reinforcement. (The clearest example was the potential trade-off between monetary reform and East–West commerce in 1982.) Generally speaking, a government's policies reflect a fairly stable coalition of domestic interests. Construction of that coalition represents a sunk cost from the point of view of domestic political entrepreneurs. To change those policies for the sake of better international coordination would often require a significant readjustment of the government's base of support and might offend the personal convictions of key government leaders. Thus, the potential gains from (or the losses avoided by) successful international coordination must be quite large to offset the domestic costs, particularly given the high uncertainty surrounding the international game.

The construction of transnational coalitions is impeded by the reluctance of most officials to search for potential allies within foreign governments. Even in the successful cases cited above, the transnational alliances were more tacit than explicit. To our knowledge, the only overt invitations for foreign pressure in summit history involved US energy policy and Japanese trade and fiscal policy prior to Bonn.[19] On the other hand, we have seen that potential transnational alliances failed to materialise on such issues as US inflation-fighting in 1978, Japanese fiscal policy in 1982, and the US budget deficit in 1983. Even among governments as well known to one another as the Western allies are, officials are often surprisingly misinformed about domestic alignments abroad, and they are sceptical of their own ability to manoeuvre effectively in a foreign game whose rules they do not fully understand.

Moreover, even when the respective negotiators are aware of internal divergences across the international table, the obstacles to transnational coordination and the risks of failure are high. Even within the intimacy of the Library Group, for example, several attempts to forge transnational alliances provoked angry protests about 'foreign interference'. One experienced summiteer spoke with some ambivalence:

If someone in Washington wanted to play one part of my government against another, I would tell him, 'Get out immediately; it's none of your business.' So I wouldn't like to interfere in any other friendly government's internal controversies. As long as it doesn't become known, okay, but once it became known, everyone would think that this was totally inappropriate.

Academic theorists of transnational politics must not underestimate the resilience of the norms of national sovereignty. Summits have not occasioned altruism. Summits cannot force unwilling leaders to cooperate. But summits can make cooperation easier, if leaders are so disposed. Dieter Hiss states the case with admirable clarity.

Of special interest is the question whether governments ever undertook any measures, occasioned by the summit, which they would not have undertaken without the summit. The answer is clear. No country violates its own interests, but the definition of its interests certainly can change through a summit, with its possible trade-offs and give-and-take. . . . The results of the summit meetings, efficaciously inserted into the domestic decision process, make it easier to steer this process in a direction which produces positive results not only from the narrower national point of view, but also in the international context, [so that] the potential for international cooperation grows and the potential for serious international economic, monetary, or trade policy conflicts and beggar-thy-neighbour policies declines.[20]

In some important instances the summit process has contributed to the resolution of policy differences among the Western countries and has served as a prophylaxis for the health of the international trading system. If no significant domestic pressure for an internationally co-operative line of policy exists, summitry cannot create it, but where such pressure does exist, leaders can use the summit process to amplify its effectiveness. It is striking that summiteers returning home have more often been criticised for the paucity of practical results than for excessive concessions to foreign pressure.[21] This no doubt reflects the fine-tuned political sensitivities of the leaders and their domestic advisors, but it also suggests that they have typically erred on the side of caution. The full potential of summitry for helping to reconcile the dilemma of sovereignty and interdependence may not yet have been explored.

The previous chapter reviewed the consequences of the first nine summits, from Rambouillet in 1975 to Williamsburg in 1983. This chapter looks ahead to the summits which will follow, from London in 1984 onwards. It briefly considers the factors that might make for change or continuity in later years. It then makes some tentative suggestions first about possible changes in the summit format, which might lead to better results, and finally about issues worthy of treatment by the heads of government.

Change and continuity

The summits, despite their institutional development, still differ greatly from any international organisation. There is no founding document – no charter, treaty, or articles – which limits the scope of their discussions. They have no headquarters and no secretariat. They have, over the years, developed a regular timetable, a customary range of subjects, and various procedural conventions. But the growth of these institutional aspects has not wholly stifled their role as the personal instruments of the leaders. The summits can still adapt rapidly to new demands from outside or to changes in the attitudes of the heads of government present – far more quickly than formal organisations like the OECD or IMF.

The summits therefore have a protean quality – an ability to change their shape as needed – which other bodies do not share. While the first four summits, in retrospect, give an appearance of continuity, each summit after Bonn appears to make a fresh start. Tokyo responded to the second oil crisis; Venice opened the decade of the 1980s; Ottawa introduced a new generation of leaders; Versailles launched a second summit cycle after each country had acted as host; and Williamsburg marked the passage from recession to recovery. Some of these changes of direction, for example at Venice and Versailles, proved more apparent than real. But they make it hard to pick out a dominant trend, while a series of only nine summits is a weak basis for extrapolation. Any forecast of their future role, let alone any prescription, is bound to be hazardous.

The economic conditions which will confront the summits of the middle to late 1980s may resemble much more closely those which faced the earliest meetings, not the most recent ones. The Rambouillet summit of 1975 took place just as recovery began from the recession following the first oil crisis, with the United States well ahead of Europe. The 1983 Williamsburg summit was held at the corresponding point in the cycle following the second oil crisis. The summits which follow Williamsburg, like the early ones, may be able to concentrate again on assuring economic recovery and giving impulses in trade and monetary matters, rather than on the austere policies necessary in the early 1980s. This will influence the choice of issues for future summits, to be considered later.

A personal instrument like the summit will also change its nature as the participating leaders change. Here, however, election results in Europe during 1983 suggested an unusual prospect of continuity. Chancellor Kohl should still be in office at the summit of 1986 and Mrs Thatcher, as well as President Mitterrand, up to 1987. Despite the choice of the Socialist Sr Craxi as Italian Prime Minister, the parliamentary arithmetic which emerged from the 1983 elections in Italy suggested no fundamental change from the pattern of previous years. With elections due before the end of 1984 in the United States, Japan, and Canada, there is much more uncertainty there. But if President Reagan should be re-elected, that would give him a run of four more summits up to 1988.

Williamsburg, however, was the first of the summits at which none of the 'founding fathers' was present. After Mr Trudeau, no leader will survive from the early formative years of the summits: Mrs Thatcher, first present at Tokyo, will be the doyenne.[1] It is worth looking briefly at how the leaders in power in 1983 differed from their predecessors, as some guide to the summit's future direction.

The first and most striking feature was the disappearance of former finance ministers. In 1977 and 1978 six out of the eight summit leaders – counting Mr Jenkins for the Commission – had previously served as finance ministers. From Tokyo onwards their numbers began to dwindle. At Williamsburg none of the leaders had experience as finance minister, and this is unlikely to change in the near future. This should mean that the contribution made by the leaders to economic discussions would derive more from their political skill and judgment and less from technical expertise and originality. It may also mean a growing interest in non-economic subjects alongside economic ones.

A second feature was an overall move to the right in the governments of the major countries. This was the experience in the United Kingdom, the United States, Germany, and even Japan since 1978. The emergence of a socialist government in France should in principle redress the balance; but one lesson of the summits since the beginning has been that a single country cannot successfully resist the prevailing trend. This political movement to the right reinforced the shift in economic philosophy already described in chapter 7. The prevailing current of thought among the summit countries favoured financial rigour, reducing government intervention, and maximum reliance on the market. This might not last indefinitely into the future. The pendulum of economic ideas could well swing back, whether or not there is any parallel political change. If there were a different administration in the United States from 1985, with a greater interest in international coordination of economic policy, this could exert a strong influence in that direction. But even then the entrenched position of the United Kingdom and Germany could delay any shift until late in the decade.

A third feature was an abiding reaction – as described in chapter 11 – against the highly structured, 'specific' summit process favoured by President Carter and his team. The drawbacks of this have been often stated: overloading the agenda, excessive bureaucratic apparatus, wordy declarations, and unreal expectations of results – all leaving too little scope for any personal contribution by the leaders themselves. But although this reaction set in from 1981, it took much longer than anyone expected to arrest the momentum of the summit process. Williamsburg was the first summit which in the view of most participants regained what they regarded as the original spirit of the summits – and even here the French remained critical. All the major participants were in favour of making the summits simpler and more personal. President Mitterrand earlier likened the ideal summit to a conclave of cardinals and President Reagan and Mrs Thatcher were known to hold similar views.[2]

The shape of future summits

Personal contact and consultation among the leaders indeed lie at the core of the summit process. Nothing can substitute for these direct exchanges as a means of enabling the leaders to understand each other better and to realise how much their policies interact. This can remain true even when the leaders do not find a close personal rapport. The regular practice of top-level consultation which has grown up with the summits should provide a direct reminder to the leaders of their common interests and should help to forestall fundamental disagreements among the Western powers. If the summits were to cease – as seemed possible for a time after Versailles – this would seriously weaken the cohesion of the West.

But the record shows that informal, personal contacts, valuable though these are, do not suffice on their own. If limited to this the summits fall short of their potential. There is not enough incentive to advance from exchanges of views and information towards consensus or agreement, with each side prepared to move from its starting-point to achieve common ground on difficult or divisive issues. The summit has only a passing effect in concentrating the minds of the participating governments – at all levels, not only at the top – on the international implications of their policies. Understandings reached among the leaders alone can prove to be of limited impact and of short duration, or even to be based on mutual misinterpretation, unless they are recorded, if possible in the form of public commitments. To attempt to reach conclusions on sensitive subjects in the short timespan of the summit itself is a risky procedure; the ground still needs to be prepared in advance, so that differences can be narrowed and subjects where the gap remains too wide can be excluded. Finally, in the effort to avoid arousing undue expectations, the summits may provide an inadequate response to the severe difficulties which beset the world.

The best format for future summits, therefore, would be one which can reconcile maximum scope for informal direct exchanges with the incentive to reach common ground on major issues and the means of expressing a consensus achieved. It is necessary to hold back the growth of bureaucratic apparatus, while creating the right framework for the leaders to exercise their unique capabilities – for integrating varied subjects, balancing domestic and external pressures, and exercising high-level political authority. The next sections of this chapter will suggest how this might be done.

The selection of economic subjects
If the summits are to achieve their full potential, the leaders ought to be able to reach joint commitments among themselves on certain subjects and to express these publicly. But in the time available the leaders can discuss in depth, and decide on, only one major problem, or at most two. It is therefore important to select with the greatest care the central problem or problems on which commitments might be sought and to limit their number rigorously; this should be a key task for the sherpas.

In some years the problem may be a single-issue one, which would dominate the summit like exchange rates at Rambouillet and energy at Tokyo. But often such single-issue problems, however important, will not make the best use of the capacities of the leaders to integrate different subjects and reconcile domestic and external considerations. The Bonn summit shows how the heads of government could strike bargains across issues and find a balance where the Americans moved in one field, the Germans in another, and the Japanese in a third. The sherpas could look deliberately for a central problem for each summit which provided similar opportunities for the leaders to achieve balancing commitments. (A number of such problems are suggested later in this chapter as meriting summit treatment later in the 1980s.) Once the sherpas have made their choice, it is essential to resist the temptation to add items to the agenda for the benefit of stimulating the bureaucratic machine lower down in the participating countries. Topics not meriting top-level treatment should be kept out, wherever possible, and discussion of a subject at the summit on one occasion – like, for example, illicit practices in trade in 1977 – should not mean that it necessarily returns to that level again.

It is impossible in practice to prevent participants from raising in the preparations, or at the summit itself, whatever subjects are closest to their preoccupations, both economic and political. Nor should the sole annual meeting of the leaders be limited to discussing a single complex of problems. The leaders would of course consider a range of other issues more informally, though this should be without the express intention that these exchanges will lead to visible commitments.

With such an approach it should be possible to lighten the work of the sherpas. The papers which used to be prepared on individual issues tended, over time, to lead to congestion at the summit itself, since each had to be matched by a passage in the declaration, whether the leaders discussed the issue or not. These subject papers could fall away and preparation be concentrated on a single 'thematic' paper, like that produced before Williamsburg. This could serve not only as a focus for discussion on those selected problems where commitments are sought but also provide background for the more informal exchanges, even though its preparation may be more difficult in future than it was before Williamsburg.

The summit declarations could similarly be lightened. Some agreed statement is necessary to give expression to the consensus reached and to provide a standard against which subsequent observance of summit commitments can be judged. But the declaration does not have to cover all economic subjects just because the responsibilities of the leaders are comprehensive. It could focus on those economic problems where new conclusions or commitments have been reached, as is the current practice with foreign policy subjects at the summits. The endorsement or repetition of known positions for the record on other issues could be omitted or reduced.

This approach could have implications for the summits' timing and location. It is difficult under present circumstances to envisage more than one seven-power summit per year, since the growth of heads-of-government meetings of all kinds already encroaches seriously on the time available to the leaders.[3] The summits have come to be held every summer, and if they are not to go beyond informal exchanges there would be no reason to change this regular annual timing. But if visible commitments are to be sought and expressed, there might be a stronger case for timing the summit at that moment in the year when the leaders could make their maximum contribution to resolving the chosen problem, in the light of international discussion in other organisations or the evolution of domestic opinion. In 1978, for example, the Germans resisted pressure to hold the Bonn summit earlier in the year than July, which would have been premature for them. In 1982 several participants thought the Versailles summit would have been more productive if held in September rather than June. For reasons like these there might be advantage in shortening the interval between fixing the date and holding the summit itself, to allow more flexibility in the timing. This would have the drawback that the host country might be prevented from choosing a special site away from the capital where all could be lodged under one roof, since such a location would probably have to be booked long in advance. But in practice the most productive summits have often been those held at work-a-day sites in capitals, like London (1977), Bonn, and Tokyo.

The treatment of political issues
Venice and Williamsburg proved both the necessity and the merit of treating political subjects at the seven-power summits in a more extensive and formal way than just by spontaneous conversations over meals. In fact, in each of the ten years since 1974, the leaders of the major Western powers took part in multilateral gatherings concerned with political and security issues. There were five NATO summits (1974, 1975, 1977, 1978, and 1982) plus the Guadeloupe four-power meeting of 1979; the remaining four years – 1976, 1980, 1981, and 1983 – were those when political discussion was particularly important at the seven-power summits. The heads of government clearly felt the need to come together at fairly frequent intervals to consider political and security issues.

The seven-power meetings provide opportunities both to combine direct personal exchanges and formal conclusions, while NATO summits do not, as chapter 9 explained. But the benefits of political discussion at the summits have been limited hitherto by the ad hoc and unpredictable procedures. Too often the leaders concentrated on the crisis of the moment, rather than on fundamental issues which deserved top-level treatment. It would be worth selecting foreign policy items in advance of the summit with the same care as economic ones. Those expected to lead to formal public conclusions should be strictly limited in number, though informal exchanges could cover a wider range. When complex or sensitive issues are to be considered, like arms control, the leaders would benefit here also from a 'thematic' paper to focus the discussion and warn them of any pitfalls. It seems strange that preparation before seven-power summits has been vestigial in this field, compared with the meticulous work in advance of NATO summits. The summits would still have to react to crises or disasters which flared up just at the time when they were meeting; but they should not leave the impression that these were the only foreign policy subjects to which they gave their attention.

Political and economic preparation for the summits should in future fit closer together. It is not possible in every summit country to have a sherpa like the British Secretary of the Cabinet, who could handle equally well economic and political items. But, whatever the national structure, the sherpas should always keep in mind the interaction and relative priorities in the two fields. The allocation of time at the summits as between economic and foreign policy subjects would vary from year to year. There might be less need for foreign policy conclusions at the seven-power summit if a NATO summit were also planned. But both the political background of the present leaders and the unsettled state of the world would suggest that the summit format for the 1980s should allow for up to half the time available being devoted to foreign policy subjects.

There is, however, a danger of the summits becoming overloaded with too many subjects. In the past, when the leaders gave substantial attention to foreign policy issues, as at Venice and Williamsburg, the economic discussions were curtailed. For this reason there is a strong case for making the summits themselves last rather longer. Two days allow barely adequate time for serious discussion. An extra day would make it easier to do justice to both economic and political questions. Past experience suggests that there should be no problem about adding a third day to the summit. In 1977, for example, most of the leaders stayed in London for four consecutive days, to cover first an economic and then a NATO summit. The US President has usually combined the summit with a bilateral visit to the host country.

On a revised timetable the leaders might gather in the late afternoon of Friday, in time for a first working session followed by dinner. They would then have two full days for discussions on Saturday and Sunday. A final session among the leaders on Monday morning would complete the texts of the declaration, and would be followed by the closing press conference. The extra time available could help to build up an easy and fruitful atmosphere for informal discussion. The timetable would allow for tête-à-tête sessions among the heads of government which are clearly welcomed by the participants; these could be followed, as at Williamsburg and in bilateral summits between European countries, by plenary meetings at which any consensus which emerged among the leaders themselves could be communicated more widely. Finally, it would be easier, with more time, to fit in the bilateral meetings which are an essential complement to the summit.

External relations

The summits of recent years seem to have lost their earlier capacity to invigorate other international organisations, tending instead to create their own special groups which duplicated the work of existing bodies. A revised summit format should seek to correct this trend, in the interests of reducing bureaucracy in the summit process, restoring morale in the existing organisations, and improving relations between the two.

As a first step, future summits could adopt the principle of fore-swearing the creation of seven-power subordinate groups. Existing groups could be wound up or merged with wider organisations. The energy group created in 1979 and 1980, for example, need not be revived – and the problem of France's absence from the IEA should be handled from within the Community. The technology group should be integrated with the OECD. The 'Quadrilateral', which brings together ministers of trade, should, if maintained, operate as necessary on the margins of the GATT. The multilateral surveillance group should be linked with the IMF.

If the summits became more active in reaching visible commitments, this could revive the anxieties of those countries not present. More extensive discussion of political and security issues could aggravate this problem, and so the summit governments should be more systematic in consulting and reassuring non-participating countries and other international organisations. In the Community the habit of holding a European Council meeting just before the summit could usefully be revived. The country holding the EC presidency should be more active in discharging its Community responsibilities instead of leaving it all to the Commission.[4] Otherwise, the host country for each summit should have a particular responsibility for keeping non-participants in touch and there should be close bilateral contacts with key governments on political as well as economic issues.

There should also be an informal but predictable cycle of consulta-tions with the OECD, IMF, GATT, and related organisations on economic issues and with NATO on relevant political and security issues. On occasion, these bodies could be called upon to help in the summit preparations. If, for example, the central problem foreseen for the summit was the single issue of energy, a report from the IEA and OECD could be a useful input. Any summit follow-up should always be entrusted to the responsible international organisations. There should be thorough briefings in each of these, covering the results of the summit and its consequences for the organisation concerned, rather than allowing the members and the staff to find out through the media what happened at the summit.

Improved public presentation of the summits would also be necessary, since over the years the summits have become, in some sense, the prisoners of the media. It would never be possible to isolate the summits from press attention; but some of the consequent problems could be mitigated, in a number of ways. One way would be to cut down the theatrical trappings of the summits, which make the media present them as spectacles rather than serious meetings. Second, the participants should recognise the danger of allowing the press to dictate events at the summit. Full advance briefing makes the most of the educative role of the summits. But it also becomes harder to modify a position in negotiation when this has already been announced in public.[5] Finally, it would be essential to avoid every suggestion that the participants regard summitry as a competitive rather than a cooperative activity. The media will inevitably reflect and exaggerate a 'winners and losers' mentality, with damaging results, as after Ottawa and Versailles. Government spokesmen must always stress that the success of the summit depends on the extent of the common ground achieved.

Issues for future summits

This chapter will not attempt a comprehensive forecast of the major issues which might come before the summits of the middle and late 1980s. Such a prediction would not be realistic in the present disturbed times. The international financial and banking system, for example, clearly faces a period of severe strain. The summits are not likely to become deeply involved in this field, as long as the focus is on financial rescue operations involving delicate, largely unpublicised negotiations between creditor and debtor governments and commercial and central banks. But the summits might have a role if leading Western governments should decide that major debt reconstruction was necessary. Similarly, energy does not seem likely to be a major summit subject for some years, while the IEA and the Community remain vigilant in reminding governments of their commitments to energy conservation and the development of new sources. But a further disruption in oil supplies, provoked by another political upheaval, might cause the summits to become deeply involved once again.

The intention is rather to identify a limited number of subjects which might deserve to be selected as the central problem for a future summit, leading to fairly precise and visible commitments by the participants. These subjects have been chosen because they provide the opportunity for bargains and balanced undertakings between different issues, which only heads of government can articulate: because they call for the reconciliation of sensitive domestic and external pressures; and because only the authority exercised by the leaders themselves could produce movement at lower levels. The first and third of the proposed subjects have been touched on by earlier summits, but now deserve more concentrated attention; the second covers issues where the summits have successfully intervened in the past. Finally, there are some suggestions for political subjects for future summits.

Sustaining economic recovery

The summits from Williamsburg onwards would have the same objective as the earliest summits: to promote and sustain a durable, non-inflationary recovery. Hitherto the summits approached this task by one of two routes: Keynesian demand management, whose zenith was in 1977 and 1978; and the monetarist approach largely prevalent since then.

The Bonn summit produced a coherent set of demand management measures, as part of a wider package. This was thrown off course by the disruption of the oil crisis and by the consequences of neglecting inflation over a longer period. But the technique of concerted action affecting demand was worked out during the first four summits (with support from the OECD and the Community) and could be revived should the prevailing economic philosophy change.

Concerted action through the monetarist approach has so far eluded the summits, because of differences, mainly between the United States and Europe, over methods rather than objectives. The multilateral surveillance group created at Versailles in 1982 probably provides a better framework than the summit itself for resolving these differences and reaching agreement on new concepts such as 'world money supply'. This is because finance ministers can meet more often than the leaders, they have more technical expertise and support, and their discussions can take place out of the public eye. However, they lack the political authority of the leaders and it is likely that the issues would have to come back to summit level again before any effective concerted action package could be agreed based on the monetarist approach.

But there is a third element in sustaining recovery which hitherto the summits have rather neglected but which deserves more attention in future. This concerns the structural adaptation of the participants' economies which would be needed to make the revival durable. This would entail, in the first place, comparative discussion of industrial support policies, including subsidies and fiscal aids, many of which could be criticised as obstacles to competition and the free market. It would also involve looking at the structures of labour markets. It is clear that somewhat faster growth would not alone absorb present levels of unemployment. Meanwhile, the financial burden of unemployment benefit is disturbing summit governments, already aware of the rising need for social spending on behalf of an ageing population. Another aspect could be the pattern of investment in the participating countries, where at present savings are attracted into financial assets at the expense of productive investment, especially in key areas like energy and high technology. Many of these structural issues involve an element of protection, whether overt or concealed, which needs to be exposed and made subject to market pressures.

Structural adaptation policies have been raised in the preparations for earlier summits and mentioned in the declarations. The Bonn summit of 1978 commended the OECD's positive adjustment programme; there were references in the Tokyo and Venice declarations to the need for structural changes; the French initiative on technology at Versailles was intended as a contribution to a debate of this kind. But structural adjustment issues have never led to clear commitments at the summits, though there are several reasons why they call for treatment at this level. They are the responsibility of many different departments in each country and bring together, sometimes under severe tension, domestic pressures and international obligations. Concerted action is needed, in that measures by several countries together, for example to reduce obstacles to competition, would benefit them all, but any one government would hesitate to act alone without the assurance that its partners were doing likewise. Finally, different actions would be needed by different countries to produce a balanced package of undertakings. Obstacles to competition in European countries, for example, often lie in the activities of public enterprises; in the United States they are found in the role of the courts and in judicial restraints; in Japan they appear in the circuits of distribution.

There are many potential difficulties. This subject would require careful handling within the Community, as many of the issues are on the borderline of Community competence. It would require more extensive preparation among the Europeans than has been the practice recently. Many of the issues are fairly new to wider international treatment. But considerable work has been done by the OECD; and one purpose of the summit's involvement could be to invigorate the OECD's role in this area – and the OECD might in its turn contribute to summit preparation. Above all, the issues are complex – even more than those of demand management or monetary control – and politically sensitive while growth is still low and unemployment high. But without the necessary structural adaptation, the economic recovery which began in 1983, and its successors, could prove weak and short-lived.

Trade and monetary negotiations

One or more future summits could take as their objective the restoration of order in the international trade and monetary system. Oil crisis and recession have made it natural to resort to short-term, de facto expedients, to prevent a total breakdown. But a return to more clearly defined rules and to respect for contractual obligations would be needed to reinforce any economic recovery.

The external counterpart of action by summit countries to remove domestic obstacles to competition could be commitments to strengthen the international trading system. Promises at successive summits to check or reverse protectionism by dismantling trade barriers have not proved adequate. A stronger and more lasting incentive to remove trade restrictions is required. This might be provided by further rounds of formal negotiations in the GATT in the course of the 1980s. These might not resemble earlier rounds. The subjects – services, high technology, agriculture – would be more complex and need more varied treatment. But they all should be brought within a contractual framework, which only the GATT could provide. For this purpose, repeated high-level pressure from the summits over several years might be needed to keep up the momentum.

The summits, as in past years, need not go deeply into the detail. But the participants could assert certain basic objectives and principles – to be converted into action through the GATT framework. In particular, they could restore the principle of non-discrimination in international trade and move away from the practice of market–sharing arrangements, which form a particular temptation to the summit countries, representing over 60 per cent of all international trade. These have often been introduced in response to competition from low-cost imports from newly industrialising countries. Exports from these countries have also been penalised if they do not offer reciprocity. But this, in the long run, is self-defeating. Necessary structural adjustment in the developed countries is delayed; and the developing countries are unable to increase the export earnings they need to service their often crippling debts and restore their financial health.

The international monetary system is also in serious need of overhaul. The regime of floating exchange rates in operation since 1973 has not fulfilled its promise. Instead of insulating countries from the effects of others' actions, it exaggerates the volatility in major exchange rates which is provoked by shifts in economic policies and performance. But the technical problems facing any attempt to restore greater order to the system are stupendous. The sheer size of international monetary movements can easily sweep away any attempts at coordinated intervention by central banks, as was demonstrated once again in August 1983. In the past decade, the dollar has moved in such huge zig-zags, appreciating by about 50 per cent against the Deutschmark between 1979 and 1983, that no one could predict what is a reasonable equilibrium level.

Here too, arguably only a push from the very top could generate the political determination necessary to grapple with these problems. The single lasting innovation on the monetary scene since 1975 – the EMS – came about because of the political resolve of President Giscard and Chancellor Schmidt. This need for a high-level impulse lay behind President Mitterrand's monetary initiative before Williamsburg. The reaction at the summit itself to this was hesitant and qualified. On the other hand, the process of multilateral surveillance may promote, over the years, a genuine convergence of policy leading to greater underlying exchange rate stability. That could give the opportunity for the summits to launch, with conviction, the movement back to a more stable monetary system based on international rules and commitments.

There is a certain symmetry between the respective positions of the Europeans and the Americans in the trade and monetary fields. The European Community has adopted a cautious, even defensive attitude to trade negotiations as compared with the Americans. The need to reconcile the differing objectives of the member states has often made it hard for the Community to take the initiative. However, this attitude to trade negotiations allows protectionist pressures to build up not only in Europe but also in the United States, where only the counter-pressure of continuous negotiation can keep them in check. In the monetary field, on the other hand, progress requires a change of heart by the United States. Throughout the period covered by the summits the Americans have been reluctant to undertake any international obligations with regard to the dollar. This has been most conspicuous in recent years. But even in 1978, when the Carter Administration adopted an active intervention policy, it made its support arrangements on a bilateral and ad hoc basis.

In this context, the idea launched before Williamsburg that trade and financial issues should on occasion be discussed together was a good one and could be important for the future. Such discussion should not be confined to the interaction of trade and debt problems for the developing countries; it should also consider the interaction of monetary instability on trade flows and investment. The procedural difficulty over Community competence in trade, but not in finance, should not be made a decisive obstacle. Since this procedure crosses normal departmental boundaries, it might need periodic encouragement in future from summit level. Furthermore, the summits themselves should consider these issues in relation to one another. The summit leaders would not only give separate impulses to trade and to monetary negotiations. They might be able to prepare a package in which European moves on trade would be matched by US moves in the monetary field, leading to a decisive advance in both areas.

The developing countries

A third central problem for a summit of the 1980s could be to work out an approach to the developing countries which matches better the nature and scale of their problems. In general, previous summits found it hard to come to grips with this inchoate subject, with its intractable difficulties both of substance and procedure.

The difficulties of substance vary by country and by region. Middle-income countries, notably in Latin America, face problems which come from trying to grow too fast – excessive levels of debt and inadequate earnings from their exports. Apart from rescheduling and other immediate financial measures, these countries need above all improved access for their exports, whether manufactures or processed agricultural products, as the only long-term prospect of relieving the burden of debt. Otherwise, continued deflation, to satisfy their creditors, would produce intolerable political strains.

The problem for low-income countries – especially in sub-Saharan Africa – has been that they are not growing at all. In the African countries population growth more than absorbed the expansion of GDP in the 1970s and will probably do so again in the 1980s.[6] Low-income countries gained negligible benefits from trade in the 1970s, and in 1981 and 1982 the prices of the commodities they export fell to their lowest level, in real terms, for 30 years. If the low-income countries are to become capable of competing internationally and to begin catching up on the road to development, they would require not only domestic adaptation of their economies but also substantial help from outside. Otherwise some will begin to disintegrate. Low-income countries can attract little foreign private capital. With oil prices falling, OPEC will no longer be a major provider. Western governments are the only available source of the help that is needed, in the form of technical advice and training as well as capital for investment.

Improved trade access and increased aid for developing countries compete with domestic demands in all the summit countries. The argument from mutual benefit carries some weight. But it is weak for the low-income countries, who have little to offer, while competition from middle-income countries is unwelcome when unemployment is high. Only the heads of government would have the capacity to balance economic, political, and humanitarian considerations and give an impulse to more generous policies, now that the strains of recession are easing. Only the leaders at the summit could make this a joint commitment of the major Western countries, reflecting a sense of responsibility to make the open economic system work not only for their own peoples, but for all, even the poorest.

There is a possibility here for balanced commitments between the various summit participants. The Europeans might be readier to respond to US suggestions for a special round of trade negotiations for the developing countries if the United States, for its part, could guarantee its contributions to the replenishments needed for the World Bank and IDA. Just as trade measures have to be negotiated multilaterally, so multilateral development finance has many advantages, in that the institutions can more easily link their funds to serious adaptation programmes than donor governments can. The summits should therefore continue to do what thay can to help US Administrations overcome their persistent difficulties with Congressional authority for multilateral contributions.

In addition, however, the summit participants might want to look for ways which would highlight and maintain their personal commitment both to improving trade access and additional aid finance and to ensuring that developing countries made good use of what was on offer. Here the summit leaders might consider seeking the direct participation of heads of state and government of developing countries themselves – thus short-circuiting the procedural difficulties which arise from the pattern of formal intergroup discussions in the North–South dialogue. The seven leaders, with the Community, might, for example, consider inviting a small group of their counterparts from developing countries to join them for part of a summit meeting. There would be controversy, inevitably, over the choice of those who came and resistance from those who argued that the only acceptable approach to the problems of the Third World was one in which all countries participated. It would be wise to involve the development institutions both at the level of practical execution and to encourage comparable efforts by other aid donors both in the OECD and in OPEC. But unless the heads of government can give a decisive lead in these issues, many developing countries may be worse off in 1990 than they were ten years before, despite their own best efforts.

Political subjects

The practice and the achievements of earlier summits are a less reliable guide to future discussions of foreign policy issues than they are for economic ones. There is simply less to go on. Nevertheless it is clear, from the experience of Venice and Williamsburg at least, that certain issues deserve treatment at summit level because of their intrinsic importance, being central to the security of the West and the search for peaceful conditions in the world at large. Because of their complexity and political sensitivity, these issues also require careful advance preparation if summit discussion is to produce clear conclusions, with a lasting impact on the attitudes of the participants and other countries.

Aspects of East–West relations clearly have a strong claim to a place on the summit agenda on these grounds and this is likely to grow stronger as the 1980s unfold. The evolution in the Japanese approach, marked at Williamsburg by a readiness to consider security subjects for the first time, has made this problem much easier to handle at the summits. There would be a recurrent need in the future to address arms control and deployment issues, in the context of INF, START, and related negotiations, so as to ensure the closest agreement between the summit countries at every stage and to reduce the opportunities for the Russians to sow discord. More generally, the summit leaders could assess at intervals the direction of Soviet foreign policy and consider the right Western approach. They should not take regional problems, such as those which arise in Eastern Europe, Central America, or the Caribbean, as the starting point, but should try to fit such problems into a picture of Soviet intentions worldwide. This could help the West to react more coherently to any future Soviet adventures like the invasion of Afghanistan, and to avoid the sort of difficulties which arose earlier over economic relations with the Soviet Union.

A second priority subject should be the Middle East, including the Arab–Israel dispute and the situation in the Gulf. This will clearly remain a highly sensitive and unsettled region. In the 1970s it was often a cause of friction within the West, for example after the war of 1973 and the Camp David agreements of 1978; there is always a danger of such friction recurring. In 1982 and 1983, however, the United States and the Europeans worked together much more closely, in Sinai and in Lebanon. Moreover, the region is of direct interest to Japan. There would be great merit in using the summit to consolidate the cooperation among the participants, and to promote the search for durable peaceful settlements.

These two subjects deserve inclusion for their political importance alone, though they may not call for conclusions from the summit every year. Other subjects should be chosen for treatment by the heads of government where economic and foreign policy considerations need to be fitted together. The summit leaders are uniquely equipped to achieve this, even though they have rarely done so in foreign policy discussion in the past. This approach would affect not only the choice of subject, but the perspective in which it is considered. This perspective is clearly relevant to the Middle East, because of the link between political instability and the disruption of oil supplies. The same perspective could be applied to debt problems, where, for example, governments of deeply indebted countries might be led into rash external adventures by the desire to distract attention from painful economic adjustment at home. There might even be a case for returning to the question of East–West economic relations on the basis of an agreed assessment of Soviet intentions.

Most important, the summit might look at the central issue of the interaction of economic and political, including security, relations among the participating countries themselves. This might help to overcome the traditional French resistance to formal foreign policy exchanges at the summit. President Mitterrand has argued, since taking office, that 'political solidarity among the seven, especially against the Soviet threat, has no sense unless based on solidarity in the economic field'.[7] Summit discussions on issues such as defence burden-sharing or extraterritoriality might be uncomfortable for all the participants. But if the leaders broach these sensitive subjects directly among themselves, this could strengthen the resistance to isolationist, inward-looking forces in the United States, Europe, or Japan in political relations, just as the economic exchanges at the summit have helped to ward off protectionist pressures.

Final reflections

The summits first began in 1975 for three different reasons, here recalled in reverse order from their initial statement in chapter 1: (a) to meet the wish of certain leaders, notably Giscard and Schmidt, to reverse the growing bureaucracy in international relations and to promote direct contacts in a limited circle; (b) to promote adaptation to the shifting power balance between the United States, Japan, and the members of the European Community, as the earlier hegemony of the United States declined; (c) to find a way to disentangle and to reconcile the conflicting pressures of foreign and domestic politics which flowed from economic interdependence. All three reasons remain valid in 1983 and are likely to remain valid for the future.

As for the first, much of the selective and personal character of the summits still survives their conversion into a regular event. They have a flexibility that other meetings cannot match. Even so, Rambouillet, the very first summit, showed that careful advance preparation was needed to produce satisfactory and lasting results. The summits, furthermore, should invigorate and not seek to replace existing organisations.

The first cycle of summits became cluttered and bureaucratic and this proved hard to correct. The danger now may be that future summits go too far in the other direction. For all the merits of personal exchanges, these can be inconclusive, transitory, and prone to misinterpretation. The objective should be to organise future summits so as to promote consensus in those areas where only the leaders can produce results and to record the outcome clearly as a standard for future action. This would ensure that the summit process remained vigorous and relevant, though none of the founding leaders survived.

As for the second reason, the adaptation process has proved uneven. One success has been to bring Japan firmly into the circle of Western consultations. This was not a steady progress, partly because Japanese leaders changed so often. But there has been a definite advance over time, most visible in political discussions at the summits, and matched by an evolution in Japanese public opinion. This greater involvement in political questions should help to avoid any temptation among the others to 'gang up' against Japan over economic differences.

The United States has adapted erratically. Presidents Ford and Carter were reconciled to the idea that the Europeans and Japan might advance, over time, towards equal status with the United States. But President Reagan is not so reconciled and seeks to restore the US leadership role. This was a welcome change after President Carter's hesitation, but it led to friction at the highest level, for example over budgetary policy and East–West economic relations. But despite some bad patches, for example the dispute over the Soviet gas pipeline, which gave Versailles a bad reputation, the summits remain an essential instrument for helping to prevent specific transatlantic differences from obscuring basic common interests.

The Europeans, for their part, have not been able to deploy as much collective strength through the summits as they hoped. This has largely been because of the difficulty of strengthening the internal cohesion of the Community. Even so, the summits have created an effective and practical link between the United States and the Community at the highest level, which provides a good basis for working together in the future.

As for the third reason for the summits, the management of inter-dependence, even by the heads of government, was bound to be diffi-cult. There were setbacks caused by the second oil crisis, while the system has been severely tested by prolonged recession. But over the years the leaders have often been able to work out mutually reinforcing approaches to economic management, whether in the form of balanced, interlocking policy actions or international solidarity in carrying through measures unpopular at home. The objectives remain durable, non-inflationary growth and the preservation of the open international economic system. In future, the summits might best contribute to these aims by promoting the structural adaptation of the participating econ-omies, especially through collective action to remove obstacles to the free market; by trying to restore greater order, through negotiations, to international trade and monetary relations; and by working out a more imaginative approach to the problems of developing countries, especi-ally the poorest.

The summits were not at first expected to play any formal role in non-economic matters and discussed them only on the side. As the external political environment grew worse, the summits became obliged to react; they did so in an ad hoc fashion, though sometimes with considerable success. A fourth justification for the summits in the

1980s, to be added to the original three, would be the need for regular high-level discussion of political and security matters, for example to reinforce solidarity among the allies in resisting Soviet encroachment and to promote the search for peace in the Middle East. A new task for the future should be to put foreign policy discussion at the summit on a more reliable footing, with more careful selection of topics and adequate preparation, comparable to what is done for economic issues. Instead of discussing foreign policy and economic issues separately, from now on the summits should do more to recognise and reflect the links between them.

Summitry all too easily attracts criticism. People inevitably expect more of their leaders than the leaders can reasonably deliver. Although the summit leaders' intentions have been good, their collective judgment has sometimes been adrift. On occasion the agreements reached have been too fragile to survive or the participants have not lived up to their commitments. But, despite all these imperfections, it would be a great setback if this practice of high-level consultation were allowed to lapse or if it failed in future to achieve its full potential. Heads of government cannot achieve miracles. If they attempt too much, they may fall short. But there are some problems which none but they can tackle and which they can only solve if they work together.

Notes

Chapter 1 Introduction

1 As quoted in David Watt, 'Pros and Cons of Political Summitry', *Financial Times*, 29 April 1977.

2 Richard N. Cooper, 'Economic Interdependence and Foreign Policy in the Seventies', *World Politics*, vol. 24 (January 1972), p. 164. Subsequent work on the political dimension of economic interdependence includes Miriam Camps, *The Management of Interdependence: A Preliminary View* (New York: Council on Foreign Relations, 1974); Andrew Shonfield and others, *International Economic Relations of the Western World, 1959–1971* (London: Oxford University Press, for the Royal Institute of International Affairs, 1976), esp. vol. 1, pp. 93–137; Robert O. Keohane and Joseph S. Nye, Jr, *Power and Interdependence: World Politics in Transition* (Boston: Little, Brown, 1977); Fred Hirsch and Michael Doyle, 'Politicization in the World Economy: Necessary Conditions for an International Economic Order', in Fred Hirsch, Michael Doyle, and Edward L. Morse, *Alternatives to Monetary Disorder* (New York: McGraw-Hill, 1977); Robert J. Gordon and Jacques Pelkmans, *Challenges to Interdependent Economies: The Industrial West in the Coming Decade* (New York: McGraw-Hill, 1979); and Miriam Camps and Catherine Gwin, *Collective Management: The Reform of Global Economic Organizations* (New York: McGraw-Hill, 1981).

3 Lester R. Brown, *World Without Borders: The Interdependence of Nations* (New York: Foreign Policy Association, Headline Series, 1972).

4 Karl Kaiser, 'Transnational Relations as a Threat to the Democratic Process', in Robert O. Keohane and Joseph S. Nye, Jr, eds, *Transnational Relations and World Politics* (Cambridge, Mass.: Harvard University Press, 1972), pp. 356–70.

5 Cooper, 'Economic Interdependence and Foreign Policy in the Seventies', p. 179.

6 The literature on this issue is quite large. See, for example, Marina v.N. Whitman, *Reflections of Interdependence: Issues for Economic Theory and U.S. Policy* (Pittsburgh: University of Pittsburgh Press, 1979); Ralph C. Bryant, *Money and Monetary Policy in Interdependent Nations* (Washington, D.C.: Brookings Institution, 1980); Richard N. Cooper, 'Economic Interdependence and Coordination of Economic Policies', in Ronald Jones and Peter B. Kenen, eds, *Handbook for International Economy* (New York: North Holland, 1984); and the works collected in Rudiger Dornbusch and Jacob A. Frenkel, eds, *International Economic Policy: Theory and Evidence* (Baltimore: Johns Hopkins University Press, 1979). Some monetarist theorists of the 'rational expectations' school are sceptical about the utility of international policy coordination.

7 Camps, *The Management of Interdependence*, p. 43, as cited in Joan Edelman Spero, *The Politics of International Economic Relations*, 2nd edn (New York: St Martin's Press, 1981), p. 14.

8 See, for example, Bryant, *Money and Monetary Policy in Interdependent*

Nations, esp. pp. 453–81; Cooper, 'Economic Interdependence and Coordination of Economic Policies', and the works cited therein; Robert O. Keohane, 'U.S. Foreign Economic Policy Toward Other Advanced Capitalist States', in Kenneth A. Oye, Donald Rothchild, and Robert J. Lieber, eds, *Eagle Entangled: U.S. Foreign Policy in a Complex World* (New York: Longman, 1979), pp. 107–9; Arthur A. Stein, 'Coordination and Collaboration: Regimes in an Anarchic World', *International Organization*, vol. 36 (Spring 1982), pp. 299–324.

9   Keohane and Nye, *Power and Interdependence*, p. 226.

10   Richard N. Cooper, *The Economics of Interdependence: Economic Policy in the Atlantic Community* (New York: McGraw-Hill, 1968), pp. 170–2.

11   The original 'prisoner's dilemma' refers to a pair of accomplices held separately, each of whom is told that if he confesses and implicates his partner, he will escape punishment, but if he is silent, while his partner confesses, he will be severely punished. If both prisoners remain silent, they will both be let off lightly, but unable to coordinate their stories, each has a powerful incentive to defect, and thus both end up being punished.

12   The classic analysis of this dilemma is Mancur Olson, *The Logic of Collective Action* (Cambridge, Mass.: Harvard University Press, 1965).

13   Charles P. Kindleberger, *The World in Depression, 1929–1939* (Berkeley, California: University of California Press, 1973), p. 305 (emphasis added). See also Marina v.N. Whitman, 'Leadership without Hegemony', *Foreign Policy*, no. 20 (1975), pp. 138–64; Robert Gilpin, *U.S. Power and the Multinational Corporation: The Political Economy of Foreign Direct Investment* (New York: Basic Books, 1975); Stephen D. Krasner, 'State Power and the Structure of International Trade', *World Politics*, vol. 28 (1976), pp. 317–47; Robert O. Keohane, 'The Theory of Hegemonic Stability and Changes in International Economic Regimes, 1967–1977', in Ole R. Holsti, Randolph M. Siverson, and Alexander L. George, eds, *Change in the International System* (Boulder, Colorado: Westview Press, 1980), pp. 131–62. See also Robert O. Keohane, *Beyond Hegemony: Cooperation and Discord in the World Political Economy* (Princeton, N.J.: Princeton University Press, 1984).

14   Norman Frohlich, Joe Oppenheimer, and Oran Young, *Political Leadership and Collective Goods* (Princeton, N.J.: Princeton University Press, 1971).

15   Richard Rosecrance, ed., *America as an Ordinary Country: U.S. Foreign Policy in the Future* (Ithaca, N.Y.: Cornell University Press, 1976). See also David P. Calleo and Benjamin M. Rowland, *America and the World Political Economy: Atlantic Dreams and National Realities* (Bloomington, Indiana: Indiana University Press, 1973).

16   This was the alternative that Charles Kindleberger, reflecting on the lessons of the 1930s, found most persuasive: *The World in Depression, 1929–1939*, p. 308.

17   Olson, *The Logic of Collective Action*, pp. 5–65, explains why small groups find it easier to solve public-goods problems than large ones.

18   On this complex issue, see Joel D. Aberbach, Robert D. Putnam, and Bert Rockman, *Bureaucrats and Politicians in Western Democracies* (Cambridge, Mass.: Harvard University Press, 1981).

19   Although the theoretical significance of international policy coordination is widely recognised, empirical scholarship on the Western summits is still rare. Relevant works include George de Menil and Anthony M. Solomon, *Economic*

Summitry (New York: Council on Foreign Relations, 1983); Elke Thiel, 'Economic Summits from Rambouillet to Venice', *Aussenpolitik*, vol. 32 (1981), pp. 3–14, and 'Economic Conflict Before and After Versailles', *Aussenpolitik*, vol. 33 (1982), pp. 356–69; Henry H. Fowler and W. Randolph Burgess, *Harmonizing Economic Policy: Summit Meetings and Collective Leadership: Report of the Atlantic Council's Working Group on Economic Policy* (Boulder, Colorado: Westview Press, 1977); Charles Robinson and William C. Turner, co-chairmen, Harald B. Malmgren, rapporteur, *Summit Meetings and Collective Leadership in the 1980s* (Washington, D.C.: Atlantic Council, 1980); J. Robert Schaetzel and H.B. Malmgren, 'Talking Heads', *Foreign Policy*, no. 39 (Summer 1980), pp. 130–42; Cesare Merlini, ed., *Western Summits and Europe: Rivalry, Cooperation, and Partnership* (London: Croom Helm, 1984). Several interesting works have appeared in German, French, and Japanese: Dieter Hiss, 'Weltwirtschaftsgipfel: Betrachtungen eines Insiders' [World Economic Summits: Observations of an Insider], in Joachim Frohn and Reiner Staeglin, eds. *Empirische Wirtschaftsforschung: Konzeptionen, Verfahren und Ergebnisse* (Berlin: Duncker and Humblot, 1980); Rainer Hellmann, *Weltwirtschaftsgipfel wozu?* [Whither Economic Summits?] (Baden-Baden: Nomos, 1982); Marie-Claude Smouts, 'Les Sommets des pays industrialisés', *Revue de Droit International*, 1980, pp. 668–85; George de Menil, 'De Rambouillet à Versailles: un bilan des sommets économiques', *Politique Étrangère*, no. 2 (June 1982), pp. 403–17; Yoichi Funabashi, *Philosophy of the Summits* [in Japanese] (Tokyo: Asahi Shinbun-sha, 1980).

Chapter 2 The Origins of the Summits

1   It is usual to refer to the major international organisations concerned with economic cooperation by their initials or other abbreviations, and this practice will be followed here. The most important are: the Organisation for Economic Cooperation and Development (OECD), the International Monetary Fund (IMF – also called 'the Fund'), and the General Agreement on Tariffs and Trade (GATT). Reference will also be made to the International Bank for Reconstruction and Development (World Bank), the International Energy Agency (IEA), the Organisation of Petroleum-Exporting Countries (OPEC), and various bodies in the United Nations (UN) family, in particular the United Nations Conference on Trade and Development (UNCTAD). The IMF and World Bank are often called the Bretton Woods institutions, after the site of the conference which created them in 1945. The role of all these bodies (except OPEC) in relation to the summits is discussed in chapter 9.

2   Henry Kissinger, *Years of Upheaval* (London: Weidenfeld, 1982), chs 5 and 16.

3   The improvement in Franco-American relations dates from mid-December 1974, when President Giscard and President Ford met at Martinique, just after the EEC summit in Paris and a bilateral meeting between Ford and Chancellor Schmidt. See below, p. 15, and George de Menil and Anthony M. Solomon, *Economic Summitry* (New York: Council on Foreign Relations, 1983), p. 13.

4   Apart from Germany, only Austria and Switzerland had single-figure inflation in 1974 and 1975, though it reached 9.5 per cent in Austria in 1974 and 9.8 per cent in Switzerland in 1975. Only Iceland, Portugal, and Turkey had higher inflation than the United Kingdom over those two years.

5   Notably Helmut Schmidt; see his article 'The Struggle for the World

Product: Politics between Power and Morals', *Foreign Affairs*, vol. 52 (1974), pp. 437–51.

6   Henry Kissinger, *The White House Years* (London: Weidenfeld, 1979), p. 958, and *Years of Upheaval*, pp. 181–6.

7   Henry Owen, 'Summitry Revisited', *Atlantic Monthly*, vol. 231, no. 3 (1973), pp. 6–7.

8   James Reston, 'A Chat with Giscard', *International Herald Tribune*, 16 June 1975.

9   Text of the Communiqué published in *The Times*, 17 December 1974.

10   Rainer Hellman, *Weltwirtschaftsgipfel wozu?* (Baden-Baden: Nomos, 1982), p. 14. See also Kissinger, *Years of Upheaval*, pp. 745–6.

11   *Le Monde*, *Financial Times*, 9 July 1975.

12   *The Times*, 28 July 1975, *Süddeutsche Zeitung*, 1 August 1975.

13   *The Times*, *Le Monde*, 2 August 1975.

14   *Japan Times*, 10 September 1975; *Financial Times*, 29 September 1975, where all the personal representatives are named.

15   Henry Kissinger, 'Saving the World Economy', *Newsweek*, 24 January 1983, p. 49.

16   *Guardian*, 15 August 1975; *New York Times*, 19 August 1975; *Le Monde*, 2 September 1975.

17   George Shultz and Kenneth Dam, *Economic Policy behind the Headlines* (New York: Norton, 1977), pp. 12–13. For contemporary references to Mr Shultz's role, see *Japan Times*, 10 September 1975, and *The Times*, 19 November 1975.

18   For a fuller analysis of the Library Group, see Robert D. Putnam, 'The Western Economic Summits: A Political Interpretation', in Cesare Merlini, ed., *Western Summits and Europe: Rivalry, Cooperation, and Partnership* (London: Croom Helm, 1984), pp. 43–89. See also Menil and Solomon, *Economic Summitry*, pp. 55–6.

19   Shultz and Dam, *Economic Policy*, p. 14.

20   Helmut Schmidt, 'Gipfeltreffen: Chancen und Gefahren', *Die Zeit*, 27 May 1983.

21   Giscard is quoted from *Figaro*, 12 November 1975, and *Economist*, 21 May 1983. See also Maurice Delarue in *Le Monde*, 18 July 1981, and Menil and Solomon, *Economic Summitry*, p. 56.

22   Schmidt is quoted from *Economist*, 29 September 1979, and *Die Zeit*, 27 May 1983. See also his introduction to *Weltwirtschaftsgipfel* (Bonn, 1983), the German translation of Menil and Solomon's book *Economic Summitry*, and *Economist*, 26 February 1983.

23   Harold Wilson, *Final Term: The Labour Government 1974–1976* (London: Weidenfeld, 1979), pp. 168, 184. Clyde Farnsworth, 'A Secret Society of Finance Ministers', *International Herald Tribune*, 8 May 1977.

24   George Shultz recalled his advice at a press conference given on 17 February 1983. See also *New York Times*, 3 November 1975.

25   Henry Kissinger, 'The Industrial Democracies and the Future', address delivered at Pittsburgh, 11 November 1975. Text in *Department of State Bulletin*, vol. 73 (July–December 1975), pp. 757–64.

26   *Le Monde*, 11 November 1975; *Japan Times*, 21 October 1975.

Chapter 3 Rambouillet and Puerto Rico, 1975–6

1   For an insider's account of this summit, see Harold Wilson, *Final Term: The Labour Government 1974—1976* (London: Weidenfeld, 1979), pp. 184–8. The UK delegation (which included the author in a lowly capacity) was allocated Napoleon's bathroom as one of its offices.

2   For reports of these preparatory meetings and their work, see George Shultz and Kenneth Dam, *Economic Policy behind the Headlines* (New York: Norton, 1977) p. 13; *Le Monde*, 8 October, 16/17 November 1975; *New York Times*, 9 November 1975; *The Times*, 12 November 1975. The New York meeting was held in the penthouse of the Carlton Hotel and the personal representatives were thereafter called the Carlton Group until the term 'sherpas' became current in 1977 (see ch. 4 below).

3   *Corriere della Sera*, 5 October 1975; *Le Monde*, 1 November 1975; *Guardian*, 12 November 1975.

4   See *New York Times*, 19, 23 November 1975; *Guardian*, 12 December 1975. For the Group of Five meeting on board the presidential yacht *Sequoia*, see *Le Monde*, 1/2 September 1975.

5   *OECD Economic Outlook*, no. 18 (December 1975), p. 9. See also ibid., no. 17 (July 1975), p. 8.

6   Quoted in *Guardian*, 19 November 1975.

7   *The Times*, 22 October 1975; *Financial Times*, 5/6, 19 November 1975.

8   'A New World Economic Order', address by President Giscard at the École Polytechnique, 28 October 1975; English text from Information Service of French Embassy, London. President Giscard's interview with *Figaro*, 12 November 1975.

9   Robert Solomon, *The International Monetary System, 1945–1981* (New York: Harper & Row, 1982), especially pp. 270–4. He explains, *inter alia*, the role of the Group of Ten, composed of those OECD countries (actually eleven in number) who have committed themselves to provide supplementary finance to the IMF under certain conditions.

10   See, for example, Martin Feldstein, Chairman of the US Council of Economic Advisors, in *Economist*, 11 June 1983, p. 92.

11   House of Commons Official Record, vol. 899 (4 November 1975), columns 222–3.

12   *Financial Times*, 17 November 1975; *Economist*, 13 December 1975.

13   See Joan Pearce, *Subsidised Export Credit* (London: Royal Institute of International Affairs, 1980), p. 45.

14   Frédérick Pottier, 'La Rencontre de Rambouillet', *Politique Etrangère*, 1976, no. 1 (1976), p. 18.

15   Mr Miki, too, had hoped to bring new Japanese proposals to the summit, but was frustrated by his Finance Ministry. See *Le Monde*, 11 November; *Japan Times*, 9, 13 November 1975.

16   For the political discussion, see Wilson, *Final Term*, p. 186. For the full text of the Declaration, see *The Times*, 18 November 1975.

17   For the reactions of Ford and Giscard, see *New York Times*, 18 November 1975; *Le Monde*, 19 November 1975.

18   Andrew Shonfield, 'Can the Western Economic System Stand the Strain?', *The World Today*, May 1976, p. 172.

19   *Le Monde*, 20 November 1975.

20   See *New York Times*, 2 June 1976, for Greenspan initiative; *Figaro*, 22/23 May and *Financial Times*, 2 June, for early soundings; *Financial Times*, 4 June, for inflation worries; *Daily Telegraph*, 1 June and *Japan Times*, 4 June 1976, for the Italian angle.

21   *The Times*, 16 June 1976; *Financial Times*, 26 June 1976.

22   Belgium, exceptionally, attended the Versailles summit in 1982, as the country holding the presidency of the European Community, since none of the regular European participants held the presidency that year.

23   *OECD Economic Outlook*, no. 19 (July 1976), p. 5 ff.

24   Full text of the Declaration is in *The Times*, 30 June 1976. For comment, see *International Herald Tribune*, *Frankfurter Allgemeine Zeitung*, 30 June 1976; *Economist*, 3 July 1976. The local *San Juan Star* for 28 June carried the headline 'Summit Leaders Endorse Ford's Economic Policy'.

25   Pearce, *Subsidised Export Credit*, p. 46.

26   *Frankfurter Allgemeine Zeitung*, *Süddeutsche Zeitung*, 29 June 1976; *Le Monde*, 30 June 1976.

27   *New York Times*, *Observer*, 18 July 1976; Brent Scowcroft in *New York Times*, 4 August 1976; Giulio Andreotti, *Diari 1976—1979* (Milan: Rizzoli, 1981), pp. 20–4. According to one story, Sr Moro was invited to the lunch and was only absent by accident. But no doubt if he had been present at the table, the other four leaders would have found some other opportunity to discuss the Italian situation among themselves.

28   After a meeting in Pisa with Sr Andreotti on 1 December, President Giscard called for a summit in mid-1977. He was at once supported by his host and, after a short delay, by Herr Schmidt and Mr Callaghan. Mr Fukuda, the new Japanese Prime Minister, said he would be delighted if the meeting were held in Japan. *The Times*, 2 December 1976; *Guardian*, 4, 14 December 1976; *Japan Times*, 24 December 1976.

29   House of Commons Official Record, vol. 914 (29 June 1976), column 197.

Chapter 4 The Summit Becomes an Institution

1   Alexander Pope, *Imitations of Horace*, satire I, book II, line 127.

2   Former Trilateral Commissioners in the new Administration included President Carter, National Security Advisor Brzezinski, Secretary of State Vance, Secretary of Defense Brown, Secretary of the Treasury Blumenthal, as well as the three senior officials responsible for summit preparations, Ambassador Henry Owen, Under-Secretary of State Richard Cooper, and Under-Secretary of the Treasury Anthony Solomon.

3   See C. Fred Bergsten, Georges Berthoin, and Kinhide Mushakoji, 'The Reform of International Institutions (1976)', Egidio Ortona, J. Robert Schaetzel, and Nobuhiko Ushiba, 'The Problem of International Consultations (1976)', and Richard N. Cooper, Karl Kaiser, and Masataka Kosaka, 'Towards a Renovated International System', all in *Trilateral Commission Task Force Reports: 9–14* (New York: New York University Press, 1978); quoted passages at pp. 139, 111, 93, 110, 142.

4   Ibid., p. 140.

5   Henry H. Fowler and W. Randolph Burgess, *Harmonizing Economic Policy: Summit Meetings and Collective Leadership: Report of the Atlantic Council's Working Group on Economic Policy* (Boulder, Colorado: Westview Press, 1977), p. 28.

6 For a similar distinction between two models of summitry, see George de Menil and Anthony M. Solomon, *Economic Summitry* (New York: Council on Foreign Relations, 1983), pp. 55–7.

7 *New York Times*, 6 May 1977.

8 Credit for coining this convenient label for those who prepare the way for the summiteers is generally given to one of the UK participants. (Real Sherpas guide climbers up the Himalayas.)

9 *Neue Züriche Zeitung*, 11 May 1977. As noted in ch. 3 above, the Rambouillet monetary accord had been prepared in detail, but this had been done by Yeo and Larosière, not by the personal representatives as a group.

10 Some participants report a similar climate in other small international committees that meet frequently, such as the Council of Permanent Representatives (COREPER) of the European Community.

11 The only exceptions were Mr Shultz for President Ford in 1976 and M. Jeanneney for President Mitterrand in 1981.

12 Consistent with their status as second-class citizens in the summit context, the European Commission has generally been restricted to a single sherpa.

13 The main exception is Germany, where the chief sherpa has usually a Finance Ministry background.

14 Giscard's personal representative after 1976, M. Bernard Clappier, was Governor of the Bank of France, but his role as sherpa was quite independent of his official post.

15 Carl J. Friedrich, *Constitutional Government and Politics* (New York: Harper, 1937), pp. 16–18.

16 The finance and foreign ministers are, of course, members of the official summit delegations, occasionally joined by other colleagues, such as the trade ministers in 1978 and the energy ministers in 1979 and 1980.

17 *New York Times*, 2 July 1978.

18 19 July 1978. The paper warned that the new procedures must not lead to the imposition of US views on Europe, but judged that this was a less serious danger under Carter than under Nixon and Kissinger.

Chapter 5 The Summits and Non-participating Countries

1 See J. Robert Schaetzel and H. B. Malmgren, 'Talking Heads', *Foreign Policy*, no. 39 (Summer 1980), pp. 130–42.

2 On certain occasions the Japanese have claimed that they will speak for their Asian neighbours, the French for Francophone Africa, and the British for the Commonwealth. There is no evidence that they ever did so.

3 Egidio Ortona, J. Robert Schaetzel, and Nobuhiko Ushiba, 'The Problem of International Consultations (1976)', in *Trilateral Commission Task Force Reports: 9–14* (New York: New York University Press, 1978), p. 136.

4 See *The Times*, 11 October 1975; *New York Times*, 3 November 1975; *Figaro*, 12 November 1975.

5 *Japan Times*, 8 August 1978; *International Herald Tribune*, 24/25 March 1979. Spain, slightly larger in terms of GNP than Australia, the Netherlands, and Belgium, showed no interest in summit membership.

6 Harold Wilson, *Final Term: The Labour Government 1974–1976* (London: Weidenfeld, 1979), p. 168.

7 There was a sharp dispute in the Community in late 1975 over whether the United Kingdom could have a separate seat at the CIEC. Although Mr

Callaghan was able to speak on his own at the opening session in December, thereafter Community procedures prevailed.

8   As quoted in *Le Monde*, 6/7 June 1976. In this context 'the Four' means France, Germany, the United Kingdom, and Italy.

9   See *The Times*, 8, 17, 19 June 1976. Mr Gaston Thorn, then Luxembourg Prime Minister, was President of the European Council at the time of the Puerto Rico summit. He told the European Parliament that after Rambouillet 'oaths were sworn by all that is holy that no one would ever attend meetings like that again'; *Debates of the European Parliament* (English version), 16 June 1976, p. 95. Mr Thorn would become President of the Commission in 1981, attending the Ottawa, Versailles, and Williamsburg summits in that capacity.

10   *The Times*, 2 December 1976, 5 January 1977.

11   By analogy with the war of Jenkins' ear between Britain and Spain in the eighteenth century.

12   *International Herald Tribune*, 18 March; *Figaro*, 26/27 March; *Le Monde*, 27/28 March 1977. Presidency Statement from the European Council in *EC Bulletin*, (1977), no. 3, pp. 27–8.

13   This conclusion is consistent with the more detailed analysis given by Gianni Bonvicini and Wolfgang Wessels, 'The European Community and the Seven', in Cesare Merlini, ed., *Western Summits and Europe: Rivalry, Co-operation, and Partnership* (London: Croom Helm, 1984), pp. 167–93.

Chapter 6 London and Bonn, 1977–8

1   The story of European Community participation in the summit is described in chapter 5.

2   *OECD Economic Outlook*, no. 20 (December 1976), p. 5; no. 22 (December 1977), p. 27.

3   'Economic Prospects and Policies in the Industrial Countries: A Tripartite Report', by sixteen economists from the European Community, Japan and America (Washington, D.C.: Brookings Institution, 1977).

4   US Congress, House, *Conduct of Monetary Policy: Hearings before the Committee on Banking, Finance, and Urban Affairs*, 95th Congress, 1st session, 2 February 1977, p. 9.

5   *Washington Post*, 26 May 1977.

6   *OECD Economic Outlook*, no. 28 (December 1980), p. 135.

7   *Financial Times*, 20 January 1978.

8   This paragraph pulls together a range of arguments put forward with varying force and in various combinations during 1977 and 1978. During this period the macroeconomic debate was phrased by both sides almost exclusively in terms of fiscal policy. Not until the summits of the 1980s would macroeconomic debates focus explicitly on the coordination of national monetary policies *per se*. Of course, exchanges of views on monetary policies continued to take place among finance ministries and central banks, as they had during the days of the Library Group.

9   *New York Times*, 2 May 1977; *Washington Post*, 9 May 1977.

10   *The Times*, 3 May 1977.

11   *Daily Telegraph*, 6 May 1977.

12   A good summary of the dispute on the eve of the summit appeared in the *New York Times*, 6 May 1977.

13   *New York Times*, 6 May 1977.

14 *Frankfurter Allgemeine Zeitung*, 9 May 1977. See also *Die Zeit*, 13 May 1977.

15 *Süddeutsche Zeitung*, 6 May 1977.

16 *International Herald Tribune*, 10 May 1977; *Neue Zürche Zeitung*, 11 May 1977.

17 *The Times*, 15 June 1978.

18 *Financial Times*, 26 May 1977.

19 *Die Zeit*, 7 July 1978; *New York Times*, 7 July 1978.

20 *New York Times*, 23 July 1978.

21 Whether the policy measures decided on at Bonn were economically advisable is a quite different question, which we shall touch briefly later.

22 For an excellent account of this episode, see I. M. Destler and Hisao Mitsuyu, 'Locomotives on Different Tracks: Macroeconomic Diplomacy, 1977–1979', in I. M. Destler and Hideo Sato, eds, *Coping with U.S.–Japanese Economic Conflicts* (Lexington, Mass.: D. C. Heath, 1982), pp. 271–93.

23 *New York Times*, 20 January 1978.

24 *Daily Telegraph*, 14 February 1978.

25 *New York Times*, 16 February 1978.

26 For an excellent, detailed account of the Schmidt–Giscard initiative and its link to the Bonn summit, see Peter Ludlow, *The Making of the European Monetary System* (London: Butterworth, 1982).

27 Robert O. Keohane, 'U.S. Foreign Economic Policy Toward Other Advanced Capitalist States', in Kenneth A. Oye, Donald Rothchild, and Robert J. Lieber, eds, *Eagle Entangled: U.S. Foreign Policy in a Complex World* (New York: Longman, 1979), p. 114.

28 See Daniel Yergin, 'US Energy Policy: Transition to What?', *The World Today*, (1979), no. 3.

29 *Guardian*, 21/22 February 1978.

30 *Der Speigel*, 10 April 1978.

31 *Frankfurter Allgemeine Zeitung*, 31 March 1978.

32 *Japan Times*, 19 April 1978.

33 *Frankfurter Allgemeine Zeitung*, 5 May 1978.

34 Interestingly, in this context, a senior German politician speaks of 'the authority of the summit', precisely the same expression used by his Japanese counterpart in discussing the analogous episode in Japan. The following account of German decision-making, though anchored at crucial points by documentary evidence, is based primarily on extensive confidential interviews with virtually all key participants in the 1978 German decisions.

35 *The Times*, 15 June 1978.

36 *Frankfurter Allgemeine Zeitung*, 8 June 1978.

37 *The Times*, 17 June 1978.

38 For the President's own account of this meeting, see Jimmy Carter, *Keeping Faith: Memoirs of a President* (New York: Bantam Books, 1982), pp. 103–4.

39 *Observer*, 9 July 1978.

40 *The Times*, 15 July 1978.

41 In a faint echo of the London discussions of nuclear energy, the Americans and Canadians gave assurances at Bonn that they would not interrupt uranium supplies to Europe.

42 Giulio Andreotti, *Diari 1976–1979* (Milan: Rizzoli, 1981), p. 224.

43 This is the consensus of several unpublished studies by various national

and international financial agencies. For a discussion of relevant methodology, see *European Economy*, November 1982, Technical Annex, pp. 186–7.

44   US Senate, Subcommittee on International Economic Policy, Committee on Foreign Relations, 'Hearings on Oversight of International Economic Issues', 24 May 1979, p. 139.

45   *Frankfurter Allgemeine Zeitung*, 19 July 1978.

46   *Financial Times*, 11 November 1978. The change in US monetary policy would be reinforced with the appointment of Paul Volcker as Chairman of the Federal Reserve in the autumn of 1979.

47   US Senate, Subcommittee on International Economic Policy, Committee on Foreign Relations, 'Hearings on Oversight of International Economic Issues', 24 May 1979, p. 139. Anthony Solomon, then US Under-Secretary of the Treasury and deputy sherpa, has subsequently argued that 'the major lost opportunity of the Bonn summit agreement was that not enough pressure was put on the United States to face squarely its inflation problem and take stronger measures early enough to bring inflation under control. . . . A more specific program of action, mirroring the quantitative undertaking of the countries which agreed to stimulate demand, should have been proposed. And it might very well have gone through.' These reflections suggest that one potential transnational coalition at Bonn went unconsumated, perhaps because the signals from the advocates of greater stringency on the American side were blurred. See Anthony M. Solomon, 'A Personal Evaluation', in George de Menil and Anthony M. Solomon, *Economic Summitry* (New York: Council on Foreign Relations, 1983), p. 48.

48   George de Menil and Anthony M. Solomon, *Economic Summitry* (New York: Council on Foreign Relations, 1983), p. 27. The embedded quotation is from Sir Kenneth Couzens, formerly of the UK Treasury.

49   *Economist*, 29 September 1979. More recently, however, Schmidt has expressed a more favourable opinion about the Bonn accords. See his introduction to *Weltwirtschaftsgipfel* (Bonn, 1983), the German translation of Menil and Solomon, *Economic Summitry*.

Chapter 7 The Summits Change Direction

1   This approach was also described as differentiated demand management by the OECD Secretariat, which had been advocating it consistently at least since 1975; see ch. 3 above, p. 29 and n. 5.

2   See R. Hellmann, *Weltwirtschaftsgipfel wozu?* (Baden-Baden: Nomos, 1982), pp. 34–6, for an analysis which matches the economic policies favoured at the summits with political shifts in the participating countries.

3   *OECD Economic Outlook*, no. 24 (December 1978), pp. v–xi. Efforts to reconcile the Keynesian and anti-inflation approaches are to be seen in the McCracken Report, 'Towards Full Employment and Price Stability' (Paris: OECD, 1977), and the programme of 'positive adjustment' introduced in 1978.

4   See *European Economy*, no. 4 (November 1979), with Michael Emerson in William Wallace, ed., *Britain in Europe* (London: Heinemann, 1980), pp. 184–6; *OECD Economic Outlook*, no. 25 (July 1979); IMF, *Annual Report, 1979*.

5   For the impact of the change in US monetary policy, see Kenneth King, *US Monetary Policy and European Responses in the 1980s*, Chatham House Paper 16 (London: Routledge, 1982), pp. 1–19.

6 *OECD Economic Outlook*, no. 32 (December 1982), pp. 8–9, shows how efforts to reduce budget deficits by cutting public spending were largely frustrated by lower tax yields, higher payments to the unemployed, and increased interest charges; ibid., no. 33 (July 1983), p. 12, explains how the relationship between the targets for money supply growth and policy objectives did not turn out as expected, partly because of changes in the velocity of circulation of money.

7 The Ottawa summit declaration spoke of 'a prospect of moderate economic growth in the coming year'. In fact GNP in the summit countries contracted by about 0.3 per cent in 1982.

8 The Common Fund negotiations, encouraged by the London and Bonn summits, are a possible exception to this, as they were not completed until June 1980. But the Common Fund itself has never come into effect.

9 As noted in the talk given by Arthur Dunkel, Director-General of the GATT, at Chatham House on 17 March 1983.

10 See the World Bank's *World Development Report 1982*, pp. 7–8. The oil-importing developing countries had an average growth of GNP of 4.6 per cent during 1973–80, while the industrial countries achieved 2.4 per cent. But low-income African countries did least well, growing by only 1.3 per cent.

11 *World Development Report 1982*, pp. 10, 25, and *1983*, p. 7.

12 Henry Kissinger, *Years of Upheaval* (London: Weidenfeld, 1982), p. 746; and see above, ch. 2, pp. 15–16.

13 *New York Times*, 3 February 1977, reporting statement by Vice-President Mondale.

14 Quoted in George de Menil and Anthony M. Solomon, *Economic Summitry* (New York: Council on Foreign Relations, 1983), p. 31. See also *Die Zeit*, 27 May 1983.

15 From the Alistair Buchan Memorial Lecture, given by Helmut Schmidt on 28 October 1977; text in *Survival*, vol. 20 (January/February 1978), pp. 2–10.

16 See *American Foreign Relations, 1978; A Documentary Record* (New York: Council on Foreign Relations, 1979), pp. 41–2, 245–53.

17 Zbigniew Brzezinski, *Power and Principle* (London: Weidenfeld, 1983), p. 294. Compare the quotation from James Reston in chapter 2 above, p. 15.

18 For accounts of this meeting and its outcome, see Jimmy Carter, *Keeping Faith: Memoirs of a President* (London: Collins, 1982), pp. 234–6; Brzezinski, *Power and Principle*, p. 420; Kurt Becker in *Die Zeit*, 12 January 1979; John Barry in *The Times*, 30 June 1983.

19 President Giscard considered calling another meeting on the Guadeloupe model in March 1980, to deal with Afghanistan, but did not pursue it; Hellmann, *Weltwirtschaftsgipfel wozu?*, p. 124.

20 *Summit Meetings and Collective Leadership in the 1980s* (Washington, D.C.: Atlantic Council, 1980), p. 58. Brzezinski in a speech at IFRI, Paris, quoted in *Power and Principle*, pp. 295–6. Karl Kaiser, Winston Lord, Thierry de Montbrial, and David Watt, *Western Security: What has Changed? What Should be Done?* (London: Royal Institute of International Affairs, 1981), pp. 44–5.

21 Arrigo Levi in *The Times*, 10 July 1980.

22 Andrew Shonfield, 'The Politics of the Mixed Economy', *International Affairs*, vol. 56, no. 1 (1980), p. 11. Shonfield was critical of the approach adopted at the Tokyo summit, in contrast to his earlier welcome for Rambouillet (see ch. 3 above, p. 37, n. 18).

Chapter 8 Tokyo and Venice, 1979–80

1   *Japan Times*, 6 February, 26 April 1979; *Financial Times*, 24 March 1979; *Le Monde*, 28 March 1979.

2   For description and analysis of the onset of the second oil crisis, see Daniel Badger and Robert Belgrave, *Oil Supply and Price: What Went Right in 1980?*, Energy Paper No. 2 in the British Institutes' Joint Energy Policy Programme (London: Policy Studies Institute, 1982), pp. 101–16; and Robert Stobaugh and Daniel Yergin, *Energy Future* (New York: Ballantine, 1981), pp. 339–51.

3   *Financial Times, New York Times*, 3 March 1979; *EC Bulletin*, (1979), no. 3, p. 9.

4   *Japan Times*, 26, 28, 30 April 1979, *Financial Times*, 1 May 1979, for energy experts; *Le Monde*, 17/18 June 1979, *Japan Times*, 18, 20 June 1979, for sherpas' meeting.

5   According to OECD calculations: see *OECD Economic Outlook*, no. 24 (December 1978), p. 118, table 57.

6   *Newsweek*, 2 July 1979, p. 11.

7   For a comparison of US, French, and German reactions to the second oil crisis, see Robert J. Lieber, 'Europe and America in the World Energy Crisis', *International Affairs*, vol. 55, no. 4 (1979), pp. 538–45.

8   *Le Monde*, 16, 17/18 June 1979; *International Herald Tribune*, 16/17 June 1979.

9   *International Herald Tribune, Le Monde*, 6 June 1979.

10   The objective of limiting Community oil imports in 1985 to their 1978 level had been endorsed by the Energy Council on 27 March 1979; see *EC Bulletin*, (1979), no. 3, p. 61.

11   Ibid., (1979), no. 6, pp. 7–13, 69–71.

12   *New York Times*, 25, 26, 27 June 1979.

13   Memorandum by Stuart Eizenstat, dated 28 June 1979, quoted on the cover of the *Economist*, 14 July 1979. For Carter's own account of his battles over energy policy, see his *Keeping Faith: Memoirs of a President* (London: Collins, 1982), pp. 91–124.

14   Published accounts of the Tokyo summit by insiders are given in Carter, *Keeping Faith*, pp. 111–14 and Giulio Andreotti, *Diari 1976–1979* (Milan: Rizzoli, 1981), pp. 342–3. For the setting, see R. Hellmann, *Weltwirtschaftsgipfel wozu?* (Baden-Baden: Nomos, 1982, pp. 62–3.

15   One calculation by the OECD was that a shortfall of 2 million barrels per day would cause average oil prices to rise by about 30 per cent – the actual increase before the mid-June OPEC meeting – which would reduce GNP by up to 1 per cent and add perhaps 2–3 per cent to the inflation rate; see *OECD Economic Outlook*, no. 25 (July 1979), p. 62.

16   For the 'Schultze group' paper, see the testimony by Henry Owen to the International Economics Sub-Committee of the US Senate Foreign Relations Committee on 24 May 1979, pp. 141, 144.

17   President Carter had written to Mr Ohira in December 1978 saying that the bilateral trade imbalance could jeopardise the success of the summit; *International Herald Tribune*, 13 February 1979. A very critical internal memorandum had circulated in the European Commission in spring 1979, describing the Japanese as 'a nation of workaholics . . . living in rabbit-hutches'.

18   Carter, *Keeping Faith*, p. 111.

19 The *Observer*, 1 July 1979, contains a circumstantial account of this breakfast. See also Wilfried Kohl, *International Institutions for Energy Management*, Energy Paper No. 7 in the British Institutes' Joint Energy Policy Programme (London: Policy Studies Institute, 1983), pp. 90–1.

20 Full text of the Declaration in *The Times*, *New York Times*, 30 June 1979.

21 For agreed IEA targets, see *Financial Times*, *New York Times*, 11 December 1979. Back in 1977 the IEA had in fact set an overall ceiling for oil imports of 26 million barrels per day in 1985, but this was not broken down by countries. The Community fixed national totals for 1985 in September and for 1980 in December, see *EC Bulletin*, (1979), no. 9, p. 48, and (1979), no. 12, pp. 63–5.

22 For the IEA reaction to the Iran–Iraq war and comparison with 1979, see Badger and Belgrave, *What Went Right in 1980?*, especially pp. 127–37.

23 The OECD targets are reached by adding the Community figure for France to the IEA totals. *OECD Economic Outlook*, no. 33 (July 1983), p. 151, table 67, contains figures for actual imports with a forecast of 18 million barrels per day in 1984. At a Chatham House briefing on 14 July 1983, David Jones, the IEA's Director for Long-Term Cooperation and Policy Analysis, outlined a possible scenario involving imports of 20 million barrels per day in 1985.

24 The Community had been setting energy dependence targets since the first oil crisis; see Kohl, *International Institutions for Energy Management*, pp. 34–5. A new set of ratios and guidelines, up to 1990, were agreed by the Energy Council in May and June 1980; see *EC Bulletin*, (1980), no. 5, pp. 23–4. For the IEA meeting, see *Financial Times*, 23 May 1980.

25 On coal, see Mrs Thatcher in *House of Commons Official Report*, vol. 987 (24 June 1980), column 235. There was some conflict in the United Kingdom between the wish to promote alternatives to oil and the need to phase out uneconomic coal production. On synthetic fuels, President Carter was seeking funds from Congress for the first stage of the $88 billion investment programme announced in July 1979.

26 Andrew Shonfield, 'The World Economy 1979', *Foreign Affairs*, vol. 58, no. 3 (1980), p. 596.

27 For OECD's expectations of recession and recovery, see *OECD Economic Outlook*, no. 27 (July 1980), p. 14 and chart C, with *Financial Times*, 3 June 1980.

28 *Le Monde*, 29 November 1979. Giscard's article in the *Economist*, 21 May 1983, pp. 26–8, explains his underlying approach.

29 *North–South: a Programme for Survival*, Report of the Independent Commission on International Development Issues under the Chairmanship of Willy Brandt (London: Pan, 1980).

30 Published in *The Times*, 19 June 1980.

31 Carter, *Keeping Faith*, pp. 486–7.

32 Ibid., pp. 535–8; Zbigniew Brzezinski, *Power and Principle* (London: Weidenfeld, 1983) pp. 309–10, 461–3. It is exceptional for a bilateral meeting to be so well documented.

33 Full texts of all four statements in *EC Bulletin*, (1980), no. 6, pp. 19–20.

34 This suggestion had been made by Dr Wilfried Guth of the Deutsche Bank at a meeting of the International Monetary Conference; see *The Times*, 4 June 1980. He withdrew it a year later.

35 *House of Commons Official Report*, vol. 987 (24 June 1980), column 242. For the text of the summit declaration, see *The Times*, 25 June 1980.

36   *OECD Economic Outlook*, no. 28 (December 1980), pp. 9–10, 24. Unemployment in the OECD area in fact rose to about 32 million by the end of 1982.
37   The various IEA scenarios are contained in IEA, *World Energy Outlook* (Paris, 1982), updated by the briefing at Chatham House by David Jones referred to in in n. 23 above.
38   *Summit Meetings and Collective Leadership in the 1980s*; J. Robert Schaetzel and H. B. Malmgren, 'Talking Heads', *Foreign Policy*, no. 39 (Summer 1980), pp. 130–42.

Chapter 9 The Summits and International Organisations

1   C. Fred Bergsten, George Berthoin, and Kinhide Mushakoji, 'The Reform of International Institutions (1976)', in *Trilateral Commission Task Force Reports: 9–14* (New York: New York University Press, 1978), pp. 114–18. The report suggests that the composition of the 'core group' could change for different issues. But it also envisages that for 'coordination across issue areas' – a particular function of the summits – 'the membership of the inner group would have to remain largely constant'.
2   See, for example, Henry H. Fowler and W. Randolph Burgess, *Harmonizing Economic Policy: Summit Meetings and Collective Leadership: Report of the Atlantic Council's Working Group on Economic Policy* (Boulder, Colorado: Westview Press, 1977), pp. 24 ff. and Miriam Camps and Catherine Gwin, *Collective Management: The Reform of Global Economic Organizations* (New York: McGraw-Hill, 1981), pp. 57–8, 226–30.
3   *Harmonising Economic Policy*, pp. 14–15, 26–33.
4   Mr Wilson's list was published in the *House of Commons Official Report*, vol. 901 (24 November 1975), columns 61–8.
5   No limited group has been created in the OECD since Working Party No. 3 of the Economic Policy Committee, with ten members, dating from 1961. An attempt to limit the numbers of the Executive Committee in Special Session, founded in the early 1970s, was unsuccessful.
6   These countries already used to meet on occasions as the EPC's 'bureau': see Camps and Gwin, *Collective Management*, p. 236, n. 39; George de Menil and Anthony M. Solomon, *Economic Summitry* (New York: Council on Foreign Relations, 1983), p. 16, n. 11.
7   Notably at the OECD's EPC meeting in November; see *The Times*, *International Herald Tribune*, 22 November 1977; and Michael Henderson, 'The OECD as an Instrument of National Policy', *International Journal*, vol. 36, no. 4 (Autumn 1981), pp. 794–7.
8   For the relative roles of the summits and the IEA, see Wilfried Kohl, *International Institutions for Energy Management*, Energy Paper No. 7 in the British Institutes' Joint Energy Policy Programme (London: Policy Studies Institute, 1983), pp. 72–84; also Robert O. Keohane 'International Agencies and the Art of the Possible: the case of the IEA', *Journal of Policy Analysis and Management*, vol. 1, no. 4 (1982), pp. 469–81.
9   Quoted from a talk by Arthur Dunkel, Director-General of the GATT, at Chatham House on 22 March 1983.
10   This distinction is made by Andrew Shonfield in *International Economic Relations of the Western World, 1959—1971* (London: Oxford University Press, for the RIIA, 1976), vol. 1, pp. 131–3.

Chapter 10 Ottawa and Versailles, 1981–2

1 See Daniel Yankelovich and Larry Kaagan, 'Assertive America', *Foreign Affairs*, vol. 59, no. 3 (1981), pp. 696–712.

2 Benjamin J. Cohen, 'An Explosion in the Kitchen? Economic Relations with Other Advanced Industrial States', in Kenneth A. Oye, Robert J. Lieber, and Donald Rothchild, eds, *Eagle Defiant: United States Foreign Policy in the 1980s* (Boston: Little, Brown, 1983), p. 117.

3 The OECD already had pointed to this danger in December 1980, as noted in chapter 7. The argument was carried further by the US economist Ronald I. McKinnon, who proposed that the major central banks adopt collective monetary targets, rather than merely national ones. The proposal is attractive economically, though perhaps naive politically. A popular version of McKinnon's argument appeared in the *New York Times*, 23, 30 January 1983. See also *OECD Economic Outlook*, no. 33 (July 1983), pp. 14–21.

4 Measuring real interest rates accurately requires an estimate, not of the current inflation rate, but of the inflation rate expected over the future term of the loan, a calculation that becomes increasingly difficult for long-term borrowing. Timing was one source of confusion in discussions of the US budget deficit. Given the economic slack in 1981–3, cutting the *current* deficit would only worsen the recession. More problematic were the very substantial deficits that were projected for future years, after the economy had recovered.

5 Another alternative would have been to erect capital controls to uncouple European from US monetary affairs, but the costs of this approach were so high, its effectiveness so doubtful, and its violation of liberal economic maxims so basic that it had very little support outside some circles in Paris and Brussels.

6 *International Herald Tribune*, 6 July 1982.

7 See Miles Kahler, 'The United States and Western Europe', in Oye *et al. Eagle Defiant*, pp. 291–2 and the works cited there.

8 *International Herald Tribune*, 18 June 1981; *New York Times*, 8 August 1981.

9 *International Herald Tribune*, 10 July 1981.

10 *Die Zeit*, 24 July 1981. In a bilateral meeting, however, Schmidt won confirmation that Reagan would soon open negotiations with the Soviets on the Euromissile question.

11 *Japan Times*, 22 July 1981.

12 Emphasis added.

13 London Press Service verbatim transcript of Thatcher press conference, 22 July 1981.

14 Under the sherpas' auspices, a group of experts had worked since Venice to draft a lengthy study of North–South issues. This exercise led to some narrowing of differences among the participants and was helpful in bringing the new Reagan Administration into the international discussion of these issues. However, it left no visible traces at Montebello and was later cited as an example of the sterile 'bureaucratisation' of the summit process.

15 See, for example, *Observer*, 26 July 1981.

16 Energy was treated only in passing, although the others were satisfied to have elicited Reagan's confirmation of the United States' IEA commitments, a kind of *acquis communautaire* of summitry.

17 *Financial Times*, 17 July 1981.

18 *Japan Times*, 22 July 1981. Prime Minister Thatcher, however, castigated Japan in her final press conference, claiming that despite the communiqué's

elliptical language, the complaints had been made clear in the summit discussions.

19 See, for example, *Japan Times*, 22 July 1981; *Daily Telegraph*, 24 July 1981; *Financial Times*, 22, 23 July 1981; *New York Times*, 22 July 1981; *Boston Globe*, 26 July 1981.

20 *New York Times*, 13 February 1982.

21 *Business Week*, 21 June 1982. As this source makes clear, Sprinkel opposed currency intervention not merely because any intervention in free markets was thought to be inefficient, but also 'because it would take the pressure off countries to control their domestic inflation problems by keeping a tight rein on money growth'.

22 *New York Times*, 19 January 1982.

23 *Guardian*, 22 May 1982.

24 As explained in chapter 5, Prime Minister Martens of Belgium was added to the EC delegation, representing the presidency.

25 *Newsweek*, 14 June 1982.

26 *Daily Telegraph*, 7 June 1982.

27 *International Herald Tribune*, 3 June 1982.

28 *Le Monde*, 6/7 June 1982; *Financial Times*, 7 June 1982. Even after the public collapse of the Versailles consensus, French officials privately expressed optimism that the monetary accord marked the beginning of a process of accommodation with the Americans.

29 *Financial Times*, 7 June 1982. To be sure, not all of Secretary Regan's many obiter dicta were so dismissive. Recalling that it had been ten years since 'the Bretton Woods agreements for fixed currencies were abandoned', he added, 'this is the first step back toward some kind of rates that will have a reasonable adjustment to each other'. The intervention study, he said, 'definitely is a first step in moving toward monetary cooperation, and I have an open mind' (*International Herald Tribune*, 5/6, 8 June 1982). Unfortunately, these more flexible remarks did not attract as much French attention as his apparent denigration of the French President's perspicacity.

30 Confusion was compounded by the fact that the sherpas had met independently overnight to work on the communiqué. A verbatim account of some of the preliminary ministerial discussions was leaked by Japanese sources and appeared in *Nihon Keizai*, 26 June 1982; reasonably comprehensive accounts of the whole dispute appeared in the *Financial Times*, 7, 8 June 1982.

31 *Frankfurter Allgemeine Zeitung*, 7 June 1982.

32 *International Herald Tribune*, 8 June 1982; *Die Zeit*, 11 June 1982.

33 *International Herald Tribune*, 15 June 1982. This interview took place on Friday 11 June, apparently just before Mitterrand entered a meeting with Prime Minister Mauroy to discuss the impending, but still secret, devaluation of the franc.

34 *International Herald Tribune*, 24, 29 June 1982; *New York Times*, 30 October 1982.

35 *International Herald Tribune*, 2 July 1982.

36 *International Herald Tribune*, 23 June 1982; *New York Times*, 29 June 1982; *Financial Times*, 30 June 1982.

37 Hormats' embattled position in Washington was well known to his colleagues; 'I think he came to see the sherpas for rest and relaxation,' said one. The only person besides Helmut Schmidt and Hans-Dietrich Genscher to have

attended all eight summits up to Versailles, Hormats resigned from the State Department shortly afterwards.

38   See the *International Herald Tribune*, 29 May, 4 June 1982, and the *Neue Zürche Zeitung*, 7 June 1982.

39   Thomas Schelling, *The Strategy of Conflict* (Cambridge, Mass.: Harvard University Press, 1960), pointed out that conspicuously blindfolding oneself can be an effective way of intimidating ones opponent in a game of 'chicken', but for both players to do so can be fatal.

40   Ironically, precisely the central ambiguity in the 1975 agreement – the meaning of 'disorderly market conditions', against which it was agreed that central banks would intervene – was one of the key ambiguities in the 1982 agreement, giving rise to the divergent press briefings of Delors and Regan.

41   The *New York Times* noted this essential fact; 'At Bonn and Tokyo, leaders were conceding what they wanted to concede. Pressure from other countries was used as a buffer against domestic opposition. At Versailles, Mr. Reagan was not looking for an excuse; he does not want to change his fiscal and monetary stance. This time the other leaders were on the same side as his domestic opposition. Similarly, Europe has no intention of reducing Soviet trade as long as unemployment remains high' (reprinted in *International Herald Tribune*, 11 June 1982).

42   A few opposition figures in France and Germany favoured tighter limits on East–West trade, but their views were no more relevant than those of Congressional Democrats who wanted lower US interest rates. The summit game is played largely within the current governing coalition. As we noted earlier, some US officials did have an open mind about occasional 'smoothing' intervention in currency markets, though none of them wanted to go as far as the French in returning to a fixed rate regime. Conversely, some French officials favoured reducing subsidisation of credit for East–West trade, but none wanted to cut back that trade or link it to political conditions, as the Americans urged.

43   *International Herald Tribune*, 26 May 1982.

44   *Handelsblatt*, 4/5 June 1982; *Der Spiegel*, 17 May 1982.

Chapter 11 Williamsburg, 1983

1   As one European diplomat reflected at the time of the Ottawa summit, 'Now all these leaders are concerned most of all with their own domestic economic problems. Before, the leaders wanted to save the West because that would help them save themselves. Now, they want to save themselves first, and only after that consider the problems of the West' (*New York Times*, 20 July 1981).

2   *Handelsblatt*, 4/5 June 1982.

3   *Frankfurter Allgemeine Zeitung*, 20 July 1981.

4   *New York Times*, 12 October 1982.

5   Shultz's background briefing was reported in the *Washington Post*, 18 February 1983.

6   A minor factor encouraging new procedures may have been turnover among the personal representatives. Of the seven national sherpas in 1983, only one had been in that post two years earlier.

7   The first session of the sherpas in 1983 was only ten weeks before the summit, compared to five months in 1981.

8   Conversely, the officials responsible for preparations on the US side were

eager to involve the White House staff at all stages, in order to forestall later recrimination.

9   Robert D. Hormats (Reagan's 1982 sherpa), *Financial Times*, 23 March 1983.

10   In this spirit, the Americans called a joint meeting of trade and finance ministers of the Seven in early May 1983, but the invitation cut across lines of jurisdiction and influence elsewhere, particularly in the European Community, and the meeting did not come off as planned. Some people saw this initiative as an effort on the part of ministers, particularly trade ministers, to horn in on summitry, and the invitation caused considerable unhappiness among some sherpas. As one participant explained, 'the summit was [the personal representatives'] thing, not any business of these ministers'.

11   For an excellent account of this set of issues, see Kurt Becker, 'The Role of the Media', in Cesare Merlini, ed., *Western Summits and Europe: Rivalry, Cooperation, and Partnership* (London: Croom Helm, 1984).

12   *International Herald Tribune*, 23 July 1981; *Financial Times*, 23 July 1981.

13   On the US media blitz at Ottawa, see *New York Times*, 22 July 1981.

14   Some non-Americans attributed the better discipline to the fact that the delegation that had been the most flagrant violator of similar understandings in the past was, as host in 1983, obliged to abide by the rules.

15   *Washington Post*, 18 February 1983.

16   *OECD Economic Outlook*, no. 30 (December 1981), p. 28; no. 33 (July 1983), p. 36.

17   *Guardian*, 14 June 1982.

18   *OECD Economic Outlook*, no. 33 (July 1983), p. 19.

19   US concern about the plight of Third World debtors was hardly pure altruism; the ten largest US banks were reported to have loans totalling more than 150 per cent of their total equity at risk in troubled LDCs (*New York Times*, 18 March 1983).

20   See, for example, *Economist*, 29 May 1982; *Observer*, 30 May 1982; *Le Monde*, 1 June 1982.

21   *New York Times*, 29 May 1983.

22   *International Herald Tribune*, 6 August 1982.

23   See, for example, *New York Times*, 18 April 1983.

24   For a full listing of the various studies, see *Financial Times*, 30 March 1983.

25   *New York Times*, 22 May 1983.

26   As discussed below, the Administration's proposed Export Administration Act did occasion some difficulties at Williamsburg.

27   *New York Times*, 27 November 1982.

28   Prime Minister Fanfani of Italy was a third newcomer. Like Thatcher, he faced national elections just after the summit, but his victory was not a foregone conclusion, and in the event, his Christian Democrats would suffer their worst defeat in 30 years.

29   *New York Times*, 21 May 1983; *Le Monde*, 11, 19 May 1983.

30   *Financial Times*, 14 May 1983; *Le Monde*, 15/16 May 1983. Mitterrand's proposal for a new Bretton Woods conference, discussed below, also fits this French strategy of seeking to widen the effective circle of participants beyond the conservative Five.

31   *Boston Globe*, 31 May 1983.

32   *Promoting World Recovery: A Statement on Global Economic Strategy* (Washington, D.C.: Institute for International Economics, 1982).

33 *Newsweek*, 24 January 1983; *Economist*, 26 February 1983; *Financial Times*, 23 March 1983; *Financial Times*, 11 May 1983; *New York Times*, 18 January 1983.

34 *New York Times*, 25 February 1983; *Financial Times*, 5 May 1983.

35 *Washington Post*, 28 May 1983.

36 'Looking Toward Williamsburg: U.S. Economic Policy', *Current Policy* (US Department of State), no. 479 (21 March 1983).

37 'When the representatives of Caterpillar Tractor, General Electric, Ingersoll-Rand, and other leading exporters tell Congress, the White House, and in some cases the President himself that they are being hurt by the overvalued dollar, there has to be some policy response' (*New York Times*, 20 May 1983).

38 See, for example, articles in the *New York Times* by Robert D. Hormats, 27 March 1983, and William D. Rogers, President Ford's top international economist, 19 April 1983, as well as a survey of views of private economists, 9 December 1982.

39 *New York Times*, 28 April 1983.

40 *New York Times*, 7 December 1982. Wittingly or not, Regan's use of the term 'viscosity' echoed Giscard's formula for greater monetary stability, prior to the 1975 Rambouillet summit.

41 *New York Times*, 29 March 1983.

42 *New York Times*, 6 April 1983.

43 Mitterrand's statement coincided with a renewed call by his predecessor, Giscard d'Estaing, for 'a "phased march" towards a new Bretton Woods' (*The Economist*, 21 May 1983).

44 *Financial Times*, 31 May 1983.

45 The limited and perhaps declining significance of such professions of free-trade faith was highlighted by the US decision just weeks after Williamsburg to impose a unilateral package of tariffs and quotas on European speciality steel exports.

46 *New York Times*, 21 April 1983.

47 Japanese participation was facilitated by the fact that Nakasone was more willing and able to engage in wide-ranging discussions in English than any of his predecessors, at least since 1978. President Reagan's participation was reportedly eased by intensive briefings and practice sessions, and the Americans now felt that the President's personality would be an asset in private discussions. After the summit, even his foreign adversaries expressed admiration for Reagan's chairmanship.

48 In the wake of the drop in oil prices, energy disappeared from the summit agenda. On North–South issues, the communiqué simply endorsed ongoing efforts to deal with the debt crisis and 'welcomed' recent signs of moderation on the part of the developing nations, though without offering any new commitments on the part of the summit countries.

49 Six weeks after the summit, the Administration predicted a 1983 current account deficit of $25 billion, far exceeding the previous record of $15 billion in 1978 (*New York Times*, 11 July 1983).

50 *Financial Times*, 31 May 1983.

51 *New York Times*, 2 June 1983.

52 *New York Times*, 18, 26 September 1983.

53 *International Herald Tribune*, 11/12 June 1983. Naturally, Mitterrand's post-summit reactions were even more critical; see *Le Monde*, 10 June 1983.

54   Two months after Williamsburg, the United States joined with other countries in a concerted intervention to try to brake the continuing rise of the dollar. Although the Europeans were pleased at this break with earlier monetarist dogma, the intervention remained small by comparison with the actions of the Europeans or previous US Administrations (*New York Times*, 3, 4 August, 8 September 1983).

55   *New York Times*, 15 April 1983.

56   *New York Times*, 2 April 1983. Strictly speaking, the Japanese request concerned only the NATO study of East–West economic security, but any response would clearly set a relevant precedent.

57   *International Herald Tribune*, 22 June 1983.

58   *New York Times*, 20 February 1983.

59   *Guardian*, 31 May 1983.

60   *Le Monde*, 31 May 1983.

61   *Financial Times*, 1 June 1983.

62   *Boston Globe*, 31 May 1983; *International Herald Tribune*, 11/12 June 1983.

63   For a fuller statment of this argument, see *OECD Economic Outlook*, no. 33 (July 1983).

64   Mitterand later conceded that 'we perhaps dreamed a little in 1981, it is true, and we underestimated the duration of the international crisis, just as I overestimated the goodwill of the Americans'. He regretted not having imposed his full programme of 'rigour' in the spring of 1982, a year earlier than he had (*New York Times*, 11 July 1983).

65   *New York Times*, 1 June 1983.

66   'A Collective Approach to East–West Economic Relations', *Current Policy* (US Department of State), no. 495 (20 June 1983).

67   *New York Times*, 28 May 1983.

68   Henry R. Nau, 'Economics and Security in Alliance and East–West Relations', United States Information Service, 1 April 1983.

69   The institutional affiliation with the IMF may impart a slight bias towards deflationary policies to this mechanism.

70   *Le Monde*, 10 June 1983.

Chapter 12   Consequences of the Summits

1   For an indication that a conversation with Schmidt was crucial to Callaghan's decision to accept the IMF's terms in 1976, see Susan Crosland, *Tony Crosland* (London: Jonathan Cape, 1982), pp. 379–80. As noted later, some Canadians believe that Schmidt also personally influenced Prime Minister Trudeau's 1978 decision to cut public spending.

2   See, for example, Thomas C. Schelling, *The Strategy of Conflict* (Cambridge, Mass.: Harvard University Press, 1960); Robert Axelrod, 'The Emergence of Cooperation among Egoists', *American Political Science Review*, vol. 75 (June 1981), pp. 306–18.

3   Anthony M. Solomon, in George de Menil and Anthony M. Solomon, *Economic Summitry* (New York: Council on Foreign Relations, 1983), p. 45.

4   On the emergence of hybrid 'political administrators' throughout the West, see Joel D. Aberbach, Robert D. Putnam, and Bert A. Rockman, *Bureaucrats and Politicians in Western Democracies* (Cambridge, Mass.: Harvard University Press, 1981), esp. pp. 16–20.

5   Robert O. Keohane, *After Hegemony: Cooperation and Discord in the World Political Economy* (Princeton, N.J.: Princeton University Press, 1984).

6   One of the most intriguing conjunctions between summitry and national policy decisions involves Prime Minister Trudeau's 1978 surprise announcement of a politically–costly austerity package immediately after his return from the Bonn summit. Even officials close to this decision offer conflicting interpretations of it. Some say that the austere tone of the discussions in Germany, particularly with Schmidt, persuaded Trudeau of the need for belt-tightening, while others say that the apparent indiscipline of the other leaders, particularly Carter, confirmed Trudeau's conviction that he would have to act alone. Similar ambiguity surrounds Trudeau's 1982 decision immediately after Versailles to impose wage restraint in the public sector. Nevertheless, both cases seem to evince at least a desire on the Prime Minister's part to delay high-stakes domestic decisions until he could act on the basis of the best possible information about the international environment.

7   Cited in Menil and Solomon, *Economic Summitry*, p. 20.

6   *Le Monde*, 20 July 1978.

9   Solomon in Menil and Solomon, *Economic Summitry*, p. 44.

10   The only important exception is the US insistence on German reflation in 1978, but by then the US economy was booming. A minor counter-example is the rather muted French attack on the US fiscal deficit in 1983. A counter-example that somewhat backfired domestically, as noted above, was the Giscard–Barre encouragement for German expansion in 1978 while following a stringent line at home.

11   This sort of international policy cooperation is sometimes termed 'co-ordination', as distinct from 'consultation', or 'positive coordination', as distinct from 'negative coordination', which involves merely the lowering of barriers to international commerce and finance. However, terminology in this area is not well specified. See Marina v.N. Whitman, *Reflections of Interdependence* (Pittsburgh: University of Pittsburgh Press, 1979), pp. 281–5; Jacques Pelkmans, 'Economic Cooperation among Western Countries', in Robert J. Gordon and Jacques Pelkmans, *Challenges to Interdependent Economies* (New York: McGraw-Hill for the Council on Foreign Relations, 1979), pp. 97–123; and Arthur A. Stein, 'Coordination and collaboration: regimes in an anarchic world', *International Organization*, vol. 36 (Spring 1982), pp. 299–324.

12   See Robert D. Tollison and Thomas D. Willett, 'An Economic Theory of Mutually Advantageous Issue Linkages in International Negotiations', *International Organisation*, vol. 33 (Autumn 1979), pp. 425–49.

13   Ibid., pp. 444–5.

14   See Schelling, *The Strategy of Conflict*; Axelrod, 'The Emergence of Co-operation among Egoists'; Russell Hardin, *Collective Action* (London: Johns Hopkins University Press, 1982).

15   *Neue Zürche Zeitung*, 4 July 1982. Of course, one reason that the Europeans use the Western summit primarily to discuss US policy is that they can debate their own policies year-round in the European Community.

16   Kenneth Waltz, *Theory of World Politics* (Reading, Mass.: Addison-Wesley, 1979), p. 63; Keohane, *After Hegemony*, ch. 1.

17   An internally divided government is not necessarily a weak government, as the example of the Schmidt government of 1978 makes plain.

18 Dieter Hiss, 'Weltwirtschaftsgipfel: Betrachtungen eines Insiders', in Joachim Frohn and Reiner Staeglin, eds, *Empirische Wirtschaftsforschung* (Berlin: Duncker and Humblot, 1980), pp. 286–7.

19 There is disagreement about whether the Germans hinted that Schmidt would welcome foreign pressure. In general, Europeans seem less ready to advertise internal disagreements than either the Americans or the Japanese.

20 Hiss, 'Weltwirtschaftsgipfel', pp. 282–4.

21 Minor exceptions include some marginal criticism of Schmidt in 1978, of Ohira and Clark in 1979, and of Mitterrand and Spadolini in 1983.

Chapter 13 Ideas for Future Summits

1 Herr Genscher, the German Foreign Minister, has been at every summit since the beginning, and could still be there in 1986. No one can match this record.

2 *New York Times*, 12 October 1982; *International Herald Tribune*, 27 May 1983; *Financial Times*, 28, 29 June 1979.

3 In a period of one year, beginning on 1 July 1981, Mrs Thatcher attended the Ottawa summit; the Melbourne Commonwealth Heads of Government meeting; the Cancun North–South summit; three European Councils; the Versailles summit; and the Bonn NATO summit. This sequence – admittedly exceptional – took up one whole month out of the twelve.

4 One of the four larger Community countries should hold the presidency in the remaining years of the 1980s, except for 1986, which should be divided between the Netherlands and Portugal, and 1989, which would split between Greece and Spain. This assumes Spain and Portugal enter the Community on schedule.

5 The French were also particularly irritated at Williamsburg when the press were given advance indication of the intention to produce a political statement. This lay behind President Mitterrand's critical remarks on French television, as recorded in *Le Monde*, 10 June 1983, and noted in chapter 11.

6 See the World Bank's *World Development Report, 1981*, pp. 21–2; *1982*, pp. 21, 37.

7 *Le Monde*, 5/6 June 1982; compare *International Herald Tribune*, 17 May, *Le Monde*, 27 May 1983 and see chapter 10 above.

Appendix

A statistical overview of the changing economic fortunes of the seven countries during the period covered by this book follows on pages 254–5.

Notes:
a) Percentage changes from previous half year, seasonally adjusted at annual rates. Data for Gross Domestic Product for France, United Kingdom, and Italy; Gross National Product for all others.
b) Percentage changes from previous half year, annual rates, not seasonally adjusted.
c) $ million. Goods, services, and all transfer payments; actual data, seasonally adjusted. Data for 1982–83 are estimates.
d) Average of daily spot rates in terms of units of national currency per US $. Comparable half-yearly data for 1975 and 1976 are unavailable.

Source: OECD *Economic Outlook*.

	1975 I	1975 II	1976 I	1976 II	1977 I	1977 II	1978 I	1978 II
Growth of real GNP/GDP[a]								
United States	−4.3	6.7	6.1	2.8	7.0	5.2	4.6	5.7
Japan	0.2	5.7	6.0	3.6	7.1	3.6	6.1	4.6
Germany	−4.3	4.4	7.5	2.9	3.0	2.2	3.8	4.0
France	−1.8	3.7	6.6	3.9	3.5	1.3	5.4	3.0
United Kingdom	−2.7	−0.5	6.2	3.2	−0.9	3.7	4.7	1.1
Italy	−6.1	2.1	8.1	5.3	2.0	−1.7	3.9	4.7
Canada	0.7	3.9	9.5	0.8	2.0	3.2	3.6	3.9
Consumer prices[b]								
United States	8.3	−7.6	4.8	5.7	7.0	6.3	7.3	9.7
Japan	11.5	7.3	11.0	8.1	10.0	4.1	3.8	3.7
Germany	7.2	4.4	5.8	2.3	5.2	2.1	3.8	1.1
France	11.6	9.3	9.7	9.8	9.0	10.1	8.1	10.7
United Kingdom	28.7	23.2	15.1	13.5	20.5	9.3	7.8	8.1
Italy	16.8	9.8	18.8	19.5	21.0	12.8	12.2	11.3
Canada	9.6	11.4	6.4	6.0	8.5	9.1	8.6	9.3
Current balances[c]								
United States	8366	9914	4246	137	−5632	−8437	−10287	−4486
Japan	516	−1198	2671	1010	4605	6315	9978	6556
Germany	3225	812	2430	1507	2154	1936	3873	5144
France	1471	1202	−1102	−2321	−1188	757	2613	4386
United Kingdom	−2216	−1151	−322	−1249	−1237	1199	618	1335
Italy	87	−667	−1545	−1274	232	2236	3028	3171
Canada	−2406	−2272	−2231	−1667	−2108	−1934	−1904	−2423
Exchange rates[d]								
United States	1.00		1.00		1.00	1.00	1.00	1.00
Japan	297		297		280	257	229	192
Germany	2.46		2.52		2.38	2.27	2.08	1.94
France	4.29		4.78		4.96	4.86	4.68	4.34
United Kingdom	0.45		0.56		0.58	0.56	0.53	0.51
Italy	653		832		884	880	862	835
Canada	1.02		0.99		1.04	1.09	1.12	1.16

1979 I	II	1980 I	II	1981 I	II	1982 I	II	1983 I
1.7	2.3	-1.2	-1.1	5.5	0.7	-3.8	-0.6	3.3
5.6	4.9	4.9	4.5	4.2	2.6	2.5	4.3	1.8
4.1	3.8	2.8	-1.5	-0.5	1.2	-2.0	-1.8	2.1
2.9	4.4	0.4	-0.9	-0.4	2.8	2.0	0.4	1.1
2.7	1.7	-4.3	-3.3	-1.1	0.4	2.7	3.7	3.5
4.0	7.0	6.2	-3.3	2.4	-0.8	2.8	-6.0	-1.0
3.3	2.1	0.4	1.2	6.8	-1.1	-6.4	-3.7	4.9
10.9	13.6	15.1	10.4	10.6	9.8	4.7	5.6	1.4
2.1	6.4	9.5	6.8	4.8	3.3	2.2	2.9	1.4
5.3	4.8	6.6	4.1	7.1	5.6	5.6	4.4	2.2
9.6	12.7	14.3	12.9	12.6	15.2	12.6	7.9	10.3
12.1	21.3	19.4	12.4	12.0	11.2	9.3	4.9	3.9
15.2	17.3	24.3	19.0	21.7	15.9	16.6	16.8	15.3
9.1	9.2	9.9	11.8	13.1	12.0	11.0	9.3	4.3
-465	-1	-2799	4319	4645	-175	3222	-11316	-13300
-401	-8353	-8633	-2112	1586	3184	3414	3436	9600
238	-6342	-6563	-9142	-6185	-316	857	2467	2600
2966	2224	-1755	-2413	-1244	-3498	-6192	-5777	-4900
-1188	-619	-63	6872	9204	2773	2568	4327	700
4765	714	-4506	-5175	-4791	-3325	-3168	-2297	900
-2650	-1587	-1438	501	-2330	-2129	422	1742	1400
1.00	1.00	1.00	1.00	1.00	1.00	1.00	1.00	1.00
210	229	238	215	213	228	239	259	239
1.87	1.79	1.79	1.84	2.18	2.34	2.36	2.49	2.44
4.32	4.19	4.18	4.27	5.14	5.73	6.14	7.01	7.06
0.49	0.46	0.44	0.42	0.46	0.54	0.55	0.59	0.63
843	819	838	875	1067	1206	1291	1414	1419
1.17	1.17	1.17	1.17	1.20	1.20	1.23	1.24	1.23

Index